Buoy Engineering

Ocean Engineering: A Wiley Series

EDITOR: MICHAEL E. McCORMICK, Ph. D.,
U. S. Naval Academy
ASSOCIATE EDITOR:
RAMESWAR BHATTACHARYYA, Dr. Ingr.,
U. S. Naval Academy

Michael E. McCormick	Ocean Engineering Wave Mechanics
John B. Woodward	Marine Gas Turbines
H. O. Berteaux	Buoy Engineering

BUOY
ENGINEERING

H. O. BERTEAUX

Woods Hole Oceanographic Institution
Woods Hole, Massachusetts

A WILEY-INTERSCIENCE PUBLICATION

JOHN WILEY & SONS, New York–London–Sydney–Toronto

Library of Congress Cataloging in Publication Data:

Berteaux, H   0
  Buoy engineering.

  (Ocean engineering, a Wiley series)
  "A Wiley-Interscience publication."
  Bibliography: p.
  Includes index.
  1. Buoys—Design and construction.   I.   Title.
TC381.B47   627'.924   75-20046
ISBN 0–471–07156–0

A Mon Père

FOREWORD

"Jack of all trades, Master of none", is an old saw that usually has a derogatory overtone. But how often in the real world of Ocean Engineering, however one wants to define that profession, the need exists for a reasonable understanding of many subjects without an exhaustive knowledge of any single one.

The design, deployment, and recovery of most buoy systems are projects which involve only a few engineers, and they must consider many factors in their task. To respond to their need, Mr. Berteaux has written this book.

The major subjects—Mechanics of Floating Bodies, Mechanics of Mooring Lines, and the Design and Implantation of Oceanographic Buoy Systems —are approached at a level that a graduate engineer can quickly comprehend, and they are capably extended to a working base. Ample references are given so that an "in depth" study can be pursued, if necessary.

Developed from a course taught in the MIT/WHOI Joint Program in Ocean Engineering, *Buoy Engineering* serves well as a textbook, but I suspect it will find a wide use in the oceanographic and engineering community as a refresher for some and a reference for many.

EARL E. HAYS
Chairman, Ocean Engineering Department
Woods Hole Oceanographic Institution

SERIES PREFACE

Ocean engineering is both old and new. It is old in that man has concerned himself with specific problems in the ocean for thousands of years. Ship building, prevention of beach erosion, and construction of offshore structures are just a few of the specialties that have been developed by engineers over the ages. Until recently, however, these efforts tended to be restricted to specific areas. Within the past decade an attempt has been made to coordinate the activities of all technologists in ocean work, calling the entire field "ocean engineering." Here we have its newness.

Ocean Engineering: A Wiley Series has been created to introduce engineers and scientists to the various areas of ocean engineering. Books in this series are so written as to enable engineers and scientists easily to learn the fundamental principles and techniques of a specialty other than their own. The books can also serve as textbooks in advanced undergraduate and introductory graduate courses. The topics to be covered in this series include ocean engineering wave mechanics, marine corrosion, coastal engineering, dyanamics of marine vehicles, offshore structure, and geotechnical or seafloor engineering. We think that this series fills a great need in the literature of ocean technology.

MICHAEL E. MCCORMICK, EDITOR
RAMESWAR BHATTACHARYYA, ASSOCIATE EDITOR

November 1972

ix

PREFACE

The art of implanting floating structures in the ocean is as old as man's history. Marker buoys, mooring buoys, and aid to navigation buoys have long been familiar sights in harbors and waterways, and along sea shores.

The relatively recent past has seen many large and sophisticated buoy arrays deployed in deep waters for a multiplicity of purposes. These constrained or free floating buoyant structures often incorporate advanced engineering knowledge from many disciplines: electrical engineering, engineering physics, machine design, and mechanical engineering to name a few.

As the interest in these offshore systems grew, so grew the need for formal training in this specialized field. A one semester graduate course entitled "Buoy Engineering" was introduced in 1970 in the joint Massachusetts Institute of Technology and Woods Hole Oceanographic Institution graduate education program in ocean engineering. This book evolved from the class notes used in the presentation of the course.

The book deals with the mechanics of floating structures and anchoring lines. Its goal is to present to students and engineers without particular training in ocean engineering and experience in buoy systems a synthesis of the analytical and practical considerations needed for the design and the selection of buoy systems components: surface and subsurface buoys, anchoring lines, anchors, ancillary equipment, and their integration in systems that hopefully can survive the difficult environment of the open seas.

The book is divided in three parts. The first part, "Mechanics of Floating Bodies," covers the statics and the dynamics of free floating bodies and the study of hydrodynamic forces on constrained floating bodies. Topics reviewed in statics are: buoyancy of immersed bodies, principle of Archimedes, center of buoyancy, waterline, metacenter, and upright stability of immersed and surface floating bodies. In the dynamics the theory of planar simple harmonic waves is first introduced. The statistical representation of irregular wave trains and the concept of sea spectra are then presented. Heave and roll response of free floating bodies to regular waves and random sea states are next considered in detail. The analysis of the resistance of immersed and surface floating constrained bodies, elementary principles of flow similitude and scale model testing, and the study of hydrodynamic forces due to wave action conclude the first part.

The second part, "Mechanics of Mooring Lines," studies the statics and the dynamics of immersed anchoring lines. The statics reviews the steady-state loads and the resulting configuration of the mooring lines. Simple models with closed loop solutions (catenaries) are first considered. Cable functions are introduced next. Finally methods for computer analysis of two- and three-dimensional cases are reviewed in detail. Two line models are considered in the dynamics of mooring lines. In the first model the line is assumed to be a continuous elastic medium. Tensions and displacements are then obtained from the solution of the wave equation with proper boundary conditions. In the second model the line is represented by a finite number of discrete masses connected by restoring and damping elements. Methods of solutions for multiple degrees of freedom systems are then reviewed.

Part III deals with the practical aspects of oceanic buoy systems: classification; design logic; buoy hulls, floats materials, and fabrication; metallic and nonmetallic anchoring lines; and anchors. A review of typical environmental problems and of current deployment and retrieval techniques concludes the third and last part of the book.

Throughout the book an effort is made to present the theoretical concepts in a progressive way starting from basic and sometimes elementary principles. Pertinent exercises illustrating these concepts are included in Parts I and II. References are grouped at the end of each part. The reader is strongly encouraged to consult these references. By doing so, he will then gain a better understanding of the growing scope of buoy engineering and of the limitations of this book.

The preparation of this book was partly supported by the Sea Grant Program of the National Oceanographic and Atmospheric Administration. The support of the Office of Naval Research of the U. S. Navy to the author over his years of involvement with the design and the implantation of buoy systems at the Woods Hole Oceanographic Institution is also gratefully acknowledged.

I express my sincere gratitude to Dr. E. Hays, Chairman of the Ocean Engineering Department, Woods Hole Oceanographic Institution, for his critical review of the manuscript.

Many thanks go to my students who through their questions, comments, and reactions have so positively contributed to the book content and presentation.

I am also very grateful to Mrs. C. Muzzey, Miss B. Davies, and Mrs. A. Henry for their secretarial assistance in the preparation of the manuscript.

HENRI O. BERTEAUX

Ker Armour
Woods Hole, Massachusetts
June 1975

CONTENTS

PART III   OCEANOGRAPHIC BUOY SYSTEMS

Buoy Engineering

MECHANICS OF FLOATING BODIES

One

STATICS OF FREE FLOATING BODIES

1.1. BUOYANCY

Principle of Archimedes

A body immersed in a fluid of density ρ_F experiences an upwards force commonly referred to as "buoyancy" or buoyancy force. The expression of this force is hereafter derived. Consider an elementary volume of base dA and height $h = h_2 - h_1$ as shown in Figure 1.1. This volume is subjected to lateral and longitudinal pressure forces. Due to symmetry the lateral forces cancel out. The resultant of the longitudinal forces on the elementary volume is

$$dF = F_2 - F_1$$

$$= (p_2 - p_1)dA$$

where p_2 is the pressure at the lower face and is equal to $g\rho_F h_2$; p_1 is the pressure at the upper face and is equal to $g\rho_F h_1$; and g is the acceleration due to gravity. Thus,

$$dF = g\rho_F(h_2 - h_1)dA$$

$$= g\rho_F dV$$

3

where dV is the volume of the elementary prism. The total force on the body is therefore given by

$$F = \int dF = g\rho_F \int \int \int dV = g\rho_F V \qquad (1.1)$$

This result, known as the principle of Archimedes (282–212 B.C.), shows that the buoyancy force experienced by the body equals the weight of the fluid displaced by the body.

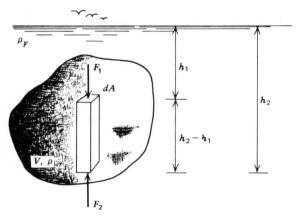

Figure 1.1.

Center of Buoyancy

The center of buoyancy, b, is defined as the center of gravity of the fluid displaced by the immersed body and the Cartesian coordinates of its location are given by

$$\bar{x}_i = \frac{\int \int \int x_i dV}{\int \int \int dV} , i = 1, 2, 3 \qquad (1.2)$$

The integrals are evaluated over the volume of displaced fluid.

1.2. STATIC EQUILIBRIUM OF FULLY IMMERSED BODIES

Resultant Gravity Force on an Immersed Body

When weight and buoyancy are the only forces applied to an immersed body, the resultant force on the body is the vector sum of these two forces (Figure 1.2). If up is positive and the sum, positive, then the body has a tendency to accelerate upwards and float; if the sum is negative, then the body has a tendency to accelerate downwards and sink. If the sum is zero, the body is said to be "neutrally buoyant," and the body is in equilibrium. A useful formula to express this resultant force, R, in the case of homogenous bodies is derived as follows:

$$R = B - W$$
$$= \rho_F g V - \rho g V$$

where ρ_F = fluid density (slugs/ft^3), ρ = body density (slugs/ft^3), V = body volume (ft^3).
Factoring $\rho g V$,

$$R = \rho g V \left(\frac{\rho_F}{\rho} - 1 \right)$$

Noting that $\rho g V$ is the weight, the resultant is then expressed as:

$$R = W \left(\frac{\rho_F}{\rho} - 1 \right) \tag{1.3}$$

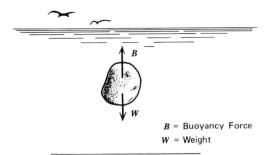

B = Buoyancy Force
W = Weight

Figure 1.2.

Stability of Immersed Bodies

When weight and buoyancy are the only forces applied to an immersed body (Figure 1.3), the body will not only accelerate, but it will also rotate about its center of gravity until the couple (Righting Moment):

$$B \, \overline{bg} \, \sin \theta = 0$$

The attitude of the body will then depend on the location of the center of gravity, g, with respect to the location of the center of buoyancy, b. If b is above g, the body will be stable upright, otherwise the body will capsize and will be stable upside down.

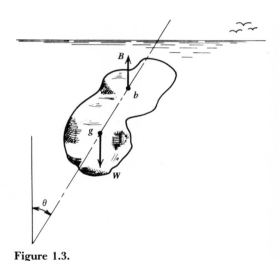

Figure 1.3.

1.3.   STATIC EQUILIBRIUM OF SURFACE FLOATING BODIES

Water Line

The condition of static equilibrium of a body floating at the surface of a fluid is derived from Archimedes principle and is expressed by

$$\int \int \int \rho_F g \, dV = \int \int \int \rho g \, dV \tag{1.4}$$

The integration of the left-hand integral is performed over the displaced volume of the fluid, whereas the integration of the right-hand integral is performed over the entire volume of the body (Figure 1.4). The intersection of the water plane and the floating body under equilibrium conditions is called the *water line*. Its location is derived from the integration results.

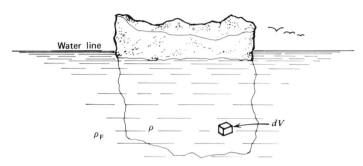

Figure 1.4.

Surface Stability of Floating Bodies

Consider the homogeneous prismatic floating body depicted in Figure 1.5*a*. When weight and buoyancy are the only forces applied, the body will float upright as indicated in Figure 1.5*b* of Figure 1.5. If an external torque is applied to the body, the body will tilt as shown in Figure 1.5*c*. When the external torque is removed, the body rotates under the action of the moment M given by

$$M = W \overline{gm}' \sin \theta \qquad (1.5)$$

where $\overline{gm}'$ is the distance from the center of gravity of the body to the intersection of the vertical above the new position b' of the center of buoyancy with the central axis of the body. (See Figure 1.5*c*.) If m' is above g, the moment will tend to upright the body (positive righting moment). If m' is below g, the body will capsize. The location of point m' when the body is upright (as point m in Figure 1.5*b*) is called the *metacenter*.

Metacentric Height

The metacentric height of a floating body is defined as:

$$gm = \lim_{\theta \to 0} gm'$$

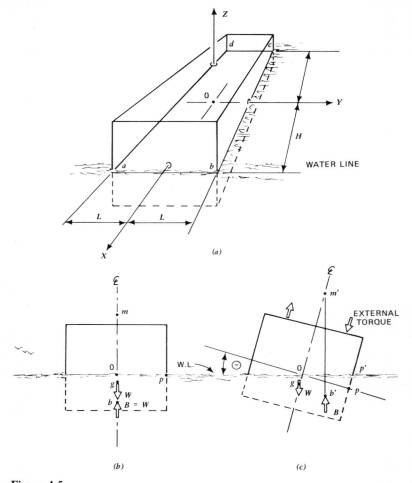

Figure 1.5.

The quantitative expression of the metacentric height is derived as follows: Two equal and opposite forces P_1 and P_2 respectively representing the gain and loss of buoyancy due to the tilt of the body are added to the original force system shown in Figure 1.5b. The moment resulting from these forces is

$$M_1 = P_1 a$$

where a is the distance between the points of application of P_1 and P_2.

To maintain a system of forces equivalent to the original system, another

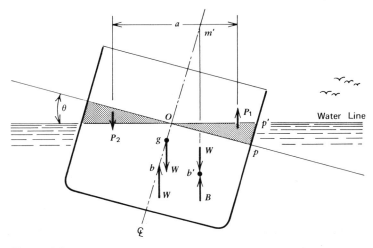

Figure 1.6.

couple of equal and opposite moment must be added. Let the equal and opposite forces of this couple be $\pm W$ applied at b and b' as shown in Figure 1.6. The condition of torque system equivalence then requires that

$$P_1 a = W \overline{bm}' \sin \theta \tag{1.6}$$

As it can be seen from Figure 1.7, the buoyancy gain due to an elementary volume of additional water displaced is given by

$$dP_1 = \rho_F \, gy \tan \theta \, dx dy$$

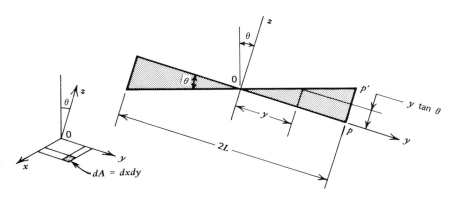

Figure 1.7.

The moment with respect to the $0x$ axis of this elementary force is

$$ydP_1 = \rho_F g \tan\theta y^2 dxdy$$

And the moment due to the buoyancy gain is

$$\int ydP_1 = \rho_F g \tan\theta \int_{-H}^{+H} \int_{0}^{L} y^2 dxdy$$

where L is the distance $0p$. A similar expression is readily obtained for the contribution of the buoyancy loss. Therefore, the moment M_1 is given by

$$P_1 a = \rho_F g \tan\theta \int_{-H}^{+H} \int_{-L}^{+L} y^2 dxdy = \rho_F g \tan\theta I \qquad (1.7)$$

where I is the second moment of area about the longitudinal axis of the body of the sectional area through the body, at the waterline, when the angle θ is zero (rectangle $abcd$, Figure 1.5a). From Eq. 1.6 and 1.7:

$$\rho_F g \tan\theta I = W \, \overline{bm}' \sin\theta$$

Also,

$$W = \rho_F g V$$

where V is the volume of water displaced by the body. Thus,

$$bm' = \frac{\tan\theta \, I}{\sin\theta \, V}$$

and the distance bm between the center of buoyancy, b, and the metacenter, m, is given by

$$bm = \lim_{\theta \to 0} bm' = \frac{I}{V} \qquad (1.8)$$

The metacentric height, $\overline{gm}$, which is the distance from the center of gravity to the metacenter, is thus finally given by

$$gm = bm \pm gb = \frac{I}{V} \pm gb \qquad (1.9)$$

Righting Moment

The righting moment for small angles of inclination is given by

$$M = W \, \overline{gm} \, \theta \qquad (1.10)$$

Note.   It should be noted that unlike immersed bodies, the condition of upright stability of surface bodies is not necessarily to have the center of buoyancy above the center of gravity, but rather to have the metacenter above the center of gravity.

The following example illustrates the basic principles of floating bodies surface stability just reviewed.

Example.   A barge, dimensions as shown on Figure 1.8, is loaded with sand up to 4 ft from the barge bottom. Find the water line, the longitudinal metacentric height, and the righting moment for $\theta = 3°$. The weight of the barge is 30,000 lb, and the unit weight of the sand is 100 lb/ft^3.

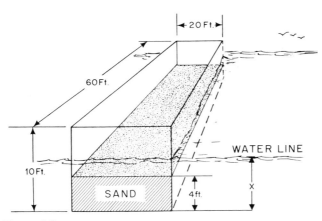

Figure 1.8.

Solution

(1)   Water Line

$$\text{Weight of sand} = 60 \times 20 \times 4 \times 100 = 480 \times 10^3 \text{ lb}$$

$$\text{Weight of barge} = \underline{\qquad\qquad 30 \times 10^3 \text{ lb}}$$

$$\text{Weight of displaced water} = \qquad 510 \times 10^3 \text{ lb}$$

The weight of displaced water is also given by

$$(60)\,(20)\rho_F g x$$

where x is the distance from the barge bottom to the water line, and $\rho_F g$ is the unit weight of sea water, 64 lb/ft^3. Solving for x,

$$x = \frac{(510) \times 10^3}{(60)(20)(64)} = 6.6 \text{ ft}$$

(2)   Metacentric Height
The moment of inertia of the water plane is given by

$$I = \tfrac{1}{12} A b^2$$

where A is the area of water plane and is equal to 60×20 or 12×10^2 ft^2, b is the rectangle base and is equal to 20 ft. Thus I is equal to

$$I = \frac{12 \times 4 \times 10^4}{12} = 4 \times 10^4 (\text{ft})^4$$

The volume of displaced water is the ratio of the weight of displaced water to the density of water. Thus

$$V = \frac{510}{64} \times 10^3 = 7.96 \times 10^3 \ (\text{ft})^3$$

Therefore,

$$\overline{bm} = \frac{I}{V} = \frac{40 \times 10^3}{7.96 \times 10^3} = 5.03 \text{ ft}$$

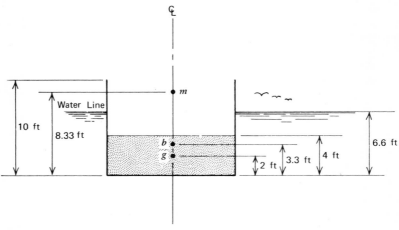

Figure 1.9.

The water line is at 6.6 ft, and, therefore, the center of buoyancy is 3.3 ft from the bottom of the barge. The center of gravity is approximately midway in the sand. The metacenter is $5.03 + 3.3 = \underline{8.33}$ ft from the bottom. These dimensions are shown in Figure 1.9. The metacenter is well above the center of buoyancy and center of gravity, and the barge is stable.

(3)   The Righting Moment is given by (1.9), that is,

$$M = W \overline{gm} \, \theta$$

where W is the weight of water displaced and is equal to 510×10^3 lb, gm is equal to $gb + bm$ or $1.3 + 5.03$ or 6.33 ft. Therefore

$$M = (510)(6.33)(0.052)10^3 = 1.67 \times 10^5 \text{ ft-lb}$$

DYNAMICS OF FREE FLOATING BODIES

2.1. OCEAN WAVES

The elementary wave form is the two-dimensional simple harmonic wave. Regular ocean waves traveling in one direction are a reasonable example of such a wave form. Irregular ocean waves can be represented by the superposition of an infinite number of simple harmonic waves of different wavelengths, directions, and amplitudes. Harmonic analysis and statistics are then used to derive the important properties of random sea states. Shallow water waves and breaking waves are beyond the scope of this discussion.

Simple Harmonic Waves

The theory of two-dimensional simple harmonic waves is hereafter briefly reviewed.

Assumptions

The following assumptions on the physical properties of the water are made: (a) The fluid is of constant density (noncompressible); and (b) the fluid is frictionless.

14

Fundamental Equations

Equation of Continuity.   The principle of mass conservation applied to an elementary volume of fluid yields the scalar equation of continuity

$$\frac{D\rho}{Dt} + \rho \nabla \cdot \vec{v} = 0 \tag{2.1}$$

where $D\rho/Dt$ is the total derivative of the fluid density, $\rho = \rho(x,y,z,t)$, and $\nabla \cdot \vec{v}$ is the divergence of the fluid particle velocity, $|\vec{v}| = v(x,y,z,t)$.

Equation of Motion (Euler).   Applying Newton's law $(\vec{F} = m\vec{a})$ to an elementary volume of fluid, the "vectorial" equation of motion of the fluid particle is obtained:

$$\vec{F}_b - \frac{1}{\rho} \nabla p = \frac{D\vec{v}}{Dt} \tag{2.2}$$

where $\vec{F}_b$ is the "body force" per unit mass due to the gravity field, ∇p is the pressure gradient, and $D\vec{v}/Dt$ is the total derivative of the fluid particle velocity.

Laplace's Equation.   When the assumption of constant density is used, expression (2.1) reduces to

$$\nabla \cdot \vec{v} = 0 \tag{2.3}$$

Furthermore, as a consequence of the second assumption, the fluid is irrotational:

$$\nabla \times \vec{v} = 0 \tag{2.4}$$

A velocity potential function $\phi = \phi(x,y,z,t)$ can, therefore, be introduced such that

$$\vec{v} = -\nabla \phi \tag{2.5}$$

Using this expression of the velocity field in the reduced equation of continuity yields the familiar Laplace's equation:

$$\nabla^2 \phi = 0 \tag{2.6}$$

The solution of this equation within the physical boundaries of the problem and with the appropriate boundary conditions will permit the derivation of the velocity field $\vec{v} = -\nabla \phi$.

The trajectories of the particles in the vicinity of their mean position can then be obtained by integration of the velocity field,

$$\vec{r} = \int_0^t \vec{v} dt$$

Solution of Laplace's Equation

Definition of the Variables.   Figure 2.1 shows a regular two-dimensional wave together with the variables used in the solution of the boundary value problem. These variables are: x, horizontal coordinate; z, vertical coordinate, positive downwards; $\xi(x,t)$ vertical displacement from mean position; H, water depth below still water level, that is, the bottom is at $z = H$; A, surface wave amplitude ($1/2$ height); L, wavelength; and $\xi_0(x,t)$, vertical displacement of the surface from a mean position (still water level).

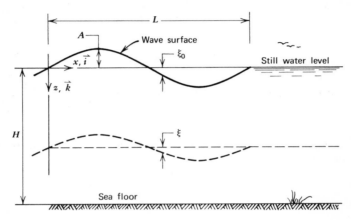

Figure 2.1.

Boundary Conditions

BOUNDARY CONDITION NO. 1.   No transport of fluid can take place through the bottom. The boundary condition at $z = H$ is, therefore,

$$w = -\frac{\partial \phi}{\partial z}\bigg|_{z=H} = 0 \qquad (2.7)$$

BOUNDARY CONDITION NO. 2.   The pressure at the wave surface is constant, and its value at the surface is arbitrarily set equal to zero, that is, $p = 0$ at $\xi = \xi_0$. An appropriate expression for this boundary condition in terms of the potential function can be obtained by integration of Euler's equation. The scalar equation of motion in the $\vec{i}$ and $\vec{k}$ directions are obtained from:

$$\vec{i} \cdot \vec{F}_b - \vec{i} \cdot \frac{1}{\rho} \nabla p = \vec{i} \cdot \frac{D\vec{v}}{Dt}$$

$$\vec{k} \cdot \vec{F}_b - \vec{k} \cdot \frac{1}{\rho} \nabla p = \vec{k} \cdot \frac{D\vec{v}}{Dt}$$

Introducing the following values for the vectorial quantities $\vec{F}_b$, $\vec{v}$, and $D\vec{v}/Dt$:

$$\vec{F}_b = g\vec{k}$$

$$\vec{v} = u\vec{i} + w\vec{k}$$

$$\frac{D\vec{v}}{Dt} = \frac{\partial \vec{v}}{\partial t} + \frac{\partial \vec{v}}{\partial x}\frac{dx}{dt} + \frac{\partial \vec{v}}{\partial z}\frac{dz}{dt}$$

or

$$\frac{D\vec{v}}{Dt} = \frac{\partial u}{\partial t}\vec{i} + \frac{\partial w}{\partial t}\vec{k} + u\left\{\frac{\partial u}{\partial x}\vec{i} + \frac{\partial w}{\partial x}\vec{k}\right\} + w\left\{\frac{\partial u}{\partial z}\vec{i} + \frac{\partial w}{\partial z}\vec{k}\right\}$$

yields

$$-\frac{1}{\rho}\frac{\partial p}{\partial x} = \frac{\partial u}{\partial t} + u\frac{\partial u}{\partial x} + w\frac{\partial u}{\partial z} \tag{2.8}$$

and

$$g - \frac{1}{\rho}\frac{\partial p}{\partial z} = \frac{\partial w}{\partial t} + u\frac{\partial w}{\partial x} + w\frac{\partial w}{\partial z} \tag{2.9}$$

Equations 2.8 and 2.9 can be written in an integrable form when the following substitutions are made:

$$\frac{\partial u}{\partial z} = \frac{\partial w}{\partial x}, \frac{\partial w}{\partial z} = \frac{\partial u}{\partial x} \quad \text{(The fluid being irrotational)}$$

$$u\frac{\partial u}{\partial x} = \frac{1}{2}\frac{\partial}{\partial x}u^2, w\frac{\partial w}{\partial x} = \frac{1}{2}\frac{\partial}{\partial x}w^2, \quad \text{and so on}$$

$$u = -\frac{\partial \phi}{\partial x}, w = -\frac{\partial \phi}{\partial z}$$

The results are

$$\frac{\partial}{\partial x}\left(-\frac{\partial \phi}{\partial t} + \frac{1}{2}(u^2 + w^2) + \frac{p}{\rho}\right) = 0$$

$$\frac{\partial}{\partial z}\left(-\frac{\partial \phi}{\partial t} + \frac{1}{2}(u^2 + w^2) + \frac{p}{\rho}\right) = g$$

Integrating

$$-\frac{\partial \phi}{\partial t} + \frac{1}{2}(u^2 + w^2) + \frac{p}{\rho} = F_1(z,t) \tag{2.10}$$

$$-\frac{\partial \phi}{\partial t} + \frac{1}{2}(u^2 + w^2) + \frac{p}{\rho} = gz + F_2(x,t) \tag{2.11}$$

The difference between these two expressions is

$$gz = F_1(z,t) - F_2(x,t)$$

This can be true for any arbitrary z, x, t only if F_2 is independent of x, that is,

$$F_2 = F_2(t)$$

Thus,

$$F_1(z,t) = gz + F_2(t)$$

When this value of F_1 is placed in (2.10), expressions (2.10) and (2.11) become identical. The integration of Euler's equation can, therefore, be uniquely expressed by

$$-\frac{\partial \phi}{\partial t} + \frac{1}{2}(u^2 + w^2) + \frac{p}{\rho} - gz = F(t) \qquad (2.12)$$

Equation 2.12 is the familiar Bernoulli's equation for time dependent two-dimensional flow of an incompressible and frictionless fluid. The choice of $F(t)$ is arbitrary, and it can be set equal to zero without loss of generality. Furthermore, if the amplitude and frequency of cyclic motion of the particles are small compared to other dimensions of the problem, then the speeds are also small and the kinetic energy term can be neglected (small amplitude wave theory). With these assumptions, the pressure is thus finally given by

$$p = \rho g z + \rho \frac{\partial \phi}{\partial t} \qquad (2.13)$$

At the surface, p is constant or equal to zero, and thus the boundary condition at the wave surface is

$$\left. \frac{\partial \phi}{\partial t} \right|_{z=\xi_0} = -g\xi_0$$

or to a good approximation

$$\left. \frac{\partial \phi}{\partial t} \right|_{z=0} = -g\xi_0 \qquad (2.14)$$

Solution of the Boundary Value Wave Problem. The boundary value problem to be solved is

$$\nabla^2 \phi = \frac{\partial^2 \phi}{\partial x^2} + \frac{\partial^2 \phi}{\partial z^2} = 0 \qquad \text{(Laplace's Equation)}$$

with the following boundary conditions

$$\frac{\partial \phi}{\partial z} = 0 \qquad \text{at } z = H$$

and

$$\frac{\partial \phi}{\partial t} = -g\xi_0 \qquad \text{at } z = 0$$

Following the classical method of separation of variables, a product solution is assumed of the form:

$$\phi = \phi(x,z,t) = X(x)Z(z)T(t)$$

Introducing this solution in Laplace's equation and dividing the result by XZT yields

$$\frac{1}{X}\frac{\partial^2 X}{\partial x^2} + \frac{1}{Z}\frac{\partial^2 Z}{\partial z^2} = 0$$

This latter expression can be split into the following two independent equations:

$$\frac{\partial^2 X}{\partial x^2} + k^2 X = 0$$

and

$$\frac{\partial^2 Z}{\partial z^2} - k^2 Z = 0$$

the sign of the constant k^2 being selected so as to insure harmonic solution in the x direction. These two equations are then readily integrated to yield

$$X = A\cos kx + B\sin kx$$

$$Z = Ce^{kz} + De^{-kz}$$

The harmonic behavior of regular waves suggests that the time dependence of the velocity potential $T(t)$ be expressed as

$$T(t) = E\sin \omega t + F\cos \omega t$$

where ω is the angular frequency

$$\omega = 2\pi f = \frac{2\pi}{T}$$

where f is the frequency and T is the wave period.

The velocity potential is thus given by

$$\phi(x,z,t) = (A\cos kx + B\sin kx)(Ce^{kz} + De^{-kz})(E\sin\omega t + F\cos\omega t)$$

The four elementary solutions obtained from this general solution are:

$$\phi_1(x,z,t) = A_1\cos kx(Ce^{kz} + De^{-kz})\cos\omega t \quad \text{and } A_1 = AF$$

$$\phi_2(x,z,t) = A_2\sin kx(Ce^{kz} + De^{-kz})\sin\omega t \quad \text{and } A_2 = BE$$

$$\phi_3(x,z,t) = A_3\cos kx(Ce^{kz} + De^{-kz})\sin\omega t \quad \text{and } A_3 = AE$$

$$\phi_4(x,z,t) = A_4\sin kx(Ce^{kz} + De^{-kz})\cos\omega t \quad \text{and } A_4 = BF$$

The Boundary Condition No. 1

$$-\frac{\partial\phi}{\partial z}\bigg|_{z=H} = 0$$

applied to the first solution yields

$$C = De^{-2kH}$$

Thus,

$$\phi_1 = A_1\cos kx(De^{-2kH}e^{kz} + De^{-kz})\cos\omega t$$

$$= 2A_1De^{-kH}\left[\frac{e^{k(z-H)} + e^{-k(z-H)}}{2}\right]\cos kx\cos\omega t$$

or

$$\phi_1 = 2A_1De^{-kH}\cosh k(z-H)\cos kx\cos\omega t \tag{2.16}$$

Boundary Condition No. 2

$$\xi_0 = -\frac{1}{g}\frac{\partial\phi}{\partial t}\bigg|_{z=0}$$

applied to ϕ_1 (2.16) yields

$$2\frac{\omega}{g}A_1De^{-kH}\cosh(kH)\cos kx\sin\omega t = \xi_0$$

But when $\cos kx\sin\omega t = 1$, $\xi_0 = A$, where A is the wave amplitude (max. ξ_0).

Therefore

$$2A_1De^{-kH} = \frac{g}{\omega}\frac{A}{\cosh(kH)}$$

and ϕ_1 becomes

$$\phi_1 = \frac{Ag\cosh[k(z-H)]}{\omega\cosh(kH)}\cos kx \cos \omega t$$

In order for ϕ_1 to be periodic in x with a wavelength L, k must be given by $k = 2\pi/L$ (wave number).
The expression of ϕ_2 derived in a similar way is

$$\phi_2 = -\frac{Ag\cosh[k(z-H)]}{\omega\cosh(kH)}\sin kx \sin \omega t$$

Any linear combination of these two solutions is also a solution of Laplace's equation. ϕ_2 can, therefore, be subtracted from ϕ_1 to give

$$\phi' = \frac{Ag\cosh[k(z-H)]}{\omega\cosh(kH)}\{\cos kx \cos \omega t + \sin kx \sin \omega t\}$$

or

$$\phi' = \frac{Ag\cosh[k(z-H)]}{\omega\cosh(kH)}\cos(kx - \omega t) \tag{2.17}$$

Equation 2.17 represents the velocity potential for a progressive wave traveling in the positive x direction.

The solution obtained in a similar way from the combination of ϕ_3 and ϕ_4 yields the velocity potential for a progressive wave traveling in the negative x direction.

$$\phi'' = \frac{Ag\cosh[k(z-H)]}{\omega\cosh(kH)}\cos(kx + \omega t) \tag{2.18}$$

The total solution of the boundary value problem is

$$\phi = \phi' + \phi''$$

Expression of the Velocity Potential in Deep Sea Applications

When H is much larger than z, as the case would be in great oceanic depths, the expression of the velocity potential ϕ is obtained by taking the limit of expression (2.17) and (2.18) as H tends to infinity.

Noting that

$$\lim_{H \to \infty} \frac{\cosh\left[k(z-H) \right]}{\cosh kH} = \lim_{H \to \infty} \frac{e^{kz}e^{-kH} + e^{-kz}e^{kH}}{e^{-kH} + e^{kH}} = e^{-kz}$$

the expression of the potential ϕ then becomes

$$\phi = \frac{Ag}{\omega} e^{-kz} \left\{ \cos(kx + \omega t) + \cos(kx - \omega t) \right\}$$
(2.19)

Wave Celerity "C"

The slope of long regular waves is small and therefore the time rate of vertical variation of the surface is approximately equal to the vertical component of the speed. In other words

$$\left. \frac{\partial \xi_0}{\partial t} \right|_{z=0} = - \left. \frac{\partial \phi}{\partial z} \right|_{z=0}$$

From Boundary Condition No. 2

$$\xi_0 = - \frac{1}{g} \frac{\partial \phi}{\partial t}$$

Thus, for $z = 0$

$$-\frac{1}{g} \frac{\partial^2 \phi}{\partial t^2} + \frac{\partial \phi}{\partial z} = 0$$
(2.20)

Introducing

$$\phi = \frac{Ag}{\omega} e^{-kz} \cos(kx - \omega t)$$

in (2.20) results in

$$gk = \omega^2$$
(2.21)

Noting that

$$\omega = 2\pi f = \frac{2\pi}{T} = \frac{2\pi C}{L} = kC$$

where L is the wave length, T is the wave period, C is the wave celerity, that is the speed of the surface deformation $C = L/T$, ω^2 is immediately given by

$\omega^2 = k^2 C^2$. This value in (2.21) yields

$$C = \sqrt{g/k} \qquad (2.22)$$

Particle Velocity

The velocity of a particle at coordinates x and z has components u and w obtained from the gradient of the velocity potential. These components are

$$u = -\frac{\partial \phi}{\partial x} = \frac{Ag}{\omega} k e^{-kz} \sin(kx - \omega t) \qquad (2.23)$$

$$w = -\frac{\partial \phi}{\partial z} = \frac{Ag}{\omega} k e^{-kz} \cos(kx - \omega t) \qquad (2.24)$$

The particle acceleration components can be obtained from the total derivative with respect to time of the velocity components.

Particle Trajectory

The parametric equations of the trajectory of a particle located at a point x, z are obtained from the integration of the particle velocity components at that point:

$$\xi = \int_0^t u\, dt = \int_0^t \frac{Ag}{\omega} k e^{-kz} \sin(kx - \omega t)\, dt$$

and

$$\zeta = \int_0^t w\, dt = \int_0^t \frac{Ag}{\omega} k e^{-kz} \cos(kx - \omega t)\, dt$$

The integration results are

$$\xi = \frac{Ag}{\omega^2} k e^{-kz} \cos(kx - \omega t)$$

$$\zeta = -\frac{Ag}{\omega^2} k e^{-kz} \sin(kx - \omega t)$$

Using relation (2.21), the horizontal and vertical displacements from the mean particle position become

$$\xi = Ae^{-kz}\cos(kx - \omega t) \tag{2.25}$$

$$\zeta = -Ae^{-kz}\sin(kx - \omega t) \tag{2.26}$$

These equations, obtained with the small amplitude approximation mentioned in the derivation, show that at any given x, z (say $x=0, z=z$), the particles describe a circle with a radius equal to Ae^{-kz}. These circles diminish with depth z (Figure 2.2). Particles do not move much at large depth z.

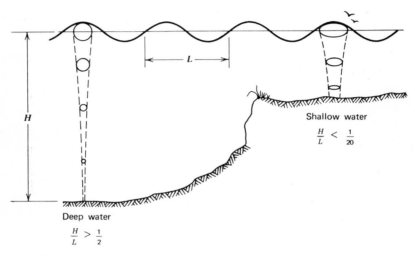

Figure 2.2.   Schematic representation of water particle trajectories.

Expression of the Surface of the Wave

The vertical displacement ζ_0 from the still water level ($z=0$) is given by (2.26) as

$$\zeta_0 = -A\sin(kx - \omega t) \tag{2.27}$$

This is the familiar equation of a wave of amplitude A traveling in the direction of positive x with a celerity $C = \omega/k$. The wave form is sketched at time $t=0$ in Figure 2.3.

Noting that $gk/\omega = \omega^2/\omega = \omega = kC$, the particle velocity components at the

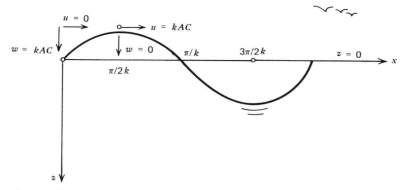

Figure 2.3.

surface can be expressed by

$$u_0 = kAC \sin (kx - \omega t) \qquad (2.28)$$

$$w_0 = kAC \cos (kx - \omega t) \qquad (2.29)$$

Pressure

In (2.13), the pressure was found to be

$$p(x,z,t) = \rho g z + \rho \frac{\partial \phi}{\partial t}$$

The first term of the sum is the hydrostatic pressure at a depth z, the second term is the pressure due to the dynamic effect of the particles motion. When the velocity potential ϕ is inserted in (2.13), the expression of the pressure becomes

$$p(x,z,t) = \rho g \left\{ z + A e^{-kz} \sin(kx - \omega t) \right\}, \quad z \geqslant 0 \qquad (2.30)$$

Due to the approximation made in the second boundary condition, this expression is valid for positive z only. This expression shows that the dynamic effect increases the hydrostatic pressure at points below the wave trough and decreases it at points below the crest that would be obtained from the instantaneous head.

Wave Energy

The energy of a wave is the sum of its potential and kinetic energy. This energy is usually expressed in terms of the average energy contained in a column of water extending to the bottom and having a horizontal area of one square unit. The average energy—potential and kinetic—is obtained by first computing the energy content in a volume of water one wavelength long by one unit of length wide and then dividing this quantity by the wavelength.

Average Potential Energy.   The potential energy of an elementary volume of water dV (one unit wide in the y direction) above the still water level (Figure 2.4) is given by:

$$d(PE) = \rho g \, dV \, \bar{\zeta}$$

where $\bar{\zeta}$ is the center of gravity of the elementary volume,

$$\bar{\zeta} = \frac{1}{2}\zeta_0$$

and

$$dV = \zeta_0 \, dx.$$

Using the expression of ζ_0 given by (2.27) and integrating over a full wavelength, say at time $t=0$,

$$\overline{PE} = \frac{\rho g}{2L} \int_x^{x+L} \zeta_0^2 \, dx$$

$$= \frac{\rho g}{2L} \int_x^{x+L} A^2 \sin^2(kx) \, dx = \frac{1}{4}\rho g A^2$$

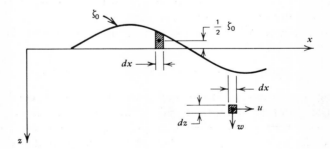

Figure 2.4.

Average Kinetic Energy.   The kinetic energy of an elementary volume $dx \, dz$ (Figure 2.4) with speed components u and w is given by

$$d(KE) = \frac{1}{2}(u^2 + w^2)\rho \, dx \, dz$$

Using the expressions of u and w given by (2.23) and (2.24) and integrating at time $t = 0$ over a wavelength

$$\overline{KE} = \frac{\rho}{2L} \int_x^{x+L} \int_0^{\infty} \left(\frac{Agk}{\omega}\right)^2 e^{-2kz} (\sin^2 kx + \cos^2 kx) \, dx \, dz$$

Noting that

$$gk = \omega^2$$

and that

$$\sin^2 kx + \cos^2 kx = 1$$

the integral reduces to

$$\overline{KE} = \left(\frac{\rho g}{2L}\right)\left(\frac{A^2}{2}\right) \int_x^{x+L} \int_0^{\infty} e^{-2kz} (2kz) \, dx \, dz$$

$$\overline{KE} = \frac{1}{4}\rho g A^2$$

Average Total Energy.   The average energy $\overline{E}$ of the wave that is the sum of the average potential and kinetic energy, is therefore given by

$$\overline{E} = \overline{PE} + \overline{KE} = \frac{1}{2}\rho g A^2 \tag{2.31}$$

Statistical Representation of Irregular Ocean Wave Trains

Regular swells are exceptional seaways, and indefiniteness of the sea surface prevails most of the time. An instantaneous profile of a train of waves will show an irregular pattern of the type depicted in Figure 2.5. A profile in any

Figure 2.5.

other direction will also show the same absence of regularity. There are, however, predominant features that will characterize a given seaway and make it different from another one. Confronted with the irregularity of the sea, one must resort to statistical analysis to describe oceanic sea states. The basic concepts necessary for the understanding of this statistical approach are hereafter presented.

Elements of Signal Theory

The following introduces certain fundamentals of signal theory. These will be useful subsequently when reviewing the statistical representation of irregular seaways. For a more complete review of the subject, the reader is referred to existing treatises on signal theory (Bendat and Piersol, 1967; Cooper and McGillem, 1967; Othes and Enochson, 1973.)

Classes of Signals.   The value that a physical variable—like a wave amplitude—may have as a function of time can be defined as a signal. Signals can be classified into two groups: deterministic and random.

DETERMINISTIC SIGNALS.   Signals that can be predicted from a knowledge of their past history are said to be deterministic. Such signals can usually be described by an explicit mathematical expression. Deterministic signals can be either periodic or nonperiodic. A signal $f(t)$ is periodic if

$$f(t+T)=f(t) \text{ for all } t.$$

T is the period, or minimum time, needed for the signal to repeat itself. The amplitude of a simple harmonic wave is a periodic deterministic signal.

RANDOM SIGNALS.   Signals that cannot be predicted before their occurrence are called random signals. A single time history—like the seaway profile depicted in Figure 2.5—of a random physical process is called a sample function $x(t)$. The collection of all possible sample functions that the physical process might have produced is a random or stochastic process, usually designated $\{x(t)\}$. The values of the sample function at some particular time t_1 is a random variable $x(t_1)$. Random variables can be discrete or continuous. Random signals can be classified according to various degrees of randomness. The wave amplitude of a confused sea is a random signal.

Description of Signals. Averages.   A certain amount of information about a given process can be obtained from averaged values of the process. Parameters of average description often encountered in practice follow.

MEAN VALUE.   The ensemble mean value $\bar{x}$ of N variables x_i is defined by

$$\bar{x} = \frac{1}{N} \sum_{i=1}^{N} x_i \tag{2.32}$$

The time average $\langle x \rangle$ of a function $x(t)$ is defined by

$$\langle x \rangle = \lim_{T \to \infty} \frac{1}{T} \int_0^T x(t)\,dt \tag{2.33}$$

Consider, for example, the collection of N wave profiles depicted in Figure 2.6 and the ensemble of variables $\{x(t_1)\}$. The mean value of the wave amplitude at time t_1 will then be

$$\overline{x(t_1)} = \lim_{N \to \infty} \frac{1}{N} \sum_{i=1}^{N} x_i(t_1) \tag{2.34}$$

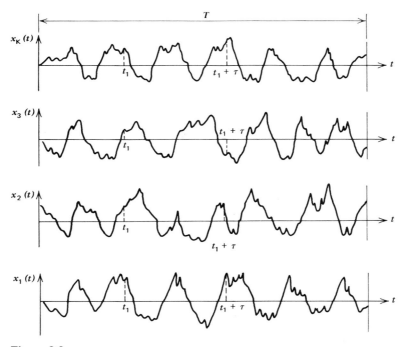

Figure 2.6.

Whereas the time average of the wave amplitude described by the sample function $x_K(t)$ is given by

$$\langle x_K \rangle = \lim_{T \to \infty} \frac{1}{T} \int_0^T x_K(t)\,dt \tag{2.35}$$

MEAN SQUARE VALUE.   The mean square value of an ensemble of N variables x_i is defined as

$$\overline{x^2} = \frac{1}{N} \sum_{i=1}^{N} x_i^2 \tag{2.36}$$

The time mean square value $\langle x^2 \rangle$ of a function $x(t)$ is given by

$$\langle x^2 \rangle = \lim_{T \to \infty} \frac{1}{T} \int_0^T x^2(t)\,dt \tag{2.37}$$

The square root of the mean square value is the familiar RMS (root mean square) value of the signal. It gives an idea of the intensity of the signal.

VARIANCE.   The variance σ^2 of a set of N variables x_i is defined by

$$\sigma^2 = \frac{1}{N} \sum_{i=1}^{N} (x_i - \bar{x})^2$$

$$= \overline{x_i^2} - (\bar{x})^2 \tag{2.38}$$

The variance of the function $x(t)$ is defined by

$$\sigma^2 = \frac{1}{T} \int_0^T (x(t) - \langle x \rangle)^2\,dt \tag{2.39}$$

$$= \frac{1}{T} \left\{ \int_0^T x^2(t)\,dt - 2\langle x \rangle \int_0^T x(t)\,dt + \langle x \rangle^2 \int_0^T dt \right\}$$

$$= \langle x^2 \rangle - 2\langle x \rangle^2 + \langle x \rangle^2$$

$$= \langle x^2 \rangle - \langle x \rangle^2 \tag{2.40}$$

The variance is the mean square value around the mean. It is equal to the mean square value minus the square of the mean value. The positive square root of the variance is called the *standard deviation*. It is a measure of the dispersion of the signal around its mean.

AUTOCORRELATION.   The ensemble average of the product of two variables is called a correlation function. When the two variables come from the same process the ensemble average

$$R_x(t_1, t_1 + \tau) = \lim_{N \to \infty} \frac{1}{N} \sum_{i=1}^{i=N} x_i(t_1)(x_i(t_1 + \tau)) \qquad (2.41)$$

is the autocorrelation function of the process. The time autocorrelation function is defined by

$$\mathcal{R}_x(\tau, K) = \lim_{T \to \infty} \frac{1}{T} \int_0^T x_K(t) x_K(t + \tau) dt \qquad (2.42)$$

The autocorrelation function provides a measure of how the value of a random variable at a time, t, will influence its value at some future time, $t + \tau$. From the definition of the mean square value, it can be seen that

$$R_x(t_1, 0) = \overline{x^2(t_1)} \qquad (2.43)$$

and

$$\mathcal{R}_x(0, K) = \langle x_K^2 \rangle \qquad (2.44)$$

STATIONARY PROCESS – ERGODIC PROCESS.   When the ensemble averages of a random process do not depend on the choice of t, the process is said to be stationary. For example, in a stationary process the mean value $\bar{x}(t_1)$ is the same for all t, that is,

$$\bar{x}(t_1) = \bar{x}$$

and similarly the autocorrelation function

$$R_x(t_1, t_1 + \tau) = R_x(\tau)$$

If in addition to be independent of time, the averages are found to be the same for all k sample functions then the process is called ergodic. In this case

$$\langle x_K \rangle = \langle x \rangle = \bar{x}$$
$$\mathcal{R}_x(\tau, K) = \mathcal{R}(\tau) = R_x(\tau)$$

for any sample function.

Process generation and time duration must be carefully considered when ascertaining the stationarity and ergodicity of a random physical process. Consider, for example, a square area of open ocean the sides of which are 10 miles long. Assume that the wind is steady and has been blowing long enough for the sea to be fully developed. If wave gauges are placed at the center of each square mile and if continuous measurements of wave heights are made during one-half hour, it is reasonable to expect the ensemble averages of the hundred records to be the same whether computed at the beginning, the middle, or the end of the measuring period. On the other hand, it would not be logical to expect the wind to remain steady and the seaway stationary over a one-week period.

Furthermore, within a 10-square-mile area of open ocean, it is reasonable to expect the random seaway to have averaged properties that are independent of the point of measurement. Therefore, the time averages of wave heights of the one-half hour hundred records should be the same for all records, and the particular seaway should be both stationary and ergodic. On the other hand, time averages obtained from measurements made over the same period, but within a 100-square-mile area, may well be found to depend on the location of the gauges.

Descriptions of irregular seaways based on single wave records $x_K(t)$ generally assume that the stochastic process is stationary and ergodic.

Description of Signals with the Help of Probability.   The probabilistic description of random signals is used to predict the mathematical expectancy of certain values or range of values of the random variable.

PROBABILITY DENSITY FUNCTION.   Consider a fraction of a sample function extending over a finite time T as shown in Figure 2.7. The probability that $x(t)$ assumes over the period T a value within the range x and $x + \Delta x$, may be expressed by the ratio T_X/T where T_X is the sum of all the periods of

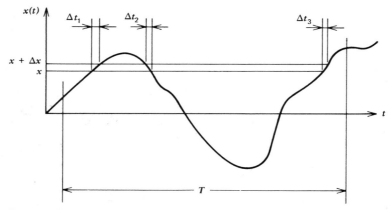

Figure 2.7.

time for which the value of $x(t)$ was in the prescribed range, that is,

$$T_X = \sum_{i=1}^{i=3} \Delta t_i$$

This ratio will approach an exact probability description of $x(t)$ as T tends to infinity, that is,

$$\text{Prob}[x < x(t) \leqslant x + \Delta x] = \lim_{T \to \infty} \frac{T_X}{T}$$

The probability density function $p(x)$ is defined as

$$p(x) = \lim_{\Delta x \to 0} \frac{\text{Prob}[x < x(t) \leqslant x + \Delta x]}{\Delta x}$$

$$p(x) = \lim_{\substack{T \to \infty \\ \Delta x \to 0}} \frac{T_X}{T\Delta x} \tag{2.45}$$

$p(x)\,dx$ is the probability that $x(t)$ lies between x and $x + dx$.

PROBABILITY DISTRIBUTION FUNCTION.   The probability $P(x)$ that the variable $x(t)$ can have a value less than or equal to a prescribed value x is given by the integral of the probability density $p(x)$ of the variable $x(t)$. Explicitly,

$$P(x) = \text{Prob}[x(t) \leqslant x] = \int_{-\infty}^{x} p(\xi)\,d\xi \tag{2.46}$$

From these definitions it follows that

$$\int_{-\infty}^{+\infty} p(\xi)\,d\xi = 1$$

$$\int_{x_1}^{x_2} p(\xi)\,d\xi = \text{Prob}[x_1 < x \leqslant x_2]$$

$$\int_{x_1}^{\infty} p(\xi)\,d\xi = \text{Prob}[x > x_1]$$

JOINT PROBABILITY DISTRIBUTION FUNCTION.   The probability for the joint occurrence of the two events,

$$x(t) \leqslant x$$

$$y(t) \leqslant y$$

is expressed by

$$P(x,y) = \text{Prob}[x(t) \leqslant x, y(t) \leqslant y]$$

$$= \int_{-\infty}^{x} du \int_{-\infty}^{y} p(u,v) \, dv \qquad (2.47)$$

where $p(u,v)$ is the joint probability density function, that is,

$$p(u,v) \, du \, dv = \text{Prob}[u \leqslant u(t) \leqslant u + du, v \leqslant v(t) \leqslant v + dv]$$

MOMENTS.   The probability density $p(x)$—when known—can be used to compute average or expected values of the random variable $x(t)$. The expected values of the function $f(x) = x^n$ are called moments. In particular,

$$\bar{x} = E[x] = \int_{-\infty}^{+\infty} x p(x) \, dx \qquad \text{is the mean value}$$

$$\overline{x^2} = E[x^2] = \int_{-\infty}^{+\infty} x^2 p(x) \, dx \qquad \text{is the mean square value}$$

$$\sigma^2 = E\big[(x - \bar{x})^2\big] = \int_{-\infty}^{+\infty} (x - \bar{x})^2 p(x) \, dx \qquad \text{is the variance}$$

The joint probability density function can, in turn, be used to compute cross moments. In particular, the autocorrelation function can be obtained from

$$R_x(t_1, t_2) = E[x_1, x_2] = \int_{-\infty}^{+\infty} dx_1 \int_{-\infty}^{+\infty} x_1 x_2 p(x_1, x_2) \, dx_2$$

Description of Signals in the Frequency Domain.   The analysis of signals and system response is often greatly simplified when the signal can be represented as a linear combination of a set of simpler elementary time functions. Such widely used "basis functions" are sinusoids. These functions are particularly convenient because of their simplicity with respect to integration, differentiation and summation. When a linear combination of sinusoidal functions is used to represent a signal $g(t)$, the resulting representation is called a Fourier series.

FOURIER SERIES.   To be represented by a Fourier series, the signal must satisfy certain conditions called the Dirichlet's conditions. These conditions are (a) the signal must be single valued; (b) the signal must have a finite number of minima, maxima, and discontinuities in any finite interval; and (c) the signal must be absolutely integrable. In other words,

$$\int_{-\infty}^{+\infty} |g(t)| \, dt < \infty$$

Consider a signal $g(t)$ satisfying the Dirichlet's conditions over a finite period, $T = t_2 - t_1$, as shown in Figure 2.8. The Fourier series representation of $g(t)$ is then given by

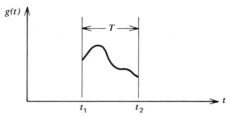

$g(t)$

t_1 t_2

Figure 2.8.

$$g(t) = \frac{a_0}{2} + \sum_{n=1}^{n=\infty} a_n \cos n\omega_0 t + b_n \sin n\omega_0 t \tag{2.48}$$

where

$$a_0 = \frac{2}{T} \int_{t_1}^{t_1 + T} g(t) \, dt \tag{2.49}$$

$$a_n = \frac{2}{T} \int_{t_1}^{t_1 + T} g(t) \cos n\omega_0 t \, dt \tag{2.50}$$

$$b_n = \frac{2}{T} \int_{t_1}^{t_1 + T} g(t) \sin n\omega_0 t \, dt \tag{2.51}$$

$$n = 1, 2, 3 \ldots$$

$$\omega_0 = \frac{2\pi}{T}$$

This representation of $g(t)$ is valid only for the time interval between t_1 and t_2. If, however, $g(t)$ is periodic with a period, $T = t_2 - t_1$, then the representation is valid for all times and not just within the interval T.

Another way to write the series is

$$g(t) = A_0 + \sum_{n=1}^{\infty} A_n \cos(n\omega_0 t - \theta_n) \tag{2.52}$$

where

$$A_0 = \frac{a_0}{2}$$

$$A_n = (a_n^2 + b_n^2)^{1/2}$$

$$\theta_n = \tan^{-1} \frac{b_n}{a_n}$$

The coefficient A_n and angle θ_n give the magnitude and phase of the sinusoids of frequency $n\omega_0$, which when added total up to $g(t)$. The explicit function $g(t)$ is the "time domain" description of the signal. The ensemble of the coefficients A_n constitute the "frequency domain" description of the signal.

COMPLEX FORM OF FOURIER SERIES.   Fourier series can be expressed in a more convenient form using the familiar complex exponential relation

$$e^{\pm jn\omega_0 t} = \cos n\omega_0 t \pm j \sin n\omega_0 t$$

where

$$j \equiv \sqrt{-1}$$

The complex form of the Fourier series is then given by

$$g(t) = \sum_{n=-\infty}^{n=+\infty} C_n e^{jn\omega_0 t} \tag{2.53}$$

with

$$C_n = \frac{1}{T} \int_{t_1}^{t_1+T} g(t) e^{-jn\omega_0 t}\, dt \tag{2.54}$$

and

$$\omega_0 = \frac{2\pi}{T}$$

FOURIER TRANSFORMS.   The representation of a nonperiodic "well behaved" signal, $g(t)$, extending over an infinite time is obtained by first considering the representation of the signal over a finite time T and then investigate the limit value of the Fourier series as $T \to \infty$. Using the complex form, the Fourier series representation of $g(t)$ over the period T is given by

$$g(t) = \sum_{n=-\infty}^{n=+\infty} C_n e^{jn\omega_0 t}$$

or

$$g(t) = \sum_{n=-\infty}^{n=+\infty} e^{jn\omega_0 t} \frac{\omega_0}{2\pi} \int_{-T/2}^{T/2} g(t) e^{-jn\omega_0 t}\, dt$$

As the period T tends to infinity, the fundamental frequency of the harmonics of the discrete series becomes a differential; the angular frequency of each component becomes the continuous variable ω; and the summation can be replaced by an integral. Thus, in the limit as $T \to \infty$

$$g(t) = \frac{1}{2\pi} \int_{-\infty}^{+\infty} g(t)e^{-j\omega t} dt \int_{-\infty}^{+\infty} e^{j\omega t} d\omega$$

or

$$g(t) = \frac{1}{2\pi} \int_{-\infty}^{+\infty} e^{j\omega t} \left\{ \int_{-\infty}^{+\infty} g(t)e^{-j\omega t} dt \right\} d\omega$$

The inner integral

$$\int_{-\infty}^{+\infty} g(t)e^{-j\omega t} dt = G(\omega) \tag{2.55}$$

is the familiar Fourier transform $G(\omega)$ of $g(t)$. In terms of its Fourier transform, $g(t)$ can be written

$$g(t) = \frac{1}{2\pi} \int_{-\infty}^{+\infty} G(\omega)e^{j\omega t} d\omega \tag{2.56}$$

This expression defines the inverse Fourier transform

$$\mathcal{F}^{-1}G(\omega) = g(t)$$

The complex form of $G(\omega)$ given by

$$G(\omega) = A(\omega)e^{j\theta(\omega)}$$

where

$$A(\omega) = |G(\omega)|$$

and

$$\theta(\omega) = \tan^{-1} \frac{\mathcal{J}mG(\omega)}{\mathcal{R}eG(\omega)}$$

introduced in (2.56) yields

$$g(t) = \frac{1}{2\pi} \int_{-\infty}^{+\infty} A(\omega)e^{j(\omega t + \theta(\omega))} d\omega \tag{2.57}$$

This last expression of $g(t)$ indicates that the function $g(t)$ is represented by the summation of a continuum of sinusoids of infinitesimal amplitude

$A(\omega)d\omega$ and of phase $\theta(\omega)$. $A(\omega)$ constitutes the amplitude spectrum of $g(t)$; whereas, $\theta(\omega)$ is the corresponding phase spectrum.

FOURIER TRANSFORM OF A RANDOM SIGNAL.   Let $x(t)$ be a sample function of a random process. A condition for this function to be Fourier transformable is that it be absolutely integrable, that is,

$$\int_{-\infty}^{+\infty}|x(t)|dt < \infty$$

This condition cannot be satisfied by any sample function of an infinitely long stationary random process. In order to obtain a Fourier transform of $x(t)$, a new sample function $x_T(t)$ must be defined such that

$$x_T(t) = x(t) \quad \text{for } |t| \leqslant T < \infty$$
$$= 0 \quad \text{for } |t| > T$$

If the usual conditions for the new truncated function $x_T(t)$ to be Fourier transformable are satisfied, then its Fourier transform will exist and will be given by

$$X_T(\omega) = \int_{-\infty}^{+\infty} x_T(t)e^{-j\omega t}\,dt \tag{2.58}$$

PARSEVAL'S THEOREM.   Consider two functions of time $f(t)$ and $g(t)$ with Fourier transforms $F(\omega)$ and $G(\omega)$. The integral of the product of these two functions can be written as

$$\int_{-\infty}^{+\infty} f(t)g(t)dt = \int_{-\infty}^{+\infty} f(t)\left[\frac{1}{2\pi}\int_{-\infty}^{+\infty} G(\omega)e^{j\omega t}d\omega\right]dt$$

$$= \frac{1}{2\pi}\int_{-\infty}^{+\infty} G(\omega)\left[\int_{-\infty}^{+\infty} f(t)e^{j\omega t}\,dt\right]d\omega$$

$$= \frac{1}{2\pi}\int_{-\infty}^{+\infty} G(\omega)F^{\star}(\omega)d\omega$$

where $F^{\star}(\omega)$ is the complex conjugate of the Fourier transform of $f(t)$. In particular, if $f(t) = g(t) = x(t)$, then

$$\int_{-\infty}^{+\infty} x(t)^2 dt = \frac{1}{2\pi}\int_{-\infty}^{+\infty} X(\omega)X(\omega)^{\star}d\omega = \frac{1}{2\pi}\int_{-\infty}^{+\infty}|X(\omega)|^2 d\omega \tag{2.59}$$

$|X(\omega)|$ being the magnitude of the Fourier transform of $x(t)$. This result is known as Parseval's theorem.

SPECTRAL DENSITY FUNCTION.   The expansion of Parseval's theorem to random variables can be used to formulate the general definition of the spectral density function.

Let $x_T(t)$ be a truncated sample function of a random process, and let $X_T(\omega)$ be its Fourier transform. Applying Parseval's theorem to this sample function, and dividing the result by $2T$ yields

$$\frac{1}{2T}\int_{-\infty}^{+\infty} x_T^2(t)\,dt = \frac{1}{4\pi T}\int_{-\infty}^{+\infty} |X_T(\omega)|^2 d\omega$$

The left-hand side of this expression would approach the mean square value of the sample function as the time interval T approached infinity. As previously stated, the Fourier transform $X_T(\omega)$ cannot be obtained as $T\to\infty$. However, it can be shown that the limit of the expected value of $|X_T(\omega)|^2/T$ as $T\to\infty$ exists (Cooper and McGillem, 1967). This result can thus be used to write

$$\lim_{T\to\infty}\frac{1}{2T}\int_{-\infty}^{+\infty} E\left[x_T^2(t)\right] dt = \lim_{T\to\infty}\frac{1}{4\pi T}\int_{-\infty}^{+\infty} E\left[X_T(\omega)|^2\right] d\omega$$

or

$$\langle \overline{x^2} \rangle = \frac{1}{2\pi}\int_{-\infty}^{+\infty}\lim_{T\to\infty}\frac{E\left[|X_T(\omega)|^2\right]}{2T}\,d\omega$$

The integrand of the right-hand side of this expression is defined as the spectral density function $S(\omega)$ of the random process, that is,

$$S(\omega) \equiv \lim_{T\to\infty}\frac{E\left[|X_T(\omega)|^2\right]}{2T}$$

The spectral density function $S(\omega)$ can be thought of as the frequency distribution of the time average of the mean square value $\langle x^2 \rangle$ of the process.

If the process is stationary, then

$$\langle \overline{x^2} \rangle \equiv \overline{x^2}$$

and the relation thus becomes

$$\overline{x^2} = \frac{1}{2\pi}\int_{-\infty}^{+\infty} S(\omega)\,d\omega \tag{2.60}$$

In this case, the quantity $S(\omega)d\omega$ represents the amount of the mean square value contained in the frequency band lying between ω and $\omega + d\omega$.

RELATION BETWEEN THE SPECTRAL DENSITY AND THE AUTOCORRELATION FUNCTION.   The spectral density $S(\omega)$ defined as

$$S(\omega) = \lim_{T \to \infty} \frac{E\left[|X_T(\omega)|^2\right]}{2T}$$

$$= \lim_{T \to \infty} \frac{E\left[X_T(\omega)x_T^{\star}(\omega)\right]}{2T}$$

can be written

$$S(\omega) = \lim_{T \to \infty} \frac{1}{2T} E\left[\int_{-\infty}^{+\infty} x_T(t_2) e^{-j\omega t_2} dt_2 \int_{-\infty}^{+\infty} x_T(t_1) e^{j\omega t_1} dt_1\right]$$

or

$$S(\omega) = \lim_{T \to \infty} \frac{1}{2T} \int_{-\infty}^{+\infty} dt_2 \int_{-\infty}^{+\infty} e^{-j\omega(t_2 - t_1)} E\left[x_T(t_1)x_T(t_2)\right] dt_1$$

Introducing

$$t_2 - t_1 = \tau$$

$$dt_2 = d\tau$$

in the above expression, yields

$$S(\omega) = \int_{-\infty}^{+\infty} \left(\lim_{T \to \infty} \frac{1}{2T} \int_{-T}^{+T} E\left[x_T(t_1)x_T(t_1 + \tau)\right] dt_1\right) e^{-j\omega \tau} d\tau$$

The quantity

$$\lim_{T \to \infty} \frac{1}{2T} \int_{-T}^{+T} E\left[x_T(t_1)x_T(t_1 + \tau)\right] dt_1$$

is recognized as the time average of the autocorrelation function of the truncated process $\langle R_x(t_1, t_1 + \tau)\rangle$. If the process is stationary, then

$$\langle R_x(t_1, t_1 + \tau)\rangle \equiv R_x(\tau)$$

and $S(\omega)$ can be written

$$S(\omega) = \int_{-\infty}^{+\infty} R_x(\tau) e^{-j\omega \tau} d\tau .$$

This interesting result shows that the spectral density $S(\omega)$ is simply the Fourier transform of the autocorrelation function of the process, that is,

$$S(\omega) = \mathfrak{F} R_x(\tau) \tag{2.61}$$

Conversely

$$R_x(\tau) = \mathfrak{F}^{-1} S(\omega) \tag{2.62}$$

Back to Ocean Waves

The physical characteristics of irregular seaways depend upon many factors: wind velocity, wind duration, fetch (distance over which the wind blows), influence of distant storms, and so forth. When these factors are held constant over a sufficient period, the sea will assume a fully developed condition, characterized by time invariant statistical averages.

A continuous record of wave amplitudes measured at one point under these steady conditions will yield a truncated sample function of the particular random sea state. The spectral density $S(\omega)$ of the stationary process can then be obtained by computation of the Fourier transform of the autocorrelation function of the record. A graphical representation of such "point spectrum" is shown in Figure 2.9. The average energy per unit area of a wave of amplitude x was shown to be proportional to x^2, namely

$$E = \tfrac{1}{2}\rho g x^2$$

Furthermore, it will be recalled from the definition of the spectral density

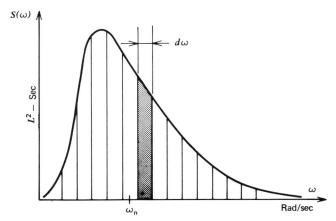

Figure 2.9.

that the area under the spectrum is proportional to the mean square value of the wave amplitudes in the record, namely

$$\overline{x^2} = \frac{1}{N} \sum_{i=1}^{N} x_i^2 = \frac{1}{2\pi} \int_0^{\infty} S(\omega) d\omega$$

These two results can therefore be combined to stipulate that:

1. The quantity $S(\omega_n) d\omega$ is proportional to the amount of average wave energy contained in a frequency band centered at the frequency ω_n.
2. The quantity

$$\lim_{d\omega \to 0} \sqrt{S(\omega_n) d\omega} \qquad (2.63)$$

is proportional to the amplitude of the elementary component wave of the spectrum with frequency ω_n.
3. The area under the spectral density curve is proportional to the average energy content of the sample record.

Wave Spectral Densities.

Several formulations of wave spectral densities have been proposed. Spectra commonly encountered in practice are:

The Amplitude Spectrum. In this spectrum the "ordinates" (as defined by Eq. (2.63)) of the spectral density are proportional to the amplitude squared of the component waves. The area S_A under the spectrum is proportional to twice the average energy E of the record, that is,

$$S_A = \int_0^{\infty} S(\omega) d\omega \propto 2E$$

The Energy Spectrum. The ordinates of the spectral density are proportional to half of the amplitude squared of the component waves. The area S_E under the spectrum is proportional to the average energy E of the record and equals $S_A/2$.

The Height Spectrum. The ordinates of the spectral density are proportional to the height squared of the component waves. The area S_H under the spectrum equals $4S_A$.

The Double Height Spectrum. The ordinates of the spectral density are proportional to twice the height squared of the component waves. The area S_{2H} under the spectrum is therefore equal to $8S_A$.
    These four types of spectrum are schematically depicted in Figure 2.10.

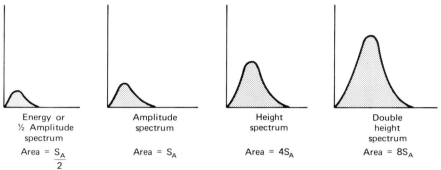

Figure 2.10.

Statistical Description of Wave Amplitudes.

The probability density function of wave amplitudes with a narrow band spectrum can be expressed by the Rayleigh distribution:

$$p(r) = \frac{2r}{\overline{r^2}} e^{-r^2/\overline{r^2}} \tag{2.64}$$

where $p(r)\,dr$ is the probability that a wave amplitude (r) lies between r and $r + dr$ and $\overline{r^2}$ is the mean square value of the wave amplitudes in the records (Longuet-Higgins, 1953). Histograms of actual wave amplitudes have been found to closely follow this theoretical distribution (Figure 2.11). This fact can therefore be used to obtain, with the help of the Rayleigh distribution, the quantitative formulation of a number of interesting statistical results.

Most Probable Wave Amplitude.   The most probable wave amplitude is the value r_m of r for which

$$\frac{d}{dr} p(r) = 0 \tag{2.65}$$

Differentiating the probability density function yields

$$\frac{d}{dr} p(r) = \frac{2}{\overline{r^2}} e^{-r^2/\overline{r^2}} \left\{ 1 - \frac{2r}{\overline{r^2}} \right\} = 0$$

Using this expression, the most probable wave amplitude r_m is found to be

$$r_m = 0.707 \sqrt{\overline{r^2}}$$

where $\sqrt{\overline{r^2}}$ is the root mean square value of the wave amplitudes in the record.

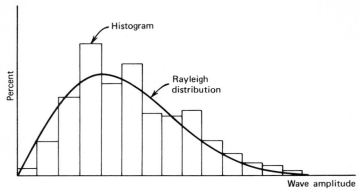

Figure 2.11.

Statistical Means.   The fraction f $(0 \leqslant f \leqslant 1)$ of wave amplitudes larger than a given amplitude r_0 is

$$f = \int_{r_0}^{\infty} p(r) \, dr \qquad (2.66)$$

The average $\bar{r}_f$ of these f highest amplitudes can in turn be found from

$$\bar{r}_f = \frac{\displaystyle\int_{r_0}^{\infty} r p(r) \, dr}{\displaystyle\int_{r_0}^{\infty} p(r) \, dr} = \frac{1}{f} \int_{r_0}^{\infty} r p(r) \, dr \qquad (2.67)$$

Example. Consider, for example, one-third of the highest waves in the record, that is, $f = 1/3$. The average amplitude of these third highest waves, called *significant* wave amplitude, is computed as follows: From (2.66)

$$f = \frac{1}{3} = \int_{r_0}^{\infty} p(r) \, dr = e^{-r_0^2 / \overline{r^2}}$$

From which

$$r_0 = \sqrt{\log_e 3} \, \sqrt{\overline{r^2}}$$

$$r_0 = 1.05 \sqrt{\overline{r^2}}$$

From (2.67)

$$\bar{r}_{1/3} = 3 \int_{r_0}^{\infty} r p(r) \, dr$$

Integrating by parts

$$\int_{r_0}^{\infty} u\,dv = uv \Big|_{r_0}^{\infty} - \int_{r_0}^{\infty} v\,du$$

with

$$u = r$$

$$du = dr$$

$$dv = p(r)\,dr$$

$$v = \int dv = \int p(r)\,dr = -e^{-r^2/\overline{r^2}}$$

yields

$$3\int_{r_0}^{\infty} rp(r)\,dr = -3re^{-r^2/\overline{r^2}}\Big|_{r_0}^{\infty} + 3\int_{r_0}^{\infty} e^{-r^2/\overline{r^2}}\,dr$$

$$= 3r_0 e^{-r_0^2/\overline{r^2}} + 3\int_{r_0}^{\infty} e^{-r^2/\overline{r^2}}\,dr$$

$$= \sqrt{\log_e 3}\ \sqrt{\overline{r^2}} + 3\int_{r_0}^{\infty} e^{-r^2/\overline{r^2}}\,dr$$

$$= 1.05\sqrt{\overline{r^2}} + 3\int_{r_0}^{\infty} e^{-r^2/\overline{r^2}}\,dr$$

The change of variable $r^2/\overline{r^2} = t^2/2$ transforms the integral term into

$$\frac{3}{\sqrt{2}}\sqrt{\overline{r^2}}\int_{t_0}^{\infty} e^{-t^2/2}\,dt$$

where

$$t_0 = \frac{\sqrt{2}\ r_0}{\sqrt{\overline{r^2}}} = \sqrt{2}\ (1.05) = 1.48$$

Multiplying and dividing by $\sqrt{2\pi}$ further transforms the integrand into the familiar standardized normal distribution function

$$\phi(t) = \frac{1}{\sqrt{2\pi}}e^{-t^2/2}$$

The integral term thus becomes

$$3\sqrt{\pi}\sqrt{\overline{r^2}}\ \frac{1}{\sqrt{2\pi}}\int_{1.48}^{\infty} e^{-t^2/2}\,dt$$

or

$$5.317\sqrt{\overline{r^2}}\left\{\frac{1}{\sqrt{2\pi}}\int_{-\infty}^{+\infty}e^{-t^2/2}dt-\frac{1}{\sqrt{2\pi}}\int_{-\infty}^{1.48}e^{-t^2/2}dt\right\}$$

which gives

$$5.317\sqrt{\overline{r^2}}\ \{1-0.93056\}=.368\sqrt{\overline{r^2}}$$

The value 0.93056 is found from published tables of the cumulative distribution function

$$F(t)=\int_{-\infty}^{t}\phi(t)\,dt=\frac{1}{\sqrt{2\pi}}\int_{-\infty}^{t}e^{-t^2/2}dt$$

Thus finally the significant wave amplitude is

$$\bar{r}_{1/3}=1.048\sqrt{\overline{r^2}}\ +0.368\sqrt{\overline{r^2}}$$

$$=1.416\sqrt{\overline{r^2}}$$

Mean Amplitude.   The mean amplitude of all the waves in the record is obtained when $f=1$ and $r_0=0$ and is given by the first moment

$$\bar{r}=\int_{0}^{\infty}rp(r)\,dr$$

Table 2.1 shows the integration results for several values of f.

TABLE 2.1. WAVE AMPLI-TUDE MEANS.

Fraction, f, of Largest Amplitudes Considered	Mean Values $\bar{r}_f/\sqrt{\overline{r^2}}$
0.01	2.359
0.10	1.800
0.333	1.416
0.50	1.256
1.00	0.886

Maximum Expected Wave Amplitude.   The expectation of the largest amplitude in a sample of N waves is found from the first moment of the probability distribution of the maximum amplitudes r_{max}. Results obtained from this computation are summarized in Table 2.2 (Longuet-Higgins, 1953).

TABLE 2.2. EXPECTED
MAXIMUM AMPLITUDES.

Number of Waves N	Maximum Wave Amplitudes $r_{max}/\sqrt{\overline{r^2}}$
50	2.12
100	2.28
500	2.61
1,000	2.78
10,000	3.13
100,000	3.47

Table 2.3 presents a useful compilation of wave heights and wave periods as a function of sea states and wind forces.

Statistical Results in Terms of the Amplitude Spectrum.

The relation between the mean square value of the wave amplitudes in the record and the amplitude spectrum was shown to be

$$\overline{r^2} = \int_{-\infty}^{+\infty} S(\omega)\,df$$

Therefore, the statistical results obtained in terms of the root mean square $\sqrt{\overline{r^2}}$ of the record can be expressed as well in terms of $\sqrt{S_A}$ where S_A is the area under the amplitude spectrum.

When dealing with a spectrum, S_i, other than an amplitude spectrum, one must exercise caution to account for the difference in the areas under the two spectra. If α is the constant associated with $\sqrt{S_A}$ (any of the constants listed in Tables 2.1 and 2.2 for example) and β the constant associated with $\sqrt{S_i}$ then β is readily found from the equality,

$$\alpha\sqrt{S_A} = \beta\sqrt{S_i} \tag{2.68}$$

TABLE 2.3 WAVE AND SEA SCALE FOR FULLY ARISEN SEA

Sea State	Sea-General Description	(Beaufort) wind force	Wind Description	Range (knots)	Wind velocity (knots)
0	Sea like a mirror.	0	Calm	<1	0
	Ripples with the appearance of scales are formed, but without foam crests.	1	Light airs	1–3	2
1	Small wavelets, short but pronounced; crests have a glassy appearance, but do not break.	2	Light breeze	4–6	5
2	Large wavelets, crests begin to break. Foam of glassy appearance. Perhaps scattered white horses.	3	Gentle breeze	7–10	8.5 10
3	Small waves, becoming larger; fairly frequent white horses.	4	Moderate breeze	11–16	12 13.5 14 16
4	Moderate waves, taking a more pronounced long form; many white horses are formed. (Chance of some spray).	5	Fresh breeze	17–21	18 19 20
5 6	Large waves begin to form; the white foam crests are more extensive everywhere. (Probably some spray).	6	Strong breeze	22–27	22 24 24.5 26 28
7	Sea heaps up and white foam from breaking waves begins to be blown in streaks along the direction of the wind. (Spindrift begins to be seen).	7	Moderate gale	28–33	30 30.5 32 34
8	Moderately high waves of greater length edges of crests break into spindrift. The foam is blown in well marked streaks along the direction of the wind. Spray affects visibility.	8	Fresh gale	34–40	36 37 38 40
	High waves. Dense streaks of foam along the direction of the wind. Sea begins to roll. Visibility affected.	9	Strong gale	41–47	42 44 46
9	Very high waves with long overhanging crests. The resulting foam is in great patches and is blown in dense white streaks along the direction of the wind. On the whole the surface of the sea takes a white appearance. The rolling of the sea becomes heavy and shock-like. Visibility is affected.	10	Whole gale	48–55	48 50 51.5 52 54
	Exceptionally high waves. Sea completely covered with long white patches of foam lying in direction of wind. Everywhere edges of wave crests are blown into froth. Visibility affected.	11	Storm	56–63	56 59.5
	Air filled with foam and spray. Sea white with driving spray; visibility very seriously affected.	12	Hurricane	64–71	>64

Table 2.3 (*Continued*)

	Wave height feet		Significant range of periods (sec)	T_{max}(Period of maximum energy of spectrum)	T(average period)	λ(average wave length)	Minimum fetch (nautical miles)	Minimum duration (hours)
Average	Significant	Average$^{1}_{10}$ highest						
0	0	0	—	—	—	—	—	—
0.05	0.08	0.10	$\leqslant 1.2$	0.7	0.5	1.0	5	18 min.
0.18	0.29	0.37	0.4–2.8	2.0	1.4	6.7	8	39 min.
0.6	1.0	1.2	0.8–5.0	3.4	2.4	20	9.8	1.7
0.88	1.4	1.8	1.0–6.0	4	2.9	27	10	2.4
1.4	2.2	2.8	1.0–7.0	4.8	3.4	40	18	3.8
1.8	2.9	3.7	1.4–7.6	5.4	3.9	52	24	4.8
2.0	3.3	4.2	1.5–7.8	5.6	4.0	59	28	5.2
2.9	4.6	5.8	2.0–8.8	6.5	4.6	71	40	6.6
3.8	6.1	7.8	2.5–10.0	7.2	5.1	90	55	8.3
4.3	6.9	8.7	2.8–10.6	7.7	5.4	99	65	9.2
5.0	8.0	10	3.0–11.1	8.1	5.7	111	75	10
6.4	10	13	3.4–12.2	8.9	6.3	134	100	12
7.9	12	16	3.7–13.5	9.7	6.8	160	130	14
8.2	13	17	3.8–13.6	9.9	7.0	164	140	15
9.6	15	20	4.0–14.5	10.5	7.4	188	180	17
11	18	23	4.5–15.5	11.3	7.9	212	230	20
14	22	28	4.7–16.7	12.1	8.6	250	280	23
14	23	29	4.8–17.0	12.4	8.7	258	290	24
16	26	33	5.0–17.5	12.9	9.1	285	340	27
19	30	38	5.5–18.5	13.6	9.7	322	420	30
21	35	44	5.8–19.7	14.5	10.3	363	500	34
23	37	46.7	6–20.5	14.9	10.5	376	530	37
25	40	50	6.2–20.8	15.4	10.7	392	600	38
28	45	58	6.5–21.7	16.1	11.4	444	710	42
31	50	64	7–23	17.0	12.0	492	830	47
36	58	73	7–24.2	17.7	12.5	534	960	52
40	64	81	7–25	18.6	13.1	590	1110	57
44	71	90	7.5–26	19.4	13.8	650	1250	63
49	78	99	7.5–27	20.2	14.3	700	1420	69
52	83	106	8–28.2	20.8	14.7	736	1560	73
54	87	110	8–28.5	21.0	14.8	750	1610	75
59	95	121	8–29.5	21.8	15.4	810	1800	81
64	103	130	8.5–31	22.6	16.3	910	2100	88
73	116	148	10–32	24.0	17.0	985	2500	101
>80	>128	>164	10–(35)	(26)	(18)			

49

Example. Obtain from the area S_{2H} under a double height spectrum the value of $\overline{H_{\frac{1}{3}}}$, the significant wave height of the record.

Solution. For an amplitude spectrum the significant wave height is given by

$$\overline{H_{\frac{1}{3}}} = 2\,\overline{a_{\frac{1}{3}}} = 2(1.416)\sqrt{S} = 2.83\sqrt{S}$$

Therefore,

$$2.83\sqrt{S} = \beta\sqrt{8S}$$

and thus

$$\beta = \frac{2.83}{\sqrt{8}} = 1$$

The significant height based on the area under the double height spectrum S_{2H} is, therefore,

$$\overline{H_{\frac{1}{3}}} = \sqrt{S_{2H}}$$

This result shows that the area under a double height spectrum directly yields the significant wave height.

Empirical Formulation of Sea Spectra.

Several empirical formulas, based on the analysis of records of wave amplitudes, have been proposed to express the spectral density of the energy spectrum as a function of the wave frequency. Either wind speed or wave significant height and period are used in these formulas.

In the first case, the spectral density $S(\omega)$ is of the form

$$S(\omega) = \frac{A}{\omega^5} e^{-B/V^4\omega^4}$$

where A and B are empirical constants, and V is the speed of the wind.

In the second case $S(\omega)$ is given by

$$S(\omega) = \frac{AH_S^2}{T_S^4\omega^5} e^{-B/T_S^4\omega^4}$$

where A and B are again empirical constants, T_S is the significant period and H_S the significant height.

Examples of Spectral Density Formulas

1.   PIERSON–MOSKOWITZ FORMULA.

$$S_{2H}(\omega) = \frac{135}{\omega^5} e^{-9.7\times 10^4/V_K^4\omega^4} \text{ ft}^2\text{-sec} \qquad (2.69)$$

where $S_{2H}(\omega)$ is the double height spectrum and V_K is the wind speed in knots.

2. BRETSCHNEIDER FORMULA

$$S_{2H}(\omega) = \frac{4200 H_S^2}{T_S^4 \omega^5} e^{-1050/T_S^4 \omega^4} \text{ ft}^2\text{-sec} \tag{2.70}$$

where H_S is in feet.

3. INTERNATIONAL SHIP STRUCTURE CONGRESS (I.S.S.C.) FORMULA

$$S_{2H}(\omega) = \frac{2760 H_S^2}{T_S^4 \omega^5} e^{-630/T_S^4 \omega^4} \text{ ft}^2\text{-sec} \tag{2.71}$$

where H_S is again in feet.

2.2. DYNAMIC RESPONSE OF FREE FLOATING BODIES TO OCEAN WAVE EXCITATION

Principle of Virtual Mass

In order to accelerate a body immersed in water not only must the body be accelerated but also the mass of a certain amount of water close to, or ahead of the body. As a result the force F' needed to accelerate the body in water is greater than the force F required to accelerate the same body in vacuum. This can be expressed by

$$F' = (m + m')a > F = ma$$

where m' is the *added* (or hydrodynamic) mass due to entrained water and the sum $m + m'$ is generally referred to as the virtual mass.

Added Mass Coefficient

The added mass is usually expressed by

$$m' = C_m \rho_F (\text{Vol}) \tag{2.72}$$

where C_m is the added mass coefficient, ρ_F is the density of the fluid (slugs/ft^3), and Vol is the volume of the fluid displaced by the immersed body (ft^3). Ideal flow theory, as shown in the following example, can be used to predict the value of the added mass coefficient for bodies of simple geometry.

Example. Added Mass Coefficient for a Sphere. The velocity potential ϕ for a nonrotating sphere moving in a straight line in an ideal fluid can be expressed (Lamb, 1932) by

$$\phi = \frac{Ua^3}{2r^2}\cos\theta \tag{2.73}$$

where U is the instantaneous velocity of the sphere, and a is the radius of the sphere.

The kinetic energy of a fluid particle of volume dV can be generally expressed by

$$d(\text{K.E.}) = \frac{1}{2}\rho_F \nabla\phi \cdot \nabla\phi \, dV$$

The total kinetic energy of the fluid is found by integrating this differential expression over the entire velocity field, namely

$$\text{K.E.} = \frac{1}{2}\rho_F \int \int \int \nabla\phi \cdot \nabla\phi \, dV$$

Using Green's theorem,

$$\int \int \phi \nabla\phi \cdot \vec{n} dS = \int \int \int \phi \nabla^2 \phi \, dV + \int \int \int \nabla\phi \cdot \nabla\phi \, dV$$

and noting that

$$\nabla^2 \phi = 0$$

for an ideal fluid, the expression of the kinetic energy becomes

$$\text{K.E.} = \frac{1}{2}\rho_F \int \int \phi \nabla\phi \cdot \vec{n} \, dS \tag{2.74}$$

Using the expression of ϕ given by (2.73) in (2.74) and integrating over the surface of the sphere yields

$$\text{K.E.} = \frac{1}{2}\rho_F \left(\frac{2}{3}\pi a^3\right)\frac{U^2}{2}$$

The time derivative of the kinetic energy of the fluid must equal the amount of work performed, per unit of time, by the sphere on the fluid. Explicitly,

$$F\frac{dx}{dt} = FU = \frac{d}{dU}(\text{K.E.})\frac{dU}{dt} = \rho_F\left(\frac{2\pi a^3}{3}\right)U\frac{dU}{dt}$$

Dividing by U, the force F accounting for the hydrodynamic mass effect is, therefore,

$$F = \rho_F \left(\frac{2\pi a^3}{3} \right) \frac{dU}{dt} = m' \frac{dU}{dt}$$

The added mass m' is thus

$$m' = \rho_F \frac{2\pi a^3}{3}$$

When this value of m' is used in relation (2.72), the added mass coefficient C_M for the sphere is found to be

$$C_M = \frac{m'}{\rho_F (\text{vol})} = \frac{1}{2} \tag{2.75}$$

Values of added mass coefficients for bodies of different shapes have been tabulated by Patton, K. T. (1965).

Heave Motion of a Cylindrical Buoy in Simple Harmonic Waves

Coordinates

(Figure 2.12). The problem coordinates are defined as follows:

1. The still water surface is selected as the level of reference.

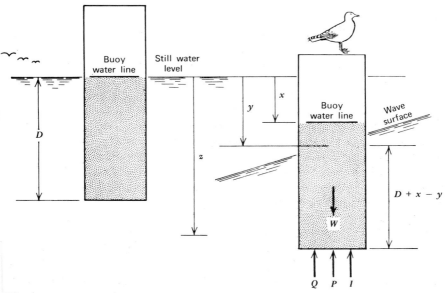

Figure 2.12.

2. x is the vertical distance, positive downwards, from this level to the water line of the buoy.
3. y is the vertical distance, positive downwards, from the level of reference to the wave surface and is given by

$$y = r \cos \omega t \tag{2.76}$$

where r is the wave amplitude, ω is the wave angular frequency,

4. z is the vertical distance, positive downwards, from the level of reference to any point in the water.

Forces.

The vertical forces acting on the buoy are

W, the weight of the buoy (downwards).

P, the pressure force on the buoy bottom (upwards).   As previously established, the pressure p at any depth z below the surface is given by

$$p = \rho g \left\{ z - y e^{-kz} \right\}$$

At the buoy bottom, $z = x + D$, D is the buoy draft. Therefore, the pressure force on the bottom area, A, is

$$P = \rho g A \left\{ x + D - y e^{-kz} \right\}$$

For buoys of small draft, z is small and the attenuation term e^{-kz} can be neglected. For buoys of larger draft, z is approximately equal to the draft D, and the attenuation term becomes e^{-kD}. Considering this latter case,

$$P = \rho g A D + \rho g A x - \rho g A y e^{-kD}$$

Q, the damping force due to water viscosity (upwards).   When linear, the damping force is assumed to be directly proportional to the relative speed between the buoy and the water. The speed of the buoy is $\dot{x}$; whereas, the vertical component of the water particle speed is $\dot{y} e^{-kz}$. If most of the damping is assumed to take place at the bottom (at $z = D$), the damping force can then be expressed by

$$Q = b \left(\dot{x} - \dot{y} e^{-kD} \right)$$

where b is the linear coefficient of friction

I, the inertial force due to the water added mass effect (upwards).   The inertial force equals the product of the added mass m' by the relative acceleration between the buoy and the water. Again, considering a buoy of large draft, and assuming that most of the inertial effect takes place on the buoy bottom, the expression of the inertial force is

$$I = m'(\ddot{x} - \ddot{y}e^{-kD})$$

Equation of Motion.

The equation of vertical motion obtained from Newton's second law of mechanics is then

$$W - \rho g A (D + x - ye^{-kD}) - b(\dot{x} - \dot{y}e^{-kD}) - m'(\ddot{x} - \ddot{y}e^{-kD}) = m\ddot{x}$$

Noting that $W = \rho g A D$, calling the restoring constant $c = \rho g A$ and the buoy virtual mass $m_v = m + m'$, and grouping the x and y terms, the equation of motion becomes

$$cx + b\dot{x} + m_v\ddot{x} = (cy + b\dot{y} + m'\ddot{y})e^{-kD}$$

Inasmuch as

$$y = r\cos\omega t$$

$$\dot{y} = -\omega r\sin\omega t$$

$$\ddot{y} = -\omega^2 r\cos\omega t$$

the right-hand side of the equation of motion can be written

$$(cy + b\dot{y} + m'\ddot{y})e^{-kD} = re^{-kD}\left\{(c - m'\omega^2)\cos\omega t - b\omega\sin\omega t\right\}$$

$$= F_0\cos(\omega t + \sigma)$$

where

$$F_0 = re^{-kD}\sqrt{(c - m'\omega^2)^2 + b^2\omega^2} \tag{2.77}$$

and

$$\sigma = \tan^{-1}\frac{-b\omega}{c - m'\omega^2} \tag{2.78}$$

F_0 is the exciting force, and σ the phase angle between the force and the wave.

The equation of motion is, thus, finally,

$$cx + b\dot{x} + m_v\ddot{x} = F_0\cos(\omega t + \sigma) \tag{2.79}$$

Buoy Heave Response.

Equation (2.79) can be written

$$\ddot{x} + 2n\dot{x} + p^2 x = \frac{F_0}{m_v} \cos(\omega t + \sigma) \qquad (2.80)$$

where

$$2n = \frac{b}{m_v}$$

and

$$p^2 = \frac{c}{m_v}$$

Equation (2.80) is the familiar equation of forced motion of a single degree of freedom mass spring system with linear damping. Standard methods of solutions to this equation can be found in textbooks of mechanics.

Natural Frequency of Heave.
The angular frequency p of free oscillation without damping is given by

$$p = \sqrt{\frac{c}{m_v}} \qquad (2.81)$$

Free Oscillations.
If the buoy is pushed down in still water and then left free to oscillate, the resulting heave motion would be described by the solution of (2.80) obtained without the exciting force. This solution is

$$x = e^{-nt} \left\{ C_1 \sin \sqrt{p^2 - n^2} \; t + C_2 \cos \sqrt{p^2 - n^2} \; t \right\} \qquad (2.82)$$

The constants of integration, C_1 and C_2, are determined by the initial conditions. The damped period of free oscillations is given by

$$T_d = \frac{2\pi}{\sqrt{p^2 - n^2}} \qquad (2.83)$$

This solution shows that the transient response is oscillatory and that the amplitude of the heave motion decays exponentially with time (Figure 2.13).The ratio of two successive amplitudes separated by a time interval equal to one damped T_d is given by

$$\frac{A_i}{A_{i+1}} = \frac{e^{-nt}}{e^{-n(t + T_d)}}$$

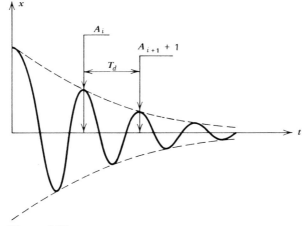

Figure 2.13.

The logarithmic decrement, δ, is thus

$$\delta = \log \frac{A_i}{A_{i+1}} = nT_d \qquad (2.84)$$

Therefore, an experimental measure of A_i, A_{i+1}, and T_d will provide a value of n. This value can be used in (2.83) to find the natural period of heave p. When p is established, the virtual mass m_v and the linear damping coefficient b can then be found from

$$p = \sqrt{\rho g A / m_v} \qquad \text{and} \qquad 2n = \frac{b}{m_v}$$

Forced Oscillations. A particular solution of

$$\ddot{x} + 2n\dot{x} + p^2 x = \frac{F_0}{m_v} \cos \omega t$$

is

$$x = \frac{F_0 / m_v}{\sqrt{\left(p^2 - \omega^2\right)^2 + 4n^2 \omega^2}} \cos\left(\omega t + \phi\right)$$

where

$$\phi = \tan^{-1} \frac{(-2n\omega)}{p^2 - \omega^2} \qquad (2.85)$$

is the phase angle between the force and the heave motion.

The heave motion is, therefore, given by

$$x = \frac{e^{-kD}r\sqrt{(c - m'\omega^2)^2 + (b\omega)^2}}{m_v\sqrt{(p^2 - \omega^2)^2 + 4n^2\omega^2}} \cos(\omega t + \phi + \sigma) \qquad (2.86)$$

The steady-state response thus consists of an harmonic oscillation of the same frequency as the wave, but of different amplitude and phase. The phase difference between heave and wave is the sum of the phase angle σ (2.78) between wave and exciting force and of the phase angle ϕ (2.85) between exciting force and heave response. It can be seen that the heave amplitude is a function of the wave frequency, ω, and of the damping coefficient n. For small dampings and at frequencies of excitation, ω, close to the natural frequency, p, of the buoy, the heave amplitude can be very large. The ratio of the heave to the wave amplitude r (magnification factor) is given by

$$\frac{x}{r} = \frac{\sqrt{(c - m'\omega^2)^2 + (b\omega)^2}}{m_v\sqrt{(p^2 - \omega^2)^2 + 4n^2\omega^2}} e^{-kD} \qquad (2.87)$$

The total response, expressed by the sum of the particular and complementary solutions is sketched in Figure 2.14.

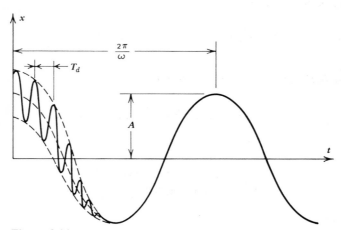

Figure 2.14.

Unresisted Rolling of a Buoy in Simple Harmonic Waves

Free Unresisted Rolling

Consider a free floating buoy forced to one side and then left free to rotate under the action of the righting moment

$$M = W \, \overline{gm} \, \sin \theta$$

where $\overline{gm}$ is the distance from the center of gravity to the metacenter, and W is the weight of the body (Figure 2.15). The instantaneous location of the axis of roll is taken as passing through the center of gravity (good approximation for bodies with the center of gravity close to the water level and true for immersed bodies).

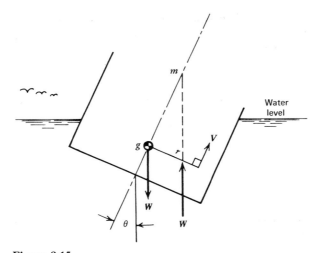

Figure 2.15.

Consider an element of volume dV of mass m at a distance $\vec{r}$ from an horizontal axis through the center of gravity and moving with a velocity, $\vec{V}$, given by

$$\vec{V} = \vec{\omega} \times \vec{r}$$

where the angular velocity $|\vec{\omega}| = d\theta / dt = \dot{\theta}$.

The inertial force on the elementary volume is in turn given by

$$d\vec{F} = \frac{d}{dt}(m\vec{V}) = m\vec{\omega} \times \vec{r}$$

The corresponding elementary torque is given by

$$d\,\vec{\mathfrak{M}} = m\vec{r}\times\vec{\omega}\times\vec{r}$$

and the total inertial torque is the integral over the entire volume of the buoy, that is,

$$\vec{\mathfrak{M}} = \int\int\int m\vec{r}\times\vec{\omega}\times\vec{r} = I\vec{\omega} = I\vec{\theta}$$

I is the moment of inertia of the entire buoy about an axis through its center of gravity.

As in the case of pure translation previously described, a certain amount of water is entrained by the body rotation. This additional inertial effect is accounted for by introducing a virtual moment of inertia I_v such that

$$I_v = I + I'$$

I' being the moment of inertia of the water entrained by the particular body. The inertial torque $I_v\ddot\theta$, thus obtained, is equal and opposite to the applied torque. Therefore,

$$I_v\ddot\theta + W\,\overline{gm}\,\sin\theta = 0$$

For small angles $\sin\theta \cong \theta$, and the equation of unresisted rolling reduces to

$$I_v\ddot\theta + W\,\overline{gm}\,\theta = 0$$

or

$$\ddot\theta + \frac{W\,\overline{gm}\,\theta}{I_v} = 0 \qquad (2.88)$$

which is the familiar differential equation for simple undamped free harmonic oscillation.

Natural Frequency of Roll.   The natural frequency of roll f_0 is given by

$$f_0 = \frac{1}{2\pi}\sqrt{W\,\overline{gm}\,/\,I_v}$$

The period of unresisted rolling is

$$T_0 = (f_0)^{-1} = 2\pi\sqrt{I_v\,/\,W\,\overline{gm}}$$

Free Unresisted Rolling.   The free unresisted rolling is given by the solution of Eq. (2.88)

$$\theta = C_1\sin\omega_0 t + C_2\cos\omega_0 t$$

where C_1 and C_2 are obtained from initial conditions.

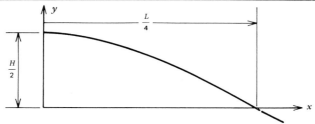

Figure 2.16.

Wave Induced Unresisted Rolling

Wave Slope.   The expression of a wave traveling in the positive x direction with origin as shown in Figure 2.16 is given by

$$y = \frac{H}{2} \cos 2\pi \left(\frac{t}{T} - \frac{x}{L} \right)$$

The slope of this wave is

$$\frac{\partial y}{\partial x} = \tan \phi = \frac{\pi H}{L} \sin 2\pi \left(\frac{t}{T} - \frac{x}{L} \right)$$

If we select to observe the slope at $x = 0$, and if the waves are long swells, the expression of the slope can be written

$$\phi \cong \tan \phi = \alpha \sin \frac{2\pi}{T} t = \alpha \sin \omega t$$

where

$$\alpha = \phi_{max} = \frac{\pi H}{L} = \frac{2\pi}{L} A = kA = \frac{\omega^2}{g} A$$

Roll Oscillation in Waves.   When the body is oscillating in waves, the righting moment is given by

$$M = W \, \overline{gm} \, \sin (\theta - \phi) \tag{2.89}$$

where θ, as in previous analysis, is the angle between the buoy center line and the vertical (roll angle) and ϕ is the wave slope. (See Figure 2.17.) For small angles θ and ϕ, expression (2.89) reduces to $M = W \overline{gm}(\theta - \phi)$, and the differential equation of motion is given by

$$I_v \ddot{\theta} + W \, \overline{gm} \, (\theta - \phi) = 0$$

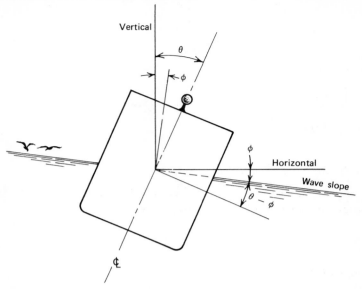

Figure 2.17.

or

$$\ddot{\theta} + \frac{W}{I_v}\,\overline{gm}\,\theta = \frac{W\,\overline{gm}}{I_v}\,\alpha\sin\omega t \tag{2.90}$$

The solution of this differential equation with initial conditions $\theta_0 = \dot{\theta}_0 = 0$ is

$$\theta = \frac{\alpha}{1 - T_0^2/T^2}\left\{\sin\omega t - \frac{T_0}{T}\sin\omega_0 t\right\}$$

where T_0 is the natural period of the buoy and T is the period of the wave. The maximum angle of roll θ_{max} is then

$$\theta_{max} = \frac{\alpha T^2}{T^2 - T_0^2} = \frac{\pi H}{L}\left(\frac{T^2}{T^2 - T_0^2}\right) \tag{2.91}$$

When the natural period T_0 of the body tends to be close to the wave period T, resonance will occur, and large values of θ will be observed. In all practical cases, damping will be present to some extent. The roll response can be studied in model or full scale tests in much the same way as heave response. In actual tests, large angles of roll will be obtained under resonance conditions.

Statistical Response of Floating Bodies to Ocean Waves Excitation

The principles of statistical analysis previously reviewed can be applied to express in terms of statistical results the dynamic response of free floating bodies when excited by random sea ways. Statistical results of interest can be, for example, the average of the one-third highest angles of roll or the most probable heave motion of a buoy of given characteristics when excited by a random sea of known amplitude spectrum.

The approach followed in this statistical analysis is to assume that the response of the body is linear or, in other words, to assume that if measurements of the response were made, their amplitudes would follow a probability density curve similar to the probability density curve of the wave amplitudes. Methods used for the analysis of the waves could then be directly applied for the analysis of the response.

Experience has shown that the heave, roll, vertical velocity, vertical acceleration, and so forth, of free floating bodies often do follow a Rayleigh distribution. In this case, the results obtained from this distribution can be used to statistically describe the response of the free floating body. It will be recalled that these statistical results are expressed in terms of the root mean square value of the record. When response measurements are available, the mean square value $\sqrt{\overline{r^2}}$ can be directly obtained from the record, and the statistical results are readily derived. For example, the average response $\bar{r}$ will be given by $\bar{r} = 0.886 \sqrt{\overline{r^2}}$.

On the other hand, if no measurements are available, and if the response is to be predicted for a given sea spectrum, then the root mean square of the response must be obtained by computation. To this end, the expression of the linear response of the body to a simple harmonic wave of unit amplitude and frequency, ω, is first established. This expression, called the Response Amplitude Operator (RAO) is usually a function $Y(\omega)$ of the different physical parameters considered in the equation of motion of particular interest and of the angular frequency ω. For example, the Response Amplitude Operator for the heave response of a cylindrical body of constant cross section is given by expression (2.87) as

$$Y(\omega) = \frac{e^{-kD}}{m_v} \frac{\sqrt{\left(c - m'\omega^2\right)^2 + \left(b\omega\right)^2}}{\sqrt{\left(p^2 - \omega^2\right)^2 + 4n^2\omega^2}}$$

The response of the body to a component wave of the spectrum with frequency ω_n will then be given by the response to a unit amplitude wave of frequency ω_n multiplied by the amplitude of the particular component wave, namely by

$$\lim_{d\omega \to 0} Y(\omega_n)\sqrt{S(\omega_n)d\omega}$$

It thus follows that the quantity

$$Y^2(\omega_n)S(\omega_n)d\omega$$

represents the mean square value of the response in the frequency band $d\omega$. The mean square value of the response of all component waves is, therefore, given by

$$\overline{r^2} = \int_0^\infty Y^2(\omega)S(\omega)d\omega = \int_0^\infty R(\omega)d\omega$$

where $R(\omega) = Y^2(\omega)S(\omega)$ is defined as the response spectral density.

Thus, the root mean square of the response can be obtained from the area under the response spectrum, namely

$$\sqrt{\overline{r^2}} = \sqrt{R}$$

where

$$R = \int_0^\infty R(\omega)d\omega$$

For example, if $S(\omega)$ is an amplitude spectrum, then the average response will be given by the product of the constant 0.886 (Table 2.1) and the area under the response spectrum, that is,

$$\bar{r} = 0.886\sqrt{R}$$

The following example illustrates the steps followed in the method.

Example. Most Probable Vertical Acceleration of a Disk Buoy. To a good approximation, a free floating disk buoy of small size follows the wave surface closely. Let this surface be expressed by

$$y = A\cos\omega t$$

where A is the wave amplitude. The buoy vertical acceleration is then given by

$$\ddot{y} = -\omega^2 y$$

The Response Amplitude Operator is, thus,

$$\text{RAO} = \frac{\ddot{y}}{y} = -\omega^2$$

and the square of the RAO is

$$(\text{RAO})^2 = \omega^4$$

If the spectrum $S(\omega)$ of the wave amplitudes is as shown in Figure 2.18a, then the acceleration response spectrum $R(\omega)$ shown in Figure 2.18c will be obtained by multiplying the ordinates of the Response Amplitude Operator squared shown in Figure 2.18b with the ordinates of $S(\omega)$.

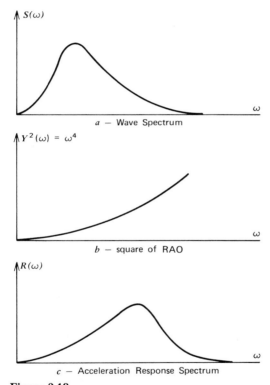

a — Wave Spectrum

b — square of RAO

c — Acceleration Response Spectrum

Figure 2.18.

The most probable acceleration of the disk buoy will then be given by

$$0.707\sqrt{R}$$

where R is the area under the response spectrum (under the curve shown in Figure 2.18c).

In addition to heave and roll, free floating bodies can also experience horizontal translation in the longitudinal (surge) and lateral (sway) directions, and rotational motion around the vertical axis (yaw) and the transverse axis (pitch).

In general, these motions are not independent from each other, and the relatively simple motions of uncoupled heave and roll just studied are limiting cases of the general theory of floating bodies dynamics. For further studies in this subject the reader is referred to the literature (Comstock, 1967, Chapter 9; McCormick, 1973, Chapter 4).

Three

HYDRODYNAMIC FORCES ON CONSTRAINED BODIES

The study of the forces induced by fluid particles on constrained structures will be considered next. The analysis of these forces and of their moments is an important input for the design of the floating structure, and for the selection of its means of attachment to the ocean floor. Forces induced by steady currents and winds are constant while forces induced by waves are time dependent.

3.1. FORCES INDUCED BY STEADY FLOW

Immersed Bodies

Let us first consider a neutrally buoyant body fully immersed in a moving fluid. As indicated in Figure 3.1, fluid particles close to the body surface exert normal and tangential forces on the body. In order to prevent the body from moving downstream, a force equal in magnitude and opposite in direction to the resultant of the forces exerted by the fluid particles, must be applied to the body. This force, which will maintain the body in static equilibrium, is called fluid resistance or drag. Similarly, in order to move a body at constant speed in a fluid at rest, a force equal and opposite to the fluid resistance must be continuously applied to the body.

How the different physical variables of the complex flow problem relate to

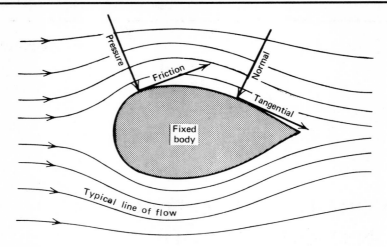

Figure 3.1.

one another can be first investigated with the help of dimensional analysis.

Observations indicate that the resistance, R, of a body immersed in an incompressible fluid does depend on the body geometry and surface roughness and on the density, viscosity, and speed of the fluid.

Therefore, one can generally write:

$$R = K(V^n \rho^x \mu^y D^z) \tag{3.1}$$

where K is a constant of proportionality, V is the speed of the fluid, ρ is the mass density of the fluid, μ is the fluid viscosity, and D is a characteristic dimension of the fluid, which can include surface roughness.

In order to be valid expression (3.1) must be dimensionally homogeneous; that is, the units of R must be the same as the units of the right-hand side of (3.1).

R is a resistance force and, therefore, is expressed in units of the product of mass by acceleration:

$$[R] = \frac{ML}{T^2} = MLT^{-2}$$

where M is the mass, L is the distance, and T is the time. The units of the mass density ρ are given by

$$[\rho] = \frac{M}{L^3} = ML^{-3}$$

The units of the speed V are in turn given by

$$[V] = \frac{L}{T} = LT^{-1}$$

Finally, viscosity units are given by

$$[\mu] = M(TL)^{-1}$$

The dimensional equation of expression (3.1) is, thus,

$$MLT^{-2} = K\left\{(LT^{-1})^n(ML^{-3})^x(MT^{-1}L^{-1})^y L^z\right\}$$

or

$$MLT^{-2} = K\left\{L^n T^{-n} M^x L^{-3x} M^y T^{-y} L^{-y} L^z\right\}$$

Equating the exponents of like dimensional quantities yields

$$1 = x + y$$
$$1 = n - 3x - y + z$$
$$-2 = -n - y$$

There are only three equations for four unknowns; therefore, one must be expressed in terms of the others. Let y be selected for this end, and write

$$x = 1 - y, z = 2 - y, n = 2 - y.$$

Thus, the expression of R given by (3.1) becomes

$$R = KV^{2-y}\rho^{1-y}\mu^y D^{(2-y)}$$

or

$$R = K\left(\frac{\mu}{D\rho V}\right)^y \rho V^2 D^2$$

Since D is any dimension of the body, D^2 may be replaced by any convenient area, A, like the projected area of the body upon a plane normal to the direction of the flow or the total immersed area.

The expression of R then becomes

$$R = K\left(\frac{\mu}{D\rho V}\right)^y A\rho V^2 \qquad (3.2)$$

This result can be rewritten in the more familiar form

$$R = \tfrac{1}{2}\rho CA V^2 \tag{3.3}$$

where

$$C = 2K \left(\frac{\mu}{D\rho V} \right)^y = f\left(\frac{D\rho V}{\mu} \right) \tag{3.4}$$

is defined as the drag coefficient.

Expression (3.3) gives the form of the relation between the resistance force and the physical variables of the problem. It states that the resistance varies as the product of the body area by the fluid density and the square of the fluid speed. No quantitative information can be obtained, however, from this expression unless the value of the drag coefficient, C, is known. Experimental measurements of the drag coefficient are therefore necessary to complement the information gained by dimensional analysis.

Expressions (3.3) and (3.4) can be combined to yield

$$C_D = \frac{R}{1/2\rho A V^2} = f\left(\frac{D\rho V}{\mu} \right)$$

This latter result indicates that the drag coefficient is a function of the dimensionless number $D\rho V/\mu$, called the Reynold's number.

It also suggests the method to follow for establishing the empirical relationship between the Reynold's number and the drag coefficients. All that is necessary is a measure of the ratio of the drag force, R, by the product $\frac{1}{2}\rho A V^2$ for increasing Reynold's numbers. Drag coefficient curves for spheres and flat plates shown in Figures 3.2 and 3.3 are examples of the numerous and widely published empirical results obtained with the help of this method (Hoerner, 1965).

Pressure and friction forces resulting from the normal and tangential stresses exerted by the fluid particles on the body surface are concurrent. Their relative magnitude depends, however, on the nature of the flow past the body. As long as the flow remains smooth, or laminar, shear stresses predominate, and the drag is essentially due to the friction of the fluid on the body immersed surface. On the other hand, when a combination of fluid speed and body shape (blunt bodies) result in the formation of an eddying wake past the body, the drag force is then essentially due to the pressure difference between the upstream and downstream sides of the body.

The resultant force obtained from the integration of the shear and pressure stresses may not necessarily be in the direction of the flow. In that case, the resultant force has two components. The one in the direction of the flow is the drag; the other in the direction normal to the flow is called the

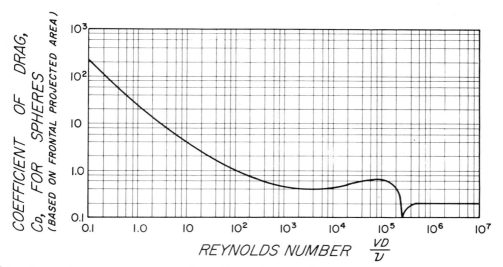

Figure 3.2. Drag coefficient versus Reynolds number for spheres.

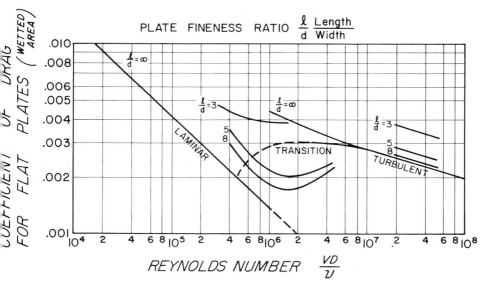

Figure 3.3. Drag coefficient versus Reynolds number for plates.

71

lift and is expressed by

$$L = \tfrac{1}{2}\rho C_L A_L V^2 \tag{3.5}$$

where C_L is the lift coefficient, and A_L is a characteristic area of the body. The mechanism of the various flow patterns that cause drag coefficients, and, therefore, the drag force on a specific body, to vary with Reynold's numbers and body shapes is described in detail in textbooks on fluid mechanics and in the literature (Lamb, 1932; McCormack and Crane, 1973; Pierson, Neumann, and James, 1960).

To summarize, the steps necessary for the computation of the resistance of a body fully immersed in a moving fluid are:

1. Establish the Reynold's number R_e for the particular fluid, fluid speed, and body shape:

$$R_e = \frac{VD\rho}{\mu} = \frac{VD}{\nu} \tag{3.6}$$

    where $\nu = \mu/\rho$ is called kinematic viscosity.
2. Find from appropriate empirical data or curves, the drag coefficient for the particular body shape and Reynold's number.
3. Use expression (3.3) or (3.5) to compute the drag and eventually the lift forces, exercising caution in the selection of the characteristic area (cross section area normal to the flow, or entire "wet" area).

A particular use of flow resistance computation is illustrated in the following example:

Example. Terminal Velocity. When a body heavier than water is left free to sink, it first accelerates under the action of gravity. As its speed increases, its immersed resistance, D, increases. Sooner or later the external forces on the body are equal, and the body sinks with a constant terminal velocity. The balance of the forces at that time, as shown in Figure 3.4, is

$$D = \tfrac{1}{2}\rho C_D A V^2 = W - B$$

where W is the weight of the body and B is the buoyancy of the body. The terminal velocity is, therefore, given by

$$V = \sqrt{\frac{2(W - B)}{\rho C_D A}}$$

When the drag coefficient for the particular body shape is highly sensitive to Reynold's number, then the problem must be solved by trial and error. The

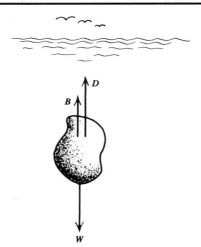

Figure 3.4.

terminal velocity is first assumed, the corresponding Reynold's number and drag coefficient C_D found, and a first computation of the terminal velocity made with this value of C_D. The process is repeated until assumed and computed terminal velocities are found to be sufficiently close.

Surface Floating Bodies

Patterns of spreading waves can be observed downstream of surface buoys set in strong currents. Such wave systems radiate kinetic and potential energy to the far reaches of the ocean. To create and maintain this energy propagation, mechanical work must constantly be done by the buoy through a force applied to the water. The equal and opposite force applied by the water to the buoy is the wave making resistance, sometimes called "wave drag." This additional form of drag interacts in a complex way with friction and pressure drags. As a result, the total flow resistance of surface piercing bodies is again best investigated when using a combination of dimensional analysis and experimentation.

Expression of the Surface Resistance

The physical variables to consider in the flow resistance of bodies floating at the surface are: ρ, mass density of the fluid (ML^{-3}); V, speed of the fluid (LT^{-1}); D, body characteristic dimension (L); μ, fluid viscosity

$(M(TL)^{-1})$; g, acceleration due to gravity (LT^{-2}); and p, absolute pressure per unit area in the fluid $(ML^{-1}T^{-2})$. Following the method of dimensional analysis previously outlined, one can write

$$R = K\left(\rho^a V^b D^c \mu^d g^e p^f\right) \tag{3.7}$$

The corresponding dimensional equation is

$$MLT^{-2} = K\left\{(ML^{-3})^a (LT^{-1})^b L^c (MT^{-1}L^{-1})^d (LT^{-2})^e (ML^{-1}T^{-2})^f\right\}$$

from which

$$a + d + f = 1$$
$$-3a + b + c + e - f = 1$$
$$b + d + 2e + 2f = 2$$

Solving for a, b, and c yields:

$$a = 1 - d - f$$
$$b = 2 - d - 2e - 2f$$
$$c = 2 - d + e$$

The resistance R can, therefore, be written as

$$R = K\rho V^2 D^2 \left(\frac{\mu}{VD\rho}\right)^d \left(\frac{Dg}{V^2}\right)^e \left(\frac{p}{\rho V^2}\right)^f$$

or

$$R = f_1\left(\frac{VD}{\nu}, \frac{V^2}{gD}, \frac{p}{\rho V^2}\right)\rho SV^2 = \tfrac{1}{2}\rho C_T SV^2 \tag{3.8}$$

where S is the wetted surface and C_T is the coefficient of total resistance, an unknown function of the three dimensionless numbers:

$$\frac{VD}{\nu} \qquad \text{Reynold's number}$$

$$\frac{V^2}{gD} \qquad \text{Froude number}$$

$$\frac{p}{\rho V^2} \qquad \text{Euler number}$$

The condition for using an expression of the form

$$R = \tfrac{1}{2}\rho C_T S V^2 \tag{3.9}$$

to compute the resistance of a surface floating body of known shape and size is that the value of C_T be the same for the body as for the model which served as a basis for the empirical derivation of C_T. In other words, the condition of flow similitude will require that the Reynolds, Froude, and Euler numbers be the same for body and model. If this were the case then the equality of Reynolds number would require that

$$\frac{V_p D_p}{\nu_p} = \frac{V_m D_m}{\nu_m}$$

where the subscripts, p, refer to the body (prototype) and the subscripts, m, refer to the model. If the fluid is the same for body and model, then

$$\frac{V_p}{V_m} = \frac{D_m}{D_p} \tag{3.10}$$

Similarly, the equality of the Froude numbers would yield

$$\frac{V_p^2}{g D_p} = \frac{V_m^2}{g D_m}$$

or

$$\frac{V_p}{V_m} = \left(\frac{D_p}{D_m}\right)^{1/2} \tag{3.11}$$

This result is obviously not in agreement with the result obtained in (3.10).

This contradiction suggests the possibility of using different fluids for model and prototype so as to preserve the equality of the Reynold's numbers. Unfortunately most ships and buoys float in water and no fluid exists, as shown in the following example, with a sufficiently small kinematic viscosity to satisfy the condition of Reynold's numbers equality.

Example. The resistance of a float 36 ft long is to be studied from tests performed on a 4 ft model. The float is to be moored in a 4 knot current. What is the condition of equality of Froude and Reynold's numbers for the model and the surface float?

Froude numbers being equal, (3.11) prevails. The model speed will, thus, be

$$V_m = \frac{V_p}{\sqrt{\lambda}}$$

where $\lambda = D_p / D_m$ is the *scale ratio*. Thus $V_m = 4\sqrt{4/36} = 1.33$ knots. For the Reynold's numbers to be equal

$$\frac{V_m D_m}{\nu_m} = \frac{V_p D_p}{\nu_p}$$

must hold. Therefore,

$$\nu_m = \left(\frac{V_m D_m}{V_p D_p} \right) \nu_p = \frac{\left(\frac{4}{3}\right)(4)}{(4)(36)} \nu_p = \frac{\nu_p}{27}$$

This indicates that the fluid of the model basin should have a kinematic viscosity ν_m 27 times smaller than the kinematic viscosity ν_p of water, which is obviously impossible.

An approach to overcome this difficulty is to separate, as suggested by Froude, the total resistance in two components, one the frictional resistance, R_F, and the other, appropriately named by naval architects the residuary resistance, R_R. The total resistance can then be written as

$$R_T = R_F + R_R$$

$$= (C_F + C_R)\tfrac{1}{2}\rho S V^2 = C_T \tfrac{1}{2}\rho S V^2 \qquad (3.12)$$

where C_F is the coefficient of friction resistance and is a function of the Reynold's number only and C_R is the coefficient of residuary resistance and is a function only of the Froude and Euler numbers. If V^2/gD and $p/\rho V^2$ are made to be the same for model and prototype then C_R is the same for both and will be given by

$$C_R = \frac{R_{RP}}{\tfrac{1}{2}\rho S_p V_p^2} = \frac{R_{RM}}{\tfrac{1}{2}\rho S_m V_m^2}$$

from which

$$\frac{R_{RP}}{R_{RM}} = \frac{S_p V_p^2}{S_m V_m^2} \qquad (3.13)$$

The bodies being geometrically similar, the areas S_m and S_p are given by

$$S_p = \alpha D_p^2$$

$$S_m = \alpha D_m^2$$

where α is a constant of proportionality, and thus

$$\frac{S_p}{S_m} = \frac{D_p^2}{D_m^2} = \lambda^2 \tag{3.14}$$

Furthermore, when body and model have the same Froude number,

$$\frac{V_p^2}{V_m^2} = \frac{D_p}{D_m} = \lambda \tag{3.15}$$

Results (3.14) and (3.15) inserted in (3.13) yield

$$R_{RP} = \lambda^3 R_{RM} \tag{3.16}$$

Thus, finally the total resistance of the body is given by

$$R_T = \tfrac{1}{2}\rho C_F S_p V_p^2 + \lambda^3 R_{RM} \tag{3.17}$$

Model Testing

In order to predict the resistance of full scale prototypes, tests are usually performed on models of similar shape but smaller dimensions. The procedure for such tests is summarized as follows:

1. Establish a scale ratio $\lambda = D_p / D_m$.
2. Determine the fluid speed relative to the model, using

$$V_m = V_p \lambda^{-\frac{1}{2}}$$

3. Tow the model at that speed, and measure the total resistance on the model R_{TM}.
4. Compute the Reynold's number for the model and the corresponding frictional resistance on the model

$$R_{FM} = \tfrac{1}{2}\rho C_{FM} S_M V_M^2$$

5. Compute the residuary resistance of the model

$$R_{RM} = R_{TM} - R_{FM}$$

6. Compute the residuary resistance of the prototype

$$R_{RP} = \lambda^3 R_{RM}$$

7. Establish the Reynold's number for the prototype and the corresponding frictional resistance on the prototype

$$R_{FP} = \tfrac{1}{2}\rho C_{FP} S_P V_P^2$$

8. The total resistance of the prototype is then obtained from

$$R_{TP} = R_{RP} + R_{FP}$$

Theoretical analysis of wave drag has progressed considerably. However, the semiempirical approach just described, of establishing the resistance of ship hulls and other floating bodies by performing scale model tests in towing basins and pressure variable water tunnels, is still very much in use.

3.2. FORCES INDUCED BY WAVES

A fixed object immersed in an oscillatory flow like a constrained structure in a seaway experiences inertial as well as drag forces. The total force at any instant is the vectorial sum of these two forces.

Inertial Force On A Fixed Object

The inertial force on a fixed structure is obtained from Newton's law and is given by

$$\vec{F} = m_v \vec{a}$$

where m_v is the virtual mass of the fluid, $\vec{a}$ is the acceleration of the fluid past the structure and is in turn given by $\vec{a} = D\vec{V}/Dt$ where $\vec{V}$, the velocity field, is a function of time and space. The virtual mass of the fluid is the mass, m, of the fluid displaced by the structure plus the added mass, m', due to the acceleration of the entrained water. (This requires some reflection. Perhaps thinking of the force needed to accelerate a neutrally buoyant body of the same form as the structure in a fluid at rest, will help visualizing the two components of the virtual mass.)

Thus, m_v, the virtual mass of the fluid flowing past the structure, is given by

$$m_v = \rho_F \mathrm{Vol}(1 + C_m) \tag{3.18}$$

where ρ_F is the mass density of the fluid (slugs/ft^3), Vol is the volume of fluid displaced by the object (ft^3), and C_m is the added mass coefficient as previously defined. The inertial force is often expressed by

$$\vec{F}_i = \rho_F C_i (\text{Vol}) \frac{D\vec{V}}{Dt}$$

where $C_i = 1 + C_m$ is defined as the coefficient of inertia. For example, in unidirectional flow, the coefficient of inertia would be 1.5 for a sphere and 2.0 for a cylinder. Actual values of coefficients of inertia for bodies of different shapes when immersed in an oscillatory flow have been investigated and published by a number of authors (Ippen, 1966; Myers et al., 1969; Yamomoto, Nath, and Sloka, 1973).

The expression for the velocity field $\vec{V}$ and the acceleration $D\vec{V}/Dt$ depends on the wave theory used for the particular application. The convective terms of the acceleration can be neglected if they turn out to be much smaller than the local acceleration term $\partial \vec{V}/\partial t$.

Drag Force On A Fixed Object

The drag force on a fixed object is given by

$$\vec{F}_D = \tfrac{1}{2} C_D \rho_F S |\vec{V}| \vec{V} \tag{3.19}$$

where $|\vec{V}|\vec{V}$ is introduced in place of V^2 in order to keep the proper sign for the drag force, and C_D, ρ_F, S have the significance previously established. The value of C_D obtained for steady unidirectional flow is often used in oscillatory flow applications because of lack of experimental data.

Forces and Moments Induced by Planar Gravity Waves

The horizontal and vertical components of wave induced forces are given by

$$\vec{F}_H = \rho_F \left[C_{iH} \text{Vol} \frac{D\vec{u}}{Dt} + \tfrac{1}{2} C_{DH} S_H |\vec{u}| \vec{u} \right] \tag{3.20}$$

$$\vec{F}_V = \rho_F \left[C_{iV} \text{Vol} \frac{D\vec{w}}{Dt} + \tfrac{1}{2} C_{DV} S_V |\vec{w}| \vec{w} \right] \tag{3.21}$$

where C_{iH} and C_{iV} are the horizontal and vertical coefficients of inertia and C_{DH} and C_{DV} the horizontal and vertical coefficients of drag.

For simple planar gravity waves in deep water the horizontal and vertical components of speed and acceleration of the water particles are given by

$$\vec{u} = \frac{Ag}{\omega} ke^{-kz} \sin(kx - \omega t)\vec{i}$$

$$\vec{w} = \frac{Ag}{\omega} ke^{-kz} \cos(kx - \omega t)\vec{k}$$

$$\frac{D\vec{u}}{Dt} \cong \frac{\partial \vec{u}}{\partial t} = -Ag\,ke^{-kz}\cos(kx - \omega t)\vec{i} \qquad (3.22)$$

$$\frac{D\vec{w}}{Dt} \cong \frac{\partial \vec{w}}{\partial t} = Ag\,ke^{-kz}\sin(kx - \omega t)\vec{k} \qquad (3.23)$$

When the object is small compared to the wave size, then the z and x dependence in the expressions for the speed and acceleration can be neglected, and the vertical and horizontal components of the wave induced force are then given directly by (3.20) and (3.21). In large structures the z and x dependence can no longer be ignored and results must be found by integration.

Example. Find the expression of the maximum horizontal component of the inertial force induced by a simple harmonic wave on a rigidly moored spar buoy of constant circular cross section (Figure 3.5).

Solution. The maximum horizontal component of inertial force on an elementary volume of the spar buoy is given by

$$dF_{iH} = (dm)_v \left.\frac{\partial u}{\partial t}\right|_{\text{max}}$$

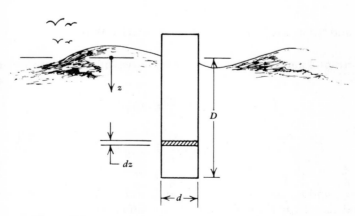

Figure 3.5.

where $(dm)_v$ the virtual mass of the fluid flowing past the elementary volume is given by

$$(dm_v) = \rho_F C_{iH} \frac{\pi}{4} d^2 dz, \qquad C_{iH} = 2$$

$$(dm_v) = \rho_F \frac{\pi}{2} d^2 dz$$

and $\partial u / \partial t$ is the horizontal component of the water particles acceleration. From (2.23)

$$u = \frac{Agk}{\omega} e^{-kz} \sin(kx - \omega t)$$

Therefore,

$$\frac{\partial u}{\partial t} = -Ag\, ke^{-kz} \cos(kx - \omega t)$$

and

$$\left. \frac{\partial u}{\partial t} \right|_{max} = Ag\, ke^{-kz}$$

The elementary force is, therefore,

$$dF_{iH} = \rho_F \frac{\pi}{2} d^2 Ag\, ke^{-kz} dz$$

The total force F_{iH} is obtained from the integration of the elementary force over the entire immersed volume, that is,

$$F_{iH}\big|_{max} = \rho_F \frac{\pi}{2} d^2 Ag \int_{z=0}^{z=D} e^{-kz} k\, dz$$

$$= \rho_F \frac{\pi}{2} d^2 Ag \left[1 - e^{-kD} \right]$$

Introducing the result

$$kg = \omega^2$$

obtained in (2.21), the force $F_{iH}\big|_{max}$ can be expressed as a function of the angular frequency, ω, as

$$F_{iH}\big|_{max} = \rho_F \frac{\pi}{2} d^2 Ag \left\{ 1 - e^{-\omega^2 D / g} \right\}$$

The moments of the horizontal and vertical forces with respect to a reference point $P(x_0, z_0)$ are given by

$$M_H = \int_{z=z_0}^{z=z} F_H z \, dz \tag{3.24}$$

$$M_V = \int_{x=x_0}^{x=x} F_V x \, dx \tag{3.25}$$

and the center of application of these forces given by

$$\bar{x} = \frac{M_V}{F_V} \tag{3.26}$$

$$\bar{z} = \frac{M_H}{F_H} \tag{3.27}$$

The detailed study of wave induced forces on fixed objects is much more complex and more difficult than the elementary and introductory concepts just reviewed. It often requires sophisticated experimentation and advanced statistical analysis. Different wave theories must be formulated for shallow water and breaking waves. The incidence of mooring line compliance, resonance conditions, and vibration induced by Karman vortices and their resulting side forces are related problems which must also be investigated.

Statistical Analysis of Forces on Constrained Structures

The principles of statistical analysis previously outlined can be used when investigating the forces induced by irregular seaways on constrained structures and floats. As usual one must recognize that this method can be used only when the relationship between the response and the forcing function is linear. The following example illustrates this approach.

Example. A cylindrical spar buoy is rigidly moored in a seaway of known spectrum $S(\omega)$. What steps should be followed to compute the average, the significant, and the most probable value of the horizontal component of the inertial force induced by the waves on the moored buoy?

Solution. The steps could be as follows:

1. First obtain an expression $F_{iH}(\omega)$ of the maximum horizontal component of inertial force induced by a wave of amplitude A and frequency ω

$$F_{iH}(\omega) = \int_0^D m_v a(z, \omega) \, dz$$

where D is the buoy draft, m_v is the virtual mass of the water, and $a(z, \omega)$ is the acceleration of the water.

2. With the help of the result thus obtained, establish the response amplitude operator $Y(\omega)$

$$Y(\omega) = \frac{F_{iH}(\omega)}{A}$$

3. Obtain the force spectrum

$$R(\omega) = Y(\omega)^2 S(\omega)$$

4. Compute the average, the significant, the most probable value of the inertial force, using

$$F = K\sqrt{R}$$

where K is the appropriate constant as previously defined and R is the area under the force response spectrum.

Linear Approximation of Drag Forces in Harmonic Motion

In this approximation the assumption is made that the actual nonlinear drag force and the equivalent linear damping force dissipate the same amount of energy per cycle.

The amount of energy, E, dissipated per cycle by any force, F, is given by

$$E = \int_0^T dE = \int_0^T F \, dl = \int_0^T FV \, dt$$

In the case of an harmonic motion,

$$x = X_0 \sin \omega t$$

the speed, V, is given by

$$V = \frac{dx}{dt} = \omega X_0 \cos \omega t$$

The energy dissipated over a cycle by a drag force, D, of the form

$$D = \tfrac{1}{2} \rho C_D A V^2 = B V^2$$

with

$$B = \tfrac{1}{2} \rho C_D A$$

is, therefore,

$$E = \int_0^T B V^3 \, dt = 4 \int_0^{T/4} B \omega^3 X_0^3 (\cos \omega t)^3 \, dt$$

or

$$E = \frac{8}{3} B X_0^3 \omega^2$$

The energy dissipated over a cycle by the equivalent damping force, D', of the form

$$D' = bV$$

where b is the linearized damping coefficient is

$$E = \int_0^T b V^2 \, dt = \int_0^T b \omega^2 X_0^2 (\cos \omega t)^2 \, dt$$

$$E = \pi b X_0^2 \omega$$

The two energies being assumed equal

$$\pi b X_0^2 \omega = \frac{8}{3} B X_0^3 \omega^2$$

from which

$$b = \frac{8}{3\pi} B X_0 \omega = \frac{4}{3\pi} \rho C_D A X_0 \omega \tag{3.28}$$

It should be noted that

$$b = b(X_0, \omega).$$

PART I
EXERCISES

EXERCISE 1
Using formula (1.4) express in terms of its "dry" weight the resultant force on a body immersed in water if

    (1)   the body is balsa wood $\rho = 7 \ \text{lb/ft}^3$

    (2)   the body is aviation gasoline $\rho = 45 \ \text{lb/ft}^3$

    (3)   the body is aluminum $\rho = 165 \ \text{lb/ft}^3$

EXERCISE 2
A dead weight anchor is to be used on a mooring line. A vertical anchoring force of 4000 lb will hold the mooring in place. Make a price estimation for two anchors: one of concrete, one of cast iron. The cost of concrete is $20/yd^3$; the density of the concrete is $150 \ \text{lb/ft}^3$; the cost of the cast iron is $.10/lb; and the density of the cast iron is $442 \ \text{lb/ft}^3$.

EXERCISE 3
A pulp log floats on its long side (Figure I.1), but a slice of this log floats on its flat side (Figure I.2). Both are cylinders with the same diameter, d, and specific gravity, γ, yet the stable position of each depends on its aspect ratio, that is, on the ratio of its height, h, to the diameter, d. Prove that the critical aspect ratio $(h/d)_c$ for which a small displacement of the cylinder from its

Figure I.1.

85

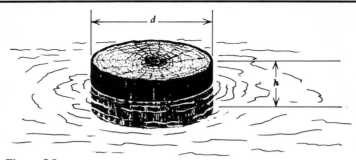

Figure I.2.

"axis vertical" position will result in a change to the horizontal and stable position, is given by

$$\left(\frac{h}{d}\right)_c = \frac{0.354}{\sqrt{(\gamma/\gamma_F)(1-\gamma/\gamma_F)}}$$

where γ is the specific gravity of wood cylinder and γ_F is the specific gravity of fluid.

EXERCISE 4
The amplitude of a regular deep sea swell is 10 ft and its length is 100 ft. *Find:* The wave period, the wave celerity, the location and magnitude of maximum wave slope; the magnitude and location of maximum horizontal and vertical components of particle speed and acceleration at the wave surface; and the pressure below the crest and the trough of the wave at a depth $z = 20$ ft below the mean level.

EXERCISE 5
Show that the celerity and the wave length of a regular (harmonic) wave of period T is given by

$$C \cong 1.6\,T \,\text{m/sec}$$

$$L \cong 1.6\,T^2 \,\text{m}$$

EXERCISE 6
Using the probability density function of wave amplitudes

$$p(r) = \frac{2r}{\overline{r^2}} e^{-r^2/\overline{r^2}}$$

where r is the wave amplitude, $p(r)\,dr$ is the probability that a wave amplitude lies in the range r and $r + dr$, and $\overline{r^2}$ is the mean square value of the wave amplitudes in the record, prove that the average wave amplitude $\bar{r}$ is given by

$$\bar{r} = 0.886\sqrt{\overline{r^2}}$$

where $\sqrt{\overline{r^2}}$ is the RMS value of the wave amplitudes.

EXERCISE 7

Consider a cylindrical buoy supporting a spherical payload as shown in Figure I.3. Using weights and dimensions indicated, find

1. the water level;
2. the righting moment for an angle of two degrees from the vertical;
3. the natural frequency of heave;
4. the natural frequency of roll (unresisted rolling).

Assume homogeneous distribution of mass in the cylinder and the sphere. Neglect the mass of the tower supporting the payload. Assume the virtual mass to be 1.2 times the mass of the buoy, and the virtual moment of inertia to be 1.2 times the buoy moment of inertia.

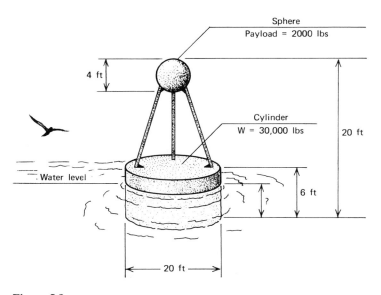

Figure I.3.

EXERCISE 8

Given the wave *slope* spectrum shown in Figure I.4, obtain the corresponding height spectrum and compute the significant acceleration (average of one-third of the highest values) of a small object closely following the surface. The wave surface is expressed by

$$y = \frac{H}{2} \cos(\omega t - kx)$$

H is the wave height and $\omega = 2\pi f$ is the angular frequency.

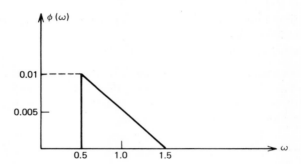

Figure I.4.

EXERCISE 9

Study of spar buoy heave response.

A spar buoy has the dimensions and weight shown in Figure I.5.

1. Find the amount of steel ballast needed for the water line to be 12 ft from either end of the 24 ft mast.
2. Find the natural period of heave taking into account the mass of the buoy structure, the mass of the steel ballast, the mass of the water stored in the water ballast tank, and the added mass. (Assume added mass of buoy hull cylinder to be the same as added mass of a sphere of same diameter. For circular plates use added mass

$$m' = \frac{8}{3} \rho_F a^3$$

where a is the plate diameter and $\rho_F = 2$ slugs/ft³).
3. Use the linearized damping coefficient, b,

$$b = \frac{4}{3\pi} \rho X_0 \omega \sum_n A_n C_n$$

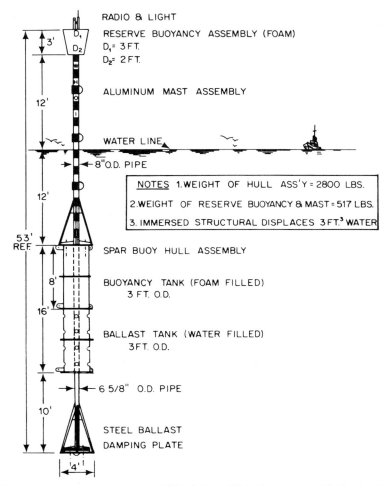

RADIO & LIGHT

RESERVE BUOYANCY ASSEMBLY (FOAM)
$D_1 = 3$ FT.
$D_2 = 2$ FT.

ALUMINUM MAST ASSEMBLY

3'

12'

WATER LINE

8"O.D. PIPE

NOTES 1. WEIGHT OF HULL ASS'Y = 2800 LBS.
2. WEIGHT OF RESERVE BUOYANCY & MAST = 517 LBS.
3. IMMERSED STRUCTURAL DISPLACES 3 FT.³ WATER

12'

53'
REF.

SPAR BUOY HULL ASSEMBLY

8'

BUOYANCY TANK (FOAM FILLED)
3 FT. O.D.

16'

BALLAST TANK (WATER FILLED)
3 FT. O.D.

6 5/8" O.D. PIPE

10'

STEEL BALLAST
DAMPING PLATE

4'

Figure I.5.   53 ft spar bouy—1972—Woods Hole Oceanographic Institution.

to determine the heave response when the buoy is excited by simple harmonic waves with amplitudes of 7 and 20 ft and periods of 12 sec and equal to the natural period.

4.   Compute the average value of the damping coefficient.

$$\bar{b} = \frac{1}{5} \sum_{i=1}^{i=5} b_i$$

where

$$b_i = \frac{4}{3\pi} \rho X_i \omega_i \sum_n A_n C_n$$

and X_i and ω_i are the average wave amplitudes and periods as given in Table 2.3 for winds of 5, 10, 20, 30, and 40 knots.

5. Use a Pierson–Moskowitz double height spectrum

$$S_{2H}(\omega) = \frac{135}{\omega^5} e^{-9.7 \times 10^4 / V_K^4 \omega^4} \ \ \text{ft}^2\text{-sec}$$

with $V_K = 40$ knots together with the value of $\bar{b}$ established in (4) to obtain (a) the significant heave response, (b) the average heave response, (c) the most frequent heave response, (d) the average of the 1/10 highest heave responses, and (e) the highest heave in 1000 waves.

EXERCISE 10

1. A 10 ft spherical buoy is ballasted as indicated on the sketch, Figure I.6. Assuming the roll motion of the sphere to follow the linear equation:

$$I_v \ddot{\theta} + b\dot{\theta} + W \overline{gm}\, \theta = \frac{\pi H}{L} W \overline{gm}\, \sin \omega t$$

or

$$\ddot{\theta} + 2n\dot{\theta} + p^2\theta = \alpha p^2 \sin \omega t$$

where $2n = b/I_v$, $Wgm/I_v = p^2$, $\alpha = \pi H/L$, H is the wave height, L is the wave length, I_v is the virtual moment of inertia equal to $1.2I$, I is the moment of inertia with respect to axis through the center of gravity of the buoy, and n/p is the damping ratio equal to 0.25, obtain the roll response amplitude operator of the buoy.

2. Use this RAO and the double roll spectrum derived from the Pierson–Moskowitz double height spectrum

$$S_{2H}(\omega) = \frac{135}{\omega^5} e^{-9.7 \times 10^4 / V_K^4 \omega^4} \ \ \text{ft}^2\text{-sec}$$

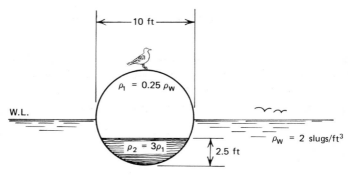

Figure I.6.

to obtain the average angle of roll $\bar{\theta}$, the significant angle of roll $\bar{\theta}_{1/3}$, and the highest roll in 1000 waves for a wind $V_k = 40$ knots.

EXERCISE 11

Compute the acceleration of a bubble of air (sphere of radius a) 10,000 ft deep, first neglecting the added mass, then taking the added mass into account. Repeat the computations when the bubble of air is close to the surface. Compare the results.

$$\text{Density of air at 10,000 ft} \quad = \rho_a = 0.65 \text{ slug/ft}^3$$

$$\text{Density of air at the surface} \quad = \rho_a = 2.4 \times 10^{-3} \text{ slug/ft}^3$$

$$\text{Density of water} \quad = \rho_w \cong \text{constant} = 2 \text{ slug/ft}^3$$

EXERCISE 12

Find the drag force on a plank 10 ft wide by 50 ft long towed in the water at a speed of 4 ft/sec. Find the drag force when the plank is across (normal to) the flow.

EXERCISE 13

What should be the specific gravity of a 3.2 ft diameter sphere for its rate of ascent in sea water at 44°F to be precisely 1.0 ft/sec. Use kinematic viscosity $\nu = 1.6 \times 10^{-5} \text{ ft}^2/\text{sec}$.

EXERCISE 14

A spherical subsurface buoy, 4 ft in diameter and made of syntactic foam (density 42 lb/ft^3), is moored in a current flowing at 2.5 ft/sec. What is the tension at the beginning of the mooring line?

EXERCISE 15

A regular swell is passing over a 1.5 ft diameter sphere held rigidly 34 ft below the "still" surface. The water depth is large enough to permit use of the theory of deep sea harmonic waves. The height of the swell is 6 ft (3 ft amplitude) and the swell period 6 sec. Find the maximum force due to wave action (amplitude and direction) on the sphere and its phase relation to the wave (i.e., when does the maximum occur?).

EXERCISE 16

Derive the expression of the moment about the lowest point of a rigidly moored spar buoy of constant diameter, d, and draft, D, resulting from the maximum horizontal inertial force induced by a regular wave of amplitude, A, and frequency, ω. Express the moment as a function of the frequency, ω.

EXERCISE 17

Study of horizontal forces on a spar buoy. Tethering.

1. Consider the spar buoy of Exercise 9. Assuming a wave amplitude of 10 ft and a period equal to the natural period of heave, compare the maximum horizontal inertial force and the maximum horizontal drag force on the buoy due to particle acceleration and velocity. The buoy is considered to be rigidly held.
2. Find the drag force on the buoy due to a 2 knots current and its point of application.
3. Find the drag force on the buoy due to a 40 knots wind and its point of application.
4. Derive the response amplitude operator for the maximum horizontal inertial force and the response amplitude operator for the moment due to this force.

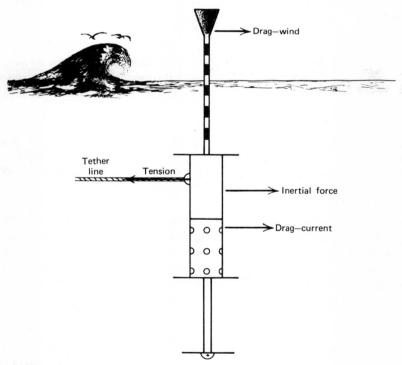

Figure I.7.

5. Use a Pierson–Moskowitz double height spectrum

$$S_{2H}(\omega) = \frac{135}{\omega^5} e^{-9.7 \times 10^4 / V_k^4 \omega^4} \ \text{ft}^2\text{-sec}$$

where $V_k = 40$ knots and the response amplitude operators obtained in (4) to compute the value of (a) significant horizontal inertial force, (b) significant moment due to this force, and (c) point of application of the significant inertial force.

6. Assuming that the spar buoy is tethered horizontally, as shown in Figure I.7, find (a) the tension in the tether line and (b) the point of attachment of the tether line for zero moment on the buoy.

REFERENCES

Attwood, E. L., and H. S. Pengelly. *Theoretical Naval Architecture*, revised edition, Longmans, Green, London, 1953.

Bendat, J. S., and A. G. Piersol. *Random Data: Analysis and Measurement Procedures*, Wiley Interscience, 1971.

Bretschneider, C. L. "Wave Forecasting," *Ocean Industry*, Vol. 2, No. 10, October 1967.

Bretschneider, C. L. "Significant Waves and Wave Spectrum," *Ocean Industry*, Vol. 3, No. 2, February 1968.

Comstock, J. P. (Ed.). *Principles of Naval Architecture*, Chapters VII and IX, The Society of Naval Architects and Marine Engineers, New York, 1967.

Cooper, G. C, and C. D. McGillem. *Methods of Signal and System Analysis*, Holt, Rinehart and Winston, New York, 1967.

Hoerner, S. F. *Fluid Dynamic Drag*, published by the author, 148 Bustead Drive, Midland Park, New Jersey, 1965.

Ippen, A. T. *Estuary and Coastline Hydrodynamics*, Chapters 1, 3, and 4, McGraw-Hill, New York, 1966.

Kinsman, B. *Wind Waves*, Chapters 1, 2, and 3, Prentice Hall, Englewood Cliffs, New Jersey, 1965.

Korvin, B. V., and Kronkovsky. *Theory of Seakeeping*, The Society of Naval Architects and Marine Engineers, New York, 1961.

Lamb, H. *Hydrodynamics*, 6th edition, Cambridge University Press, New York, 1932.

Longuet-Higgins. "On the Statistical Distribution of the Heights of Sea Waves," *Journal of Marine Research*, Vol. XI, p. 245, 1953.

Marks, W. "The Application of Spectral Analysis and Statistics to Seakeeping," Technical & Research Bulletin No. 1-24, The Society of Naval Architects and Marine Engineers, New York, 1963.

McCormack, P. D., and L. Crane. *Physical Fluid Dynamics*, Academic, New York, 1973.

McCormick, M. E. *Ocean Engineering Wave Mechanics*, Wiley, New York, 1973.

Michel, W. H. "How to Calculate Wave Forces and Their Effects," *Ocean Industry*, May and June issues, 1967.

Myers, J. J., et al. *Handbook of Ocean Engineering*, Section 12, McGraw-Hill, New York, 1969.

Neumann, G., and W. T. Pierson. *Principals of Physical Oceanography*, Chapters 12 and 15, Prentice-Hall, Englewood Cliffs, New Jersey, 1966.

Otnes, R. K., and L. Enochson. *Digital Time Series Analysis*, Wiley, New York, 1973.

Patton, K. T., "Tables of Hydrodynamics Mass Factors for Translational Motion," ASME Annual Conference, Winter, 1965.

Shapiro, A. H. *Shape and Flow*, Anchor Books, Doubleday, Garden City, New York, 1961.

Pierson, W. J., G. Neumann, and R. W. James. "Observing and Forecasting Ocean Waves," Hydrographic Office Publication No. 603, 1960.

Simonetti, P. "An Investigation of Various Forms for a Tuned Oceanographic Platform" (unpublished O. E. Thesis), Massachusetts Institute of Technology, Cambridge, Massachusetts, May 1973.

Tucker, M. J. "Analysis of Records of Sea Waves," National Institute of Oceanography, Wormley, England, 1962.

Wiegel, R. L. *Oceanographic Engineering*, Chapter II, Prentice-Hall, Englewood Cliffs, New Jersey, 1964.

Yamomoto, T., J. Nath, and L. Sloka. "Wave Forces on Horizontal Submerged Cylinders," Oregon State University, Corvallis, Oregon, Bulletin No. 47, 1973.

MECHANICS OF MOORING LINES

Chapter

Four

STATICS OF MOORING LINES

Mooring lines are hereby defined as the flexible mechanical members that connect and attach the floating structure to its anchoring points. The statics of mooring lines is the study of the loads and of their resulting effects under steady-state conditions. This study allows one to predict the geometry of the mooring and the steady-state distribution of stresses along the line.

The analysis of cable systems hereafter presented assumes perfect cable flexibility or, in other words, that cables cannot transfer moments.

4.1. STATICS OF SINGLE POINT MOORED BUOY SYSTEMS

The buoy systems hereafter considered are restricted to a very simple configuration: one float, one line, one anchor, and possibly some ancillary equipment. Even for this simple system, the analytical solutions are surprisingly numerous and complex. As in other engineering problems, the validity of their use depends on the degree of correspondence between the real conditions and the stated assumptions. In this respect mooring lines have a number of specific "weighting" factors (length, stretch, weight to drag ratio) that must be taken into account when selecting a method of solution. Figure 4.1 suggests a possible classification of the different static solutions encountered in practice.

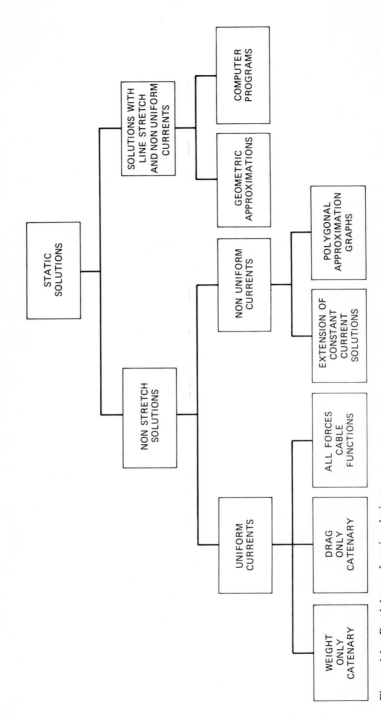

Figure 4.1. Breakdown of static solutions.

Mooring Lines Without Elasticity

In this class of solutions, the elasticity of the mooring line is not considered. Different solutions are obtained for uniform flow and for currents varying with depth.

Constant Currents

Assumptions. (*a*) The cable does not stretch under tension (i.e., elongation can be neglected). (*b*) The current direction has no vertical component. Furthermore, current direction and cable path remain coplanar. (*c*) The current magnitude is constant (i.e., does not vary with depth).

Forces. The forces to consider for the study of mooring lines immersed in steady-state currents are gravity forces, fluid drag, and line tension.

GRAVITY FORCES. The gravity forces may act up or down, the direction being given by the principle of Archimedes. Buoyant parts of buoy systems are the floats and, in certain cases, the mooring line. Nonbuoyant parts are, for example, steel wire rope mooring lines and instrument packages. If only small currents are present, the mooring line of a surface buoy hangs almost vertically from the buoy, the tension at any point in the line being approximately equal to the immersed weight of the line and equipment below that point. Only a small anchor is needed and the amount of water displaced by the surface float nearly equals the total immersed weight of the suspended hardware. In oceanic applications, however, strong currents are often present. Considerable drag forces are then applied to the mooring line, which assumes a new equilibrium configuration. Tension increases and strong anchoring becomes necessary.

The gravity force per unit of length of line is given by

$$P = W - B \quad \text{(lb/ft)} \tag{4.1}$$

where W is the weight per foot of the line and B is the weight of the water displaced by one foot of the line.

FLUID DRAG. The hydrodynamic resistance due to the flow past a cable element of diameter, d, and length, ds, when normal to the flow as shown in Figure 4.2 is given by

$$R ds = \tfrac{1}{2} \rho C_{DN} d V^2 ds \tag{4.2}$$

where C_{DN} is the coefficient of normal drag and V is the current speed. The resistance on a cable element making an angle ϕ with the direction of the flow can be considered to be made of two parts: one normal and one tangential to the cable element.

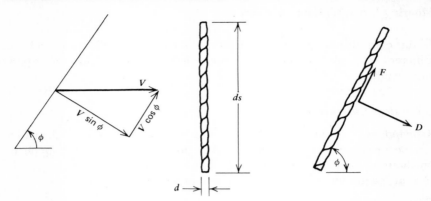

Figure 4.2.

The normal component Dds is then given by

$$Dds = \tfrac{1}{2}\rho C_{DN} d (V_N)^2 ds$$

where $V_N = V\sin\phi$ is the velocity component normal to the cable element, and thus

$$D = \tfrac{1}{2}\rho C_{DN} dV^2 \sin^2\phi$$

$$D = R\sin^2\phi \qquad (4.3)$$

where R is the resistance defined by (4.2). The tangential component Fds is in turn given by

$$Fds = \tfrac{1}{2}\rho C_{DT}\pi dV_T^2 \cos^2\phi \qquad (4.4)$$

where $C_{DT} = \gamma C_{DN}$ is the coefficient of tangential drag, $(\pi d)ds$ is the area "wetted" by longitudinal flow and $V_T = V\cos\phi$ is the velocity component tangential to the cable element.

Thus,

$$F = \tfrac{1}{2}\rho\gamma C_{DN} (\pi d) V^2 \cos^2\phi$$

$$F = \pi\gamma R \cos^2\phi \qquad (4.5)$$

Normal and tangential drag coefficients vary with Reynold's number and type of cable. For a smooth cable, and below the critical Reynold's number, the value of C_{DN} is between 0.9 and 1.2. For a rough or stranded cable, this value increases to 1.4. Finally, if strumming induced by vortices is present, a value as high as 1.8 may be appropriate.

Figure 4.3 shows the normal ($\phi = 90°$) and tangential ($\phi = 0$) drag

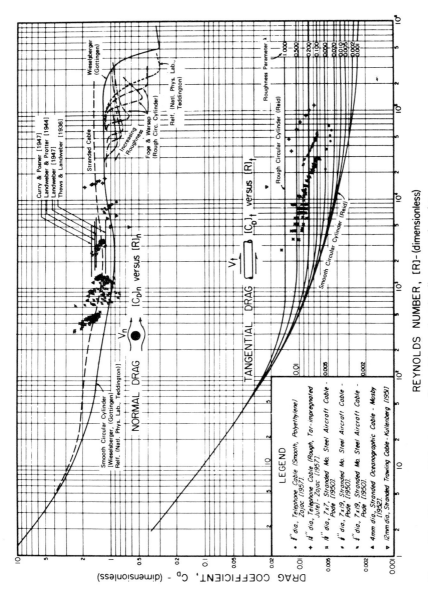

Figure 4.3. Drag coefficient versus Reynolds number for flow normal and tangential to smooth and rough circular cylinders (Wilson, 1960).

101

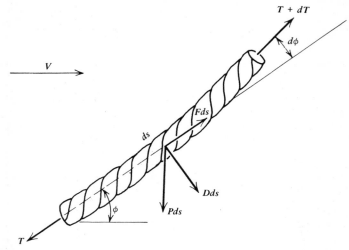

Figure 4.4. Forces on cable element; T, tension; dT, change of tension over cable element length, ds; Dds, normal pressure drag on cable element; Fds, tangential friction drag on cable element; Pds, gravity force per length, ds; ϕ, angle with flow direction, $\vec{V}$; $d\phi$, change in angle ϕ over cable element length; and ds, length of cable element.

coefficients for different types of cylinders and cables. It may be seen that the value of the tangential drag coefficient is but a small percent of the value of the normal drag coefficient, that is,

$$0.01 \leqslant \gamma \leqslant 0.03$$

Equations of Static Equilibrium. The static forces on a cable element of length ds are shown in Figure 4.4. Under static equilibrium, the vector sum of these forces must be zero. Applying this condition to the normal and tangential components of these forces yields:
In the normal direction:

$$(T+dT)\sin d\phi - Dds - P\cos\phi ds = 0$$

or for $\sin d\phi \cong d\phi$, $dTd\phi \cong 0$

$$Td\phi = (D + P\cos\phi)ds \tag{4.6}$$

In the tangential direction,

$$-T+(T+dT)\cos d\phi - P\sin\phi ds + Fds = 0$$

or

$$dT = (P\sin\phi - F)ds \qquad (4.7)$$

Integration of the Equilibrium Equations

CASE I. HEAVY AND SHORT CABLES (CATENARY). Consider a short mooring line made of heavy material (chain, steel wire rope) with a drag force applied at the buoy end only. In that case, the gravity force is predominant and the resistance terms of the cable equilibrium equation can be neglected, that is,

$$P \gg D \text{ and } F$$

Expressions (4.6) and (4.7) are therefore reduced to

$$Td\phi = P\cos\phi\, ds \qquad (4.8)$$

and

$$dT = P\sin\phi\, ds \qquad (4.9)$$

Therefore,

$$\frac{dT}{T} = \tan\phi\, d\phi$$

Integrating from $\phi = 0$ to $\phi = \phi$ yields

$$\log\frac{T}{T_0} = \int_{\phi=0}^{\phi=\phi} \tan\phi\, d\phi = \log\sec\phi$$

or

$$T_H = T\cos\phi = T_0 \qquad (4.10)$$

where T_0 is the tension at the origin $\phi = 0$ (See Figure 4.5). This result shows that the horizontal component of the tension, T_H, is *constant*. Inserting (4.10) in (4.8) yields

$$\frac{T_0 d\phi}{\cos^2\phi} = Pds$$

Integrating over the same domain gives

$$T_0\tan\phi = Ps \qquad (4.11)$$

or

$$T_V = T\sin\phi = Ps \qquad (4.12)$$

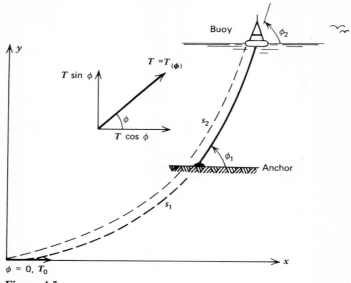

Figure 4.5.

This result shows that the vertical component of the tension, T_V, equals the immersed weight of the cable length between the origin and the point $P(\phi)$. The tension at this point is given by

$$T = \left(T_H^2 + T_V^2 \right)^{1/2}$$

$$T = \left(T_0^2 + (Ps)^2 \right)^{1/2} \tag{4.13}$$

The coordinates x and y of any point $P(\phi)$ along the mooring line are obtained in the following way:

$$x = \int dx = \int ds \cos \phi$$

From (4.10)

$$\cos \phi = \frac{T_0}{T}$$

From (4.13)

$$\frac{T_0}{T} = \left[1 + \left(\frac{Ps}{T_0} \right)^2 \right]^{-1/2}$$

Therefore,

$$dx = \frac{ds}{\sqrt{1 + (Ps/T_0)^2}}$$

Integrating,

$$x = \int_0^{s=s} dx = \frac{T_0}{P} \sinh^{-1}\left(\frac{Ps}{T_0}\right) \tag{4.14}$$

From this result,

$$s = \frac{T_0}{P} \sinh\left(\frac{Px}{T_0}\right) \tag{4.15}$$

Finally,

$$\frac{dx}{dy} = \tan\phi$$

From (4.11)

$$\tan\phi = \frac{Ps}{T_0}$$

Thus,

$$dy = \left(\frac{P}{T_0} s\right) dx$$

Using (4.15)

$$dy = \sinh\frac{Px}{T_0} dx$$

Integrating again,

$$y = \int dy = \frac{T_0}{P}\left[\cosh\left(\frac{Px}{T_0}\right) - 1\right] \tag{4.16}$$

In summary, the coordinates of any point along the mooring line are given by (4.14) and (4.16), the arc length from the origin to this point is given by (4.15), and the tension at that point, by (4.13). Results for mooring lines with an anchoring point not at the origin can be obtained from the values computed at the end points of the line (for example $s = s_2 - s_1$).

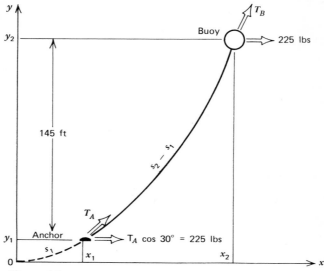

Figure 4.6.

Example. (See Figure 4.6). A surface float is moored with a chain weighing 2.5 lb/ft. The depth is 145 ft and the drag on the float is 225 lb. What should be the minimum length of chain if the allowable maximum angle of the mooring line with the horizontal is 30° at the anchor? What is then the tension at the anchor and at the buoy? What is the excursion of the buoy downstream?

Solution.

(1)   Horizontal tension = 225 lb = constant = T_0.
(2)   Tension at anchor = 225/cos 30° = 260 lb = T_A.
(3)   The vertical component of the tension at the anchor equals the weight of the fictitious chain to the origin; therefore,

$$s_1 = \frac{T_A \sin \phi_A}{P} = \frac{(260)^{1/2}}{2.5} = 52 \text{ ft}$$

(4)   This result is used to find x_1. From (4.14)

$$x_1 = \frac{225}{2.5} \sinh^{-1} \frac{130}{225} = 49.5 \text{ ft}$$

(5)   Using (4.16)

$$y_2 - y_1 = 145 \text{ ft} = \frac{225}{2.5}\left[\cosh \frac{2.5}{225} x_2 - \cosh \frac{(2.5)(49.5)}{225} \right]$$

from which

$$x_2 = 151 \text{ ft}$$

(6)   The buoy excursion downstream is thus

$$x_2 - x_1 = 101.5 \text{ ft}$$

(7)   From (4.16)

$$s_2 = \frac{225}{2.5} \sinh \frac{(2.5)(151)}{225} = 231 \text{ ft}$$

The required length of chain to the anchor is therefore,

$$s = s_2 - s_1 = 231 - 52 = 179 \text{ ft}$$

(8)   The vertical component of tension at the buoy equals the weight of the chain from the buoy to the origin, that is,

$$T_B \sin \phi_B = P s_2 = (231)(2.5) = 577 \text{ lb}$$

Note: The same result can be obtained by adding the weight of the actual length of chain and the vertical component of the tension at the anchor.

$$T_{BV} = (2.5)(179) + 130 = 577 \text{ lb}$$

(9)   Tension at the buoy is, therefore,

$$T_B = \left[(225)^2 + (577)^2 \right]^{1/2} = 618 \text{ lb}$$

CASE II. NEUTRALLY BUOYANT CABLES. The gravity force, P, and *tangential* drag, F, terms can be neglected for neutrally buoyant cables of relatively short length. In that case, Eq. (4.6) and (4.7) reduce to

$$T d\phi = D ds$$

or using (4.3)

$$T d\phi = R \sin^2 \phi \, ds \qquad (4.17)$$

and

$$\frac{dT}{ds} = 0 \qquad (4.18)$$

From (4.18)

$$T = T_0 = \text{constant} \qquad (4.19)$$

This result indicates that if the tension is known at some point in the line, then it is known at all points. From (4.17) and (4.19)

$$ds = \frac{T_0 \, d\phi}{R \sin^2 \phi}$$

The horizontal and vertical projections of the cable elements are

$$dx = ds \cos \phi = \frac{T_0}{R} \frac{\cos \phi}{\sin^2 \phi} \, d\phi$$

$$dy = ds \sin \phi = \frac{T_0}{R} \frac{d\phi}{\sin \phi}$$

The integral from one point $P_1(\phi)$ to another point $P_2(\phi)$ of these three differential equations give the length of the cable, and the horizontal and vertical distances between the two points.

The results are

$$s = \frac{T_0}{R} \left\{ \cot \phi_1 - \cot \phi_2 \right\} \tag{4.20}$$

$$x = -\frac{T_0}{R} \left\{ \operatorname{cosec} \phi_2 - \operatorname{cosec} \phi_1 \right\} \tag{4.21}$$

$$y = \frac{T_0}{R} \left\{ \log_e \left(\tan \frac{\phi_2}{2} \right) - \log_e \left(\tan \frac{\phi_1}{2} \right) \right\} \tag{4.22}$$

Example. (See Figure 4.7). A surface buoy is to be set in a uniform current of two knots with a 0.5 in. neutrally buoyant mooring line. The drag on the buoy is estimated to be 400 lb. The depth of the water is 656 ft. If the tension is not to exceed 1000 lb, what is the minimum length of line required? (Use $C_{DN} = 1.5$.)

Solution.

1.   A free body diagram at the buoy gives

$$1000 \cos \phi_2 = 400$$

Thus, $\phi_2 = 66°24'$, $\phi_2 / 2 = 33°12'$

2.   When the cable is normal to the flow, the hydrodynamic resistance per unit of cable length, R, is given by

$$R = \frac{1}{2} \rho C_{DN} dV^2 = \frac{1}{2} \frac{64}{32} (1.5) \frac{1}{2} \left(\frac{1}{12} \right) (3.38)^2$$

$$= 0.713 \text{ lb/ft}$$

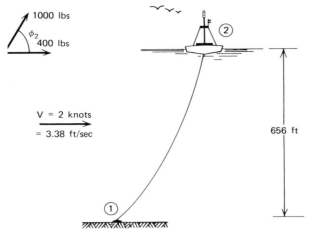

Figure 4.7.

3. From (4.22)

$$y = 656 = \frac{1000}{0.713} \log_e \frac{\tan \dfrac{\phi_2}{2}}{\tan \dfrac{\phi_1}{2}}$$

therefore,

$$\frac{\tan \dfrac{\phi_2}{2}}{\tan \dfrac{\phi_1}{2}} = \text{Napierian antilog} \frac{656(0.713)}{1000}$$

The antilog of $0.468 = 1.6$. Thus

$$\tan \frac{\phi_1}{2} = \frac{\tan(33°12')}{1.6} = 0.408$$

$$\frac{\phi_1}{2} = \tan^{-1}(0.408) = 22°12'$$

$$\phi_1 = 44°24'$$

4. From (4.20)

$$s = \frac{1000}{0.713} \left[\cot(44°24') - \cot(66°24') \right]$$

$$s = 1400(1.024 - 0.437) = 820 \text{ ft}$$

CASE III. ALL FORCES CONSIDERED—CABLE FUNCTIONS.   When the cables are long and gravity forces are important, all static forces must be considered. When this is done, the equilibrium differential equations (4.6) and (4.7) can no longer be explicitly integrated and numerical integration techniques must be used.

Tables of integration results have been obtained and published, different expression for the tangential component of the hydrodynamic drag leading to different tables.

1.   Constant Tangential Drag. Pode's Analysis.   In 1951, Pode (1951) published a set of valuable tables covering, among other applications, the problem of single point moored structures. In this analysis, the tangential component of drag, F, is considered constant. The resulting equilibrium differential equations are then

$$dT = (P \sin \phi - F) \, ds \tag{4.23}$$

$$T d\phi = (R \sin^2 \phi + P \cos \phi) \, ds \tag{4.24}$$

The ratio of these two equations is

$$\frac{dT}{T} = \frac{\dfrac{P}{R} \sin \phi - \dfrac{F}{R}}{\sin^2 \phi + \dfrac{P}{R} \cos \phi} \, d\phi$$

Integrating the expression from a point $P(\phi_0)$ to a point $P(\phi)$, the result is

$$\frac{T}{T_0} = \exp \int_{\phi_0}^{\phi} \frac{\dfrac{P}{R} \sin \phi - \dfrac{F}{R}}{\sin^2 \phi + \dfrac{P}{R} \cos \phi} \, d\phi \tag{4.25}$$

T being the tension at $P(\phi)$ and T_0 at $P(\phi_0)$. Furthermore from (4.24)

$$ds = \frac{T d\phi}{R \sin^2 \phi + P \cos \phi}$$

or, using the value of T obtained in (4.25)

$$ds = \frac{T_0 \exp \displaystyle\int_{\phi_0}^{\phi} \dfrac{\dfrac{P}{R} \sin \phi - \dfrac{F}{R}}{\sin^2 \phi + \dfrac{P}{R} \cos \phi} \, d\phi}{R \left(\sin^2 \phi + \dfrac{P}{R} \cos \phi \right)}$$

which, when integrated, gives

$$
\frac{Rs}{T_0} = \int_{\phi_0}^{\phi} \frac{\exp \int_{\phi_0}^{\phi} \dfrac{\dfrac{P}{R}\sin\phi - \dfrac{F}{R}}{\sin^2\phi + \dfrac{P}{R}\cos\phi}\, d\phi}{\sin^2\phi + \dfrac{P}{R}\cos\phi}\, d\phi
\tag{4.26}
$$

Using

$$
dx = ds \cos\phi
$$

$$
dy = ds \sin\phi
$$

the expressions for the horizontal distance and the vertical distance between the two points $P(\phi_0)$ and $P(\phi)$ at the limits of the integration domain are

$$
\frac{Rx}{T_0} = \int_{\phi_0}^{\phi} \frac{\exp \int_{\phi_0}^{\phi} \dfrac{\dfrac{P}{R}\sin\phi - \dfrac{F}{R}}{\sin^2\phi + \dfrac{P}{R}\cos\phi}\, d\phi}{\sin^2\phi + \dfrac{P}{R}\cos\phi}\, \cos\phi\, d\phi
\tag{4.27}
$$

$$
\frac{Ry}{T_0} = \int_{\phi_0}^{\phi} \frac{\exp \int_{\phi_0}^{\phi} \dfrac{\dfrac{P}{R}\sin\phi - \dfrac{F}{R}}{\sin^2\phi + \dfrac{P}{R}\cos\phi}\, d\phi}{\sin^2\phi + \dfrac{P}{R}\cos\phi}\, \sin\phi\, d\phi
\tag{4.28}
$$

Relations (4.25), (4.26), (4.27), and (4.28) are the cable functions τ, σ, ξ, η defined by Pode. Tabulated integration results are used for computing the cable shape and cable tension when in static equilibrium. The numerical value of these definite nondimensional integrals depends on:

1. Choice of origin, that is, ϕ_0;
2. Extent of the integration domain, that is, $\phi - \phi_0$;
3. Values of the parameters P/R and F/R.

In other words, if the origin is given, and values of P/R and F/R are known, a particular series of values of the four cable functions is obtained by successive computations of the four integrals over the intervals $\phi - \phi_0$ $= 1, 2, 3, \ldots$ degrees. There can be as many such series as the product of the number of values chosen for P/R by the number of values chosen for F/R.

Obviously, some limitation must be placed on these numbers. In Pode's tables, the values of F/R are confined to $F/R = 0.01, 0.02, 0.03$.

The limitation in the number of values of the parameter P/R is provided by the "critical angle" concept. When the cable hangs with one free end, its configuration is a straight line at an angle ϕ_c (critical) with the direction of the stream. The angle does not vary along the cable and $d\phi/ds = 0$. Relation (4.24) then becomes

$$R \sin^2 \phi_c + P \cos \phi_c = 0 \qquad (4.29)$$

It is clear that the range of values of ϕ_c is

$$0 < \phi_c < \frac{\pi}{2}$$

and that there is an infinite number of angles and therefore values of P/R, which satisfy (4.29) in this range.

The selection of P/R values for computing the table is arbitrary; the larger the number, the heavier and better the tables.

Pode selected values of ϕ_c from $0°$ to $85°$ by intervals of $5°$. For intermediate values, results are obtained by interpolation.

It should be noted that for physical and mathematical obvious reasons, the domain of integration must exclude the critical angle.

The results of the integration for values of F/R and P/R are grouped in four tables, with different origins leading to different tables.

In most practical cases, the points of interest on the cable are not the points of reference on which the tables are based, and, therefore, equations relating the tabulated cable functions with the cable parameters at the points of interest must be formulated.

Tension. Suppose the points of interest are P_1 and P_2 as shown in Figure 4.8. The tension at P_1 is given by

$$T_1 = \tau_1 T_0$$

where τ_1 is the tabulated value of the tension cable function and is the result of integration of expression (4.25) from the origin ϕ_0 to the point $P(\phi_1)$ for the given F/R and critical angle.

Similarly the tension at $P(\phi_2)$ is given by

$$T_2 = \tau_2 T_0$$

and, therefore,

$$\frac{T_1}{T_2} = \frac{\tau_1}{\tau_2}$$

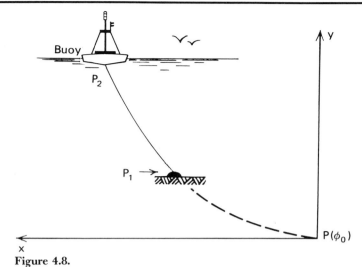

Figure 4.8.

from which

$$T_1 = T_2 \frac{\tau_1}{\tau_2} \text{ and } T_2 = T_1 \frac{\tau_2}{\tau_1} \tag{4.30}$$

Thus, if the value of the tension is known at one point, the tension at any other point is readily obtained from values of τ_1 and τ_2 found in the tables.

Cable length.   The length of the cable from the origin to the point $P(\phi_1)$ is given by

$$s_1 = \frac{T_0}{R} \sigma_1$$

where σ_1 is the tabulated value of the cable function and is the result of the integration of expression (4.26) from ϕ_0 to ϕ_1, for the particular values of ϕ_c and F/R.

Similarly the length of cable from origin to P_2 is given by

$$s_2 = \frac{T_0}{R} \sigma_2$$

The length of cable from P_1 to P_2 is, therefore,

$$s = s_2 - s_1 = \frac{T_0}{R} (\sigma_2 - \sigma_1)$$

But

$$T_0 = \frac{T_1}{\tau_1} = \frac{T_2}{\tau_2}$$

and, therefore,

$$s = \frac{T_1(\sigma_2 - \sigma_1)}{R\tau_1} = \frac{T_2(\sigma_2 - \sigma_1)}{R\tau_2} \qquad (4.31)$$

Cartesian coordinates. The horizontal and vertical distances between the points $P(\phi_2)$ and $P(\phi_1)$ are easily found using a similar approach and are given by

$$x = \frac{T_1(\xi_2 - \xi_1)}{R\tau_1} = \frac{T_2(\xi_2 - \xi_1)}{R\tau_2} \qquad (4.32)$$

$$y = \frac{T_1(\eta_2 - \eta_1)}{R\tau_1} = \frac{T_2(\eta_2 - \eta_1)}{R\tau_2} \qquad (4.33)$$

Example. (see Figure 4.9). A surface buoy is moored in 2000 ft of water. The diameter of the mooring line is 0.315 in., and its line density 0.124 lb/ft. The speed of the uniform current is 4.54 ft/sec. Anchoring limitations request that the line angle at the anchor be 30° (150°) and the tension no more than 3000 lb at the anchor. The pressure drag coefficient is 1.8 ($C_{DN} = 1.8$). Using Pode's tables find the length of the cable and the tension at the buoy (tangential drag to normal drag ratio is 0.02).

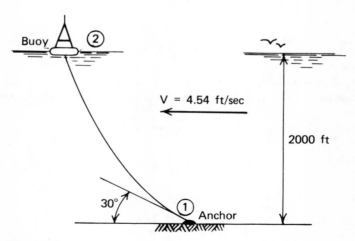

Figure 4.9.

Solution.

1. Normal Drag R

$$R = \tfrac{1}{2}\rho C_{DN} dV^2 = \left(\frac{64}{32}\right)\left(\frac{1.8}{2}\right)\left(\frac{0.315}{12}\right)(4.54)^2 \cong 1 \text{ lb/ft}$$

2. Critical angle ϕ_c. From (4.29)

$$\cos^2\phi_c - \frac{P}{R}\cos\phi_c - 1 = 0$$

Thus

$$\cos\phi_c = \tfrac{1}{2}\left[0.124 - \sqrt{.0154 + 4}\ \right] = -0.9405$$

Thus the critical angle

$$\phi_c = 20°$$

Entering the tables with

$$\phi_1 = 30° \ (150°)$$

$$\phi_c = 20°$$

and

$$\frac{F}{R} = 0.02$$

in Table 4.1 the corresponding cable functions are found to be

$$\tau_1 = 1.0176 \quad \xi_1 = -2.7405$$
$$\sigma_1 = 2.8342 \quad \eta_1 = 0.5971$$

3. From (4.33)

$$y = \frac{T_1}{R\tau_1}(\eta_2 - \eta_1) = 2000 \text{ ft}$$

And, thus,

$$\eta_2 = 0.5971 + \frac{(2000)(1)(1.0176)}{3000} = 1.2755$$

The closest value of η_2 found in the tables for the same ϕ_c is 1.2829 and the corresponding cable functions are

$$\tau_2 = 1.0828$$

$$\sigma_2 = 3.8432$$

$$\xi_2 = -3.4638$$

and the angle at the buoy is

$$\phi_2 = 61°$$

Therefore,

$$s = \frac{T_1}{R}\left(\frac{\sigma_2 - \sigma_1}{\tau_1}\right) = 2,977 \text{ ft}$$

and

$$T_2 = \frac{\tau_2}{\tau_1} T_1 = 3,190 \text{ lb}$$

More precision can be gained using interpolation.

Pode's tables are useful in applications where the physical assumptions of constant tangential drag, uniformity of current, and stiffness of the line are reasonable. Towing problems and certain buoy configurations fall into this category.

Pode's tables have been extended to include more values of P/R and to cover the case of neutrally buoyant cables with constant tangential drag by Thorne et al. (1962, 1963).

2.   Variable Tangential Drag. Wilson's Analysis.   Wilson (1960) published a set of graphs and tables of cable functions obtained from the numerical integration of the differential equations

$$dT = (P\sin\phi - \pi\gamma R\cos^2\phi)\,ds$$

$$T\,d\phi = (R\sin^2\phi + P\cos\phi)\,ds$$

These tables list the values of the following cable parameters:

$$\text{Scope} = \frac{s}{h}$$

where s is the arc length of mooring and h is the depth of the sea floor;

$$\text{Excursion} = \frac{l}{h}$$

where l is the horizontal distance between the two end points of the cable;

$$\text{Tension} = \frac{T}{ph}$$

TABLE 4.1. EXCERPT FROM "TABLES FOR COMPUTING THE
EQUILIBRIUM CONFIGURATION OF A FLEXIBLE CABLE
IN A UNIFORM STREAM" BY PODE, (1951).

	$\phi_c = 20°$					
	τ			σ		
$180° - \phi$	$f = 0.01$	$f = 0.02$	$f = 0.03$	$f = 0.01$	$f = 0.02$	$f = 0.03$
0	1.0000	1.0000	1.0000	0.0000	0.0000	0.0000
1	0.9988	0.9974	0.9960	0.1400	0.1399	0.1398
2	0.9978	0.9950	0.9923	0.2792	0.2788	0.2784
3	0.9972	0.9930	0.9889	0.4171	0.4162	0.4153
4	0.9969	0.9913	0.9859	0.5530	0.5515	0.5500
5	0.9968	0.9900	0.9832	0.6866	0.6842	0.6819
6	0.9971	0.9889	0.9809	0.8173	0.8139	0.8106
7	0.9976	0.9882	0.9789	0.9448	0.9403	0.9359
8	0.9984	0.9877	0.9772	1.0688	1.0631	1.0574
9	0.9994	0.9875	0.9758	1.1890	1.1820	1.1750
10	1.0006	0.9876	0.9748	1.3054	1.2969	1.2884
11	1.0020	0.9879	0.9740	1.4177	1.4076	1.3977
12	1.0036	0.9884	0.9734	1.5359	1.5143	1.5028
13	1.0054	0.9891	0.9731	1.6300	1.6168	1.6037
14	1.0073	0.9900	0.9730	1.7300	1.7151	1.7004
15	1.0093	0.9911	0.9731	1.8261	1.8095	1.7931
16	1.0115	0.9923	0.9734	1.9183	1.9000	1.8819
17	1.0137	0.9936	0.9739	2.0066	1.9866	1.9668
18	1.0160	0.9950	0.9745	2.0913	2.0696	2.0481
19	1.0184	0.9966	0.9753	2.1725	2.1490	2.1259
20	1.0209	.9982	0.9761	.2.2503	2.2251	2.2004
21	1.0234	1.0000	0.9770	2.3249	2.2980	2.2716
22	1.0259	1.0017	0.9781	2.3964	2.3679	2.3398
23	1.0285	1.0036	0.9793	2.4649	2.4348	2.4052
24	1.0311	1.0055	0.9805	2.5307	2.4990	2.4678
25	1.0338	1.0074	0.9818	2.5939	2.5606	2.5278
26	1.0364	1.0094	0.9831	2.6546	2.6197	2.5854
27	1.0391	1.0114	0.9846	2.7129	2.6765	2.6407
28	1.0417	1.0135	0.9860	2.7691	2.7311	2.6939
29	1.0444	1.0156	0.9875	2.8231	2.7837	2.7450

Table 4.1 (*Continued*)

180° − φ	$\phi_c = 20°$					
	τ			σ		
	$f=0.01$	$f=0.02$	$f=0.03$	$f=0.01$	$f=0.02$	$f=0.03$
30	1.0471	1.0176	0.9891	2.8751	2.8342	2.7941
31	1.0497	1.0198	0.9906	2.9253	2.8830	2.8415
32	1.0524	1.0219	0.9922	2.9736	2.9300	2.8871
33	1.0550	1.0240	0.9939	3.0204	2.9753	2.9312
34	1.0577	1.0261	0.9955	3.0655	3.0191	2.9737
35	1.0603	1.0283	0.9972	3.1092	3.0615	3.0147
36	1.0630	1.0304	0.9988	3.1514	3.1024	3.0545
37	1.0656	1.0326	1.0005	3.1924	3.1421	3.0929
38	1.0682	1.0347	1.0022	3.2320	3.1805	3.1302
39	1.0708	1.0368	1.0040	3.2705	3.2178	3.1663
40	1.0734	1.0390	1.0057	3.3079	3.2540	3.2013
41	1.0760	1.0411	1.0074	3.3442	3.2892	3.2353
42	1.0785	1.0433	1.0091	3.3795	3.3233	3.2684
43	1.0811	1.0454	1.0109	3.4139	3.3566	3.3005
44	1.0836	1.0475	1.0126	3.4474	3.3890	3.3318
45	1.0861	1.0496	1.0144	3.4801	3.4205	3.3623
46	1.0886	1.0518	1.0161	3.5119	3.4513	3.3921
47	1.0911	1.0539	1.0179	3.5430	3.4813	3.4211
48	1.0936	1.0560	1.0196	3.5734	3.5106	3.4494
49	1.0961	1.0581	1.0214	3.6031	3.5393	3.4771
50	1.0985	1.0602	1.0231	3.6321	3.5674	3.5042
51	1.1010	1.0623	1.0249	3.6606	3.5948	3.5307
52	1.1034	1.0643	1.0266	3.6885	3.6217	3.5566
53	1.1059	1.0664	1.0284	3.7158	3.6481	3.5820
54	1.1083	1.0685	1.0301	3.7426	3.6740	3.6070
55	1.1107	1.0705	1.0319	3.7690	3.6994	3.6315
56	1.1131	1.0726	1.0336	3.7949	3.7243	3.6555
57	1.1155	1.0747	1.0353	3.8203	3.7488	3.6791
58	1.1178	1.0767	1.0371	3.8454	3.7730	3.7024
59	1.1202	1.0788	1.0388	3.8700	3.7967	3.7252

Table 4.1 (*Continued*)

180° − φ	τ			σ		
	f = 0.01	f = 0.02	f = 0.03	f = 0.01	f = 0.02	f = 0.03
			φ_c = 20°			
60	1.1226	1.0808	1.0406	3.8943	3.8201	3.7478
61	1.1249	1.0828	1.0423	3.9183	3.8432	3.7700
62	1.1273	1.0849	1.0441	3.9419	3.8659	3.7919
63	1.1296	1.0869	1.0458	3.9652	3.8884	3.8135
64	1.1320	1.0889	1.0475	3.9883	3.9105	3.8348
65	1.1343	1.0909	1.0493	4.0111	3.9324	3.8559
66	1.1366	1.0930	1.0510	4.0336	3.9541	3.8767
67	1.1389	1.0950	1.0527	4.0559	3.9755	3.8973
68	1.1413	1.0970	1.0545	4.0780	3.9968	3.9177
69	1.1436	1.0990	1.0562	4.0998	4.0178	3.9379
70	1.1459	1.1010	1.0579	4.1215	4.0386	3.9580
71	1.1482	1.1030	1.0597	4.1431	4.0593	3.9778
72	1.1505	1.1051	1.0614	4.1644	4.0799	3.9976
73	1.1528	1.1071	1.0631	4.1857	4.1002	4.0171
74	1.1551	1.1091	1.0649	4.2068	4.1205	4.0366
75	1.1574	1.1111	1.0666	4.2277	4.1406	4.0559
76	1.1597	1.1131	1.0684	4.2486	4.1607	4.0752
77	1.1620	1.1151	1.0701	4.2694	4.1806	4.0943
78	1.1644	1.1171	1.0719	4.2901	4.2005	4.1134
79	1.1667	1.1192	1.0736	4.3108	4.2203	4.1324
80	1.1690	1.1212	1.0754	4.3314	4.2401	4.1513
81	1.1713	1.1232	1.0771	4.3519	4.2598	4.1703
82	1.1736	1.1252	1.0789	4.3725	4.2795	4.1891
83	1.1760	1.1273	1.0806	4.3930	4.2992	4.2080
84	1.1783	1.1293	1.0824	4.4135	4.3188	4.2269
85	1.1806	1.1314	1.0842	4.4340	4.3385	4.2457
86	1.1830	1.1334	1.0859	4.4546	4.3582	4.2646
87	1.1853	1.1355	1.0877	4.4752	4.3779	4.2835
88	1.1877	1.1375	1.0895	4.4958	4.3977	4.3024
89	1.1901	1.1396	1.0913	4.5165	4.4175	4.3214
90	1.1924	1.1417	1.0931	4.5373	4.4374	4.3404

Table 4.1 (*Continued*)

	ξ			η		
$180° - \phi$	$f=0.01$	$f=0.02$	$f=0.03$	$f=0.01$	$f=0.02$	$f=0.03$
0	0.0000	0.0000	0.0000	0.0000	0.0000	0.0000
1	−0.1400	−0.1399	−0.1398	0.0012	0.0012	0.0012
2	−0.2792	−0.2788	−0.2784	0.0049	0.0049	0.0048
3	−0.4169	−0.4160	−0.4151	0.0109	0.0108	0.0108
4	−0.5526	−0.5510	−0.5495	0.0192	0.0191	0.0190
5	−0.6857	−0.6833	−0.6810	0.0296	0.0295	0.0294
6	−0.8158	−0.8125	−0.8092	0.0422	0.0419	0.0417
7	−0.9425	−0.9381	−0.9336	0.0566	0.0562	0.0559
8	−1.0654	−1.0593	−1.0541	0.0728	0.0723	0.0717
9	−1.1844	−1.1773	−1.1704	0.0905	0.0898	0.0891
10	−1.2991	−1.2907	−1.2823	0.1097	0.1088	0.1078
11	−1.4095	−1.3996	−1.3897	0.1302	0.1290	0.1277
12	−1.5156	−1.5041	−1.4927	0.1518	0.1502	0.1487
13	−1.6172	−1.6041	−1.5912	0.1743	0.1724	0.1705
14	−1.7145	−1.6998	−1.6853	0.1977	0.1954	0.1931
15	−1.8075	−1.7912	−1.7750	0.2217	0.2190	0.2163
16	−1.8963	−1.8783	−1.8606	0.2463	0.2431	0.2400
17	−1.9810	−1.9614	−1.9420	0.2714	0.2677	0.2641
18	−2.0618	−2.0405	−2.0196	0.2969	0.2927	0.2886
19	−2.1388	−2.1159	−2.0933	0.3226	0.3179	0.3133
20	−2.2121	−2.1876	−2.1635	0.3486	0.3433	0.3381
21	−2.2820	−2.2559	−2.2302	0.3747	0.3688	0.3630
22	−2.3485	−2.3209	−2.2937	0.4009	0.3944	0.3880
23	−2.4119	−2.3827	−2.3541	0.4271	0.4200	0.4130
24	−2.4722	−2.4416	−2.4115	0.4534	0.4456	0.4300
25	−2.5297	−2.4976	−2.4661	0.4796	0.4712	0.4629
26	−2.5845	−2.5510	−2.5181	0.5057	0.4966	0.4877
27	−2.6367	−2.6018	−2.5676	0.5317	0.5219	0.5124
28	−2.6865	−2.6503	−2.6148	0.5576	0.5472	0.5369
29	−2.7339	−2.6964	−2.6597	0.5834	0.5722	0.5613

$\phi_c = 20°$

Table 4.1 (*Continued*)

	ξ			η		
$180° - \phi$	$f = 0.01$	$f = 0.02$	$f = 0.03$	$f = 0.01$	$f = 0.02$	$f = 0.03$

<table>
<tr><td colspan="7" align="center">$\phi_c = 20°$</td></tr>
<tr><td>30</td><td>−2.7792</td><td>−2.7405</td><td>−2.7025</td><td>0.6090</td><td>0.5971</td><td>0.5855</td></tr>
<tr><td>31</td><td>−2.8224</td><td>−2.7825</td><td>−2.7433</td><td>0.6345</td><td>0.6219</td><td>0.6095</td></tr>
<tr><td>32</td><td>−2.8637</td><td>−2.8225</td><td>−2.7822</td><td>0.6598</td><td>0.6464</td><td>0.6334</td></tr>
<tr><td>33</td><td>−2.9031</td><td>−2.8608</td><td>−2.8193</td><td>0.6848</td><td>0.6708</td><td>0.6570</td></tr>
<tr><td>34</td><td>−2.9407</td><td>−2.8973</td><td>−2.8548</td><td>0.7098</td><td>0.6950</td><td>0.6805</td></tr>
<tr><td>35</td><td>−2.9767</td><td>−2.9322</td><td>−2.8886</td><td>0.7345</td><td>0.7189</td><td>0.7037</td></tr>
<tr><td>36</td><td>−3.0111</td><td>−2.9656</td><td>−2.9209</td><td>0.7590</td><td>0.7427</td><td>0.7268</td></tr>
<tr><td>37</td><td>−3.0440</td><td>−2.9975</td><td>−2.9519</td><td>0.7834</td><td>0.7663</td><td>0.7497</td></tr>
<tr><td>38</td><td>−3.0755</td><td>−3.0279</td><td>−2.9814</td><td>0.8075</td><td>0.7897</td><td>0.7723</td></tr>
<tr><td>39</td><td>−3.1056</td><td>−3.0571</td><td>−3.0097</td><td>0.8315</td><td>0.8129</td><td>0.7948</td></tr>
<tr><td>40</td><td>−3.1345</td><td>−3.0850</td><td>−3.0367</td><td>0.8553</td><td>0.8359</td><td>0.8171</td></tr>
<tr><td>41</td><td>−3.1621</td><td>−3.1118</td><td>−3.0626</td><td>0.8788</td><td>0.8588</td><td>0.8392</td></tr>
<tr><td>42</td><td>−3.1885</td><td>−3.1374</td><td>−3.0873</td><td>0.9023</td><td>0.8814</td><td>0.8611</td></tr>
<tr><td>43</td><td>−3.2139</td><td>−3.1619</td><td>−3.1110</td><td>0.9255</td><td>0.9039</td><td>0.8828</td></tr>
<tr><td>44</td><td>−3.2382</td><td>−3.1854</td><td>−3.1337</td><td>0.9485</td><td>0.9262</td><td>0.9044</td></tr>
<tr><td>45</td><td>−3.2615</td><td>−3.2079</td><td>−3.1555</td><td>0.9714</td><td>0.9483</td><td>0.9257</td></tr>
<tr><td>46</td><td>−3.2838</td><td>−3.2294</td><td>−3.1763</td><td>0.9941</td><td>0.9702</td><td>0.9469</td></tr>
<tr><td>47</td><td>−3.3052</td><td>−3.2501</td><td>−3.1963</td><td>1.0167</td><td>0.9920</td><td>0.9680</td></tr>
<tr><td>48</td><td>−3.3257</td><td>−3.2699</td><td>−3.2154</td><td>1.0391</td><td>1.0136</td><td>0.9889</td></tr>
<tr><td>49</td><td>−3.3454</td><td>−3.2889</td><td>−3.2338</td><td>1.0613</td><td>1.0351</td><td>1.0096</td></tr>
<tr><td>50</td><td>−3.3643</td><td>−3.3072</td><td>−3.2514</td><td>1.0834</td><td>1.0564</td><td>1.0302</td></tr>
<tr><td>51</td><td>−3.3824</td><td>−3.3246</td><td>−3.2682</td><td>1.1054</td><td>1.0776</td><td>1.0506</td></tr>
<tr><td>52</td><td>−3.3997</td><td>−3.3414</td><td>−3.2844</td><td>1.1272</td><td>1.0987</td><td>1.0709</td></tr>
<tr><td>53</td><td>−3.4164</td><td>−3.3574</td><td>−3.2999</td><td>1.1489</td><td>1.1196</td><td>1.0911</td></tr>
<tr><td>54</td><td>−3.4323</td><td>−3.3728</td><td>−3.3147</td><td>1.1704</td><td>1.1404</td><td>1.1112</td></tr>
<tr><td>55</td><td>−3.4476</td><td>−3.3876</td><td>−3.3289</td><td>1.1919</td><td>1.1610</td><td>1.1311</td></tr>
<tr><td>56</td><td>−3.4623</td><td>−3.4017</td><td>−3.3425</td><td>1.2132</td><td>1.1816</td><td>1.1509</td></tr>
<tr><td>57</td><td>−3.4763</td><td>−3.4152</td><td>−3.3556</td><td>1.2344</td><td>1.2021</td><td>1.1706</td></tr>
<tr><td>58</td><td>−3.4898</td><td>−3.4282</td><td>−3.3681</td><td>1.2556</td><td>1.2224</td><td>1.1902</td></tr>
<tr><td>59</td><td>−3.5027</td><td>−3.4406</td><td>−3.3800</td><td>1.2766</td><td>1.2427</td><td>1.2097</td></tr>
</table>

Table 4.1 (*Continued*)

	ξ			η		
$\phi_c = 20°$						
$180° - \phi$	$f=0.01$	$f=0.02$	$f=0.03$	$f=0.01$	$f=0.02$	$f=0.03$
60	−3.5150	−3.4525	−3.3914	1.2975	1.2628	1.2291
61	−3.5268	−3.4638	−3.4024	1.3184	1.2829	1.2485
62	−3.5381	−3.4747	−3.4128	1.3391	1.3029	1.2677
63	−3.5488	−3.4851	−3.4228	1.3598	1.3228	1.2869
64	−3.5591	−3.4949	−3.4323	1.3805	1.3426	1.3059
65	−3.5689	−3.5044	−3.4414	1.4010	1.3624	1.3250
66	−3.5783	−3.5134	−3.4500	1.4215	1.3821	1.3439
67	−3.5872	−3.5219	−3.4582	1.4420	1.4018	1.3628
68	−3.5956	−3.5300	−3.4661	1.4624	1.4214	1.3817
69	−3.6036	−3.5377	−3.4735	1.4827	1.4409	1.4005
70	−3.6112	−3.5450	−3.4805	1.5030	1.4605	1.4192
71	−3.6184	−3.5520	−3.4871	1.5233	1.4800	1.4380
72	−3.6252	−3.5585	−3.4934	1.5436	1.4994	1.4567
73	−3.6316	−3.5646	−3.4993	1.5638	1.5189	1.4753
74	−3.6376	−3.5703	−3.5048	1.5841	1.5383	1.4940
75	−3.6432	−3.5757	−3.5100	1.6043	1.5577	1.5126
76	−3.6484	−3.5807	−3.5148	1.6245	1.5771	1.5313
77	−3.6533	−3.5854	−3.5192	1.6447	1.5965	1.5499
78	−3.6577	−3.5897	−3.5234	1.6649	1.6159	1.5685
79	−3.6619	−3.5937	−3.5272	1.6852	1.6353	1.5871
80	−3.6656	−3.5973	−3.5306	1.7054	1.6548	1.6058
81	−3.6690	−3.6005	−3.5337	1.7257	1.6742	1.6244
82	−3.6720	−3.6034	−3.5365	1.7460	1.6937	1.6431
83	−3.6747	−3.6060	−3.5390	1.7664	1.7132	1.6618
84	−3.6770	−3.6082	−3.5411	1.7867	1.7327	1.6805
85	−3.6790	−3.6101	−3.5429	1.8072	1.7523	1.6993
86	−3.6806	−3.6116	−3.5444	1.8277	1.7719	1.7181
87	−3.6819	−3.6128	−3.5456	1.8482	1.7916	1.7369
88	−3.6828	−3.6137	−3.5464	1.8686	1.8114	1.7559
89	−3.6833	−3.6142	−3.5469	1.8895	1.8312	1.7748
90	−3.6835	−3.6144	−3.5471	1.9103	1.8511	1.7939

where p is the immersed weight of the cable per unit of length.

ψ_n is the angle at the cable upper end,

ψ_{n-1} is the angle at the cable lower end.

These parameters are grouped according to the values of the ratio, γ, of longitudinal to normal drag coefficients and of the hydrodynamic constant, μ, defined as the ratio p/R of the immersed weight per unit of length to the normal resistance per unit of length.

Values of μ and γ used in the tables are

$$\mu = 100, 10, 5, 2, 1, 0.5, 0.2, 0.1, 0.01$$

$$\gamma = 0.1, 0.05, 0.025, 0.01, 0.00$$

The definite advantages of Wilson's tables are to directly yield the parameters of interest, to include the variation of the tangential friction drag as a function of inclination and to cover a wider range of weight to drag ratios and of normal to tangential drag ratios.

The following example illustrates the use of the Wilson tables.

Example. (see Figure 4.10). A surface buoy is moored with a 0.25 in. diameter wire rope of line density 0.1 lb/ft in 2600 m. The speed of the uniform current is 2.5 ft/sec. What is the length of the cable resulting in minimum excursion of the buoy if the tension at the buoy is not to exceed 2500 lb? What is then the excursion and the tension at the anchor? (Assume $\gamma = 0.01$ and $C_{DN} = 1.54$.)

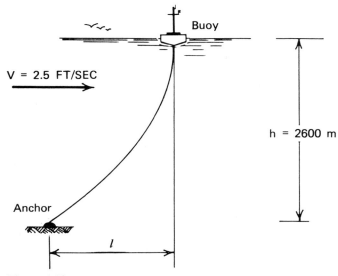

Figure 4.10.

Solution.

1. $R = \dfrac{1}{2}\rho C_{DN} dV^2 = (\dfrac{1}{2})(\dfrac{64}{32})(1.54)\dfrac{1}{4}\dfrac{1}{12}(2.5)^2 = 0.2 \text{ lb/ft}$

2. $\mu = \dfrac{p}{R} = \dfrac{0.1}{0.2} = 0.5$

3. Enter Wilson tables for $\mu = 0.5$ and $\gamma = 0.01$ (Wilson, 1960, p. 111)

$$\frac{T_B}{ph} = \frac{T_N}{Wh} = \frac{2500}{(0.1)8540} = 2.93$$

The value close to 2.93 and with minimum, l/h, yields:

$$\psi_2 = 35.9 \qquad \text{angle at anchor}$$

$$\psi_1 = 90° \qquad \text{angle at buoy}$$

$$\frac{T_A}{ph} = \frac{T_{N-1}}{Wh} = 1.94$$

Minimum $l/h = 0.493$ and $s/h = 1.162$. Therefore

$$s = (1.162)h = (1.162)(2600) = 3020 \text{ m}$$

$$l = (0.493)h = (0.493)(2600) = 1280 \text{ m}$$

$$T_A = (1.94) ph = (1.94)(0.1)(2600)(3.28) = 1650 \text{ lb}$$

Variable Currents

The assumption of current uniformity applies to a limited number of practical cases. In most oceanographic applications the current force and direction are a function of depth. Simplified "current profiles" are often used to represent planar flow (steps and linear or exponential decrease).

Solutions for the study of line statics in variable currents can be based on simple or elaborate models. Simple models will yield approximate solutions of sufficient validity for certain practical cases, in particular when current profiles and drag coefficients are not well established.

Complex solutions for the analysis of stiff cables in variable currents have been presented (Wilson, 1961). However, when better models are formulated and computer techniques are used, little difficulty is added by including the elastic properties of the line to obtain a more realistic solution.

Simple Extension of Uniform Current Analysis.   This extension is based on the assumption of current uniformity over a portion of the water depth and absence of current over the remaining part. The method of analysis for the two regions depends on the nature of the mooring line. For example, with a wire rope, all static forces could be considered in the current region whereas in still water the cable would assume the shape of a catenary. On the other hand, with a neutrally buoyant line, a solution neglecting the gravity forces would be used for the current region, the part of the line in still water being a straight line.

The immediate boundary condition at the interface of the two current zones is continuity of tension and line angle.

Polygonal Approximation.   In this approach the current profile is represented by a series of steps of uniform current. Gravity forces and drag forces on the cable are evaluated in each step and the resulting tension vector determined at point of current changes (nodes). The geometry of the mooring line is then approximated by constructing a polygonal line following the tensions vector from one node to the next (see Figure 4.11).

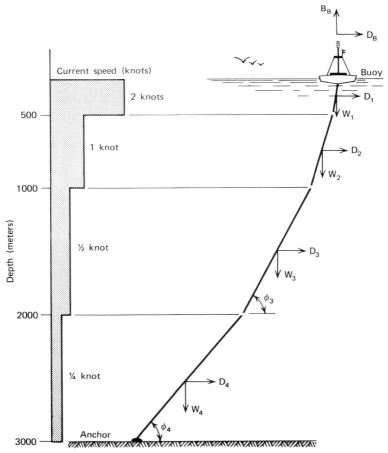

Figure 4.11.   Polygonal approximation

The tension T_i and the angle ϕ_i with the horizontal at any node, i, are then given by

$$T_i = \left[\left(B_B - \sum_{n=1}^{n=i} P_n l_n \right)^2 + \left(D_B + \sum_{n=1}^{n=i} D_n \right)^2 \right]^{1/2} \qquad (4.34)$$

and

$$\phi_i = \tan^{-1} \frac{B_B - \sum_{n=1}^{n=i} P_n l_n}{D_B + \sum_{n=1}^{n=i} D_n} \qquad (4.35)$$

where B_B is the weight of water displaced by the buoy; $P_n l_n$ is the immersed weight of segment n of length l; D_B is the drag on the buoy; and

$$D_n = \tfrac{1}{2}\rho C_{Dn} d_n h_n V_n^2$$

is the drag on segment n of diameter d_n and drag coefficient C_{Dn}, h_n being the width of the step n.

SURFACE BUOY. It can be seen from the free body diagram of a surface buoy (Figure 4.12) that the conditions of static equilibrium of the buoy are

$$B_B = W + T_V - R_V \qquad (4.36)$$

$$D_B = T_H \qquad (4.37)$$

where B_B is the weight of the water displaced by the buoy; W is the weight of the buoy; T_V is the vertical component of the tension; T_H is the horizontal component of the tension; R_V is the vertical component of the resistance, R, on the buoy (lift); $D_B = R_H$ is the horizontal component of the resistance R on the buoy (drag). If the tension and the resistance at the buoy are known then the shape of the mooring line and the tension distribution can easily be established.

When the vertical component of tension is not given, then other physical constraints must be specified (like buoy excursion or mooring length). The problem is then solved by iteration. A buoyancy force B_B is assumed, the line geometry is established and then compared with the physical constraints. (The horizontal projection of the segment lengths must be compared with the given buoy excursion, for example.) The assumed force is then corrected and the process repeated until sufficient agreement is obtained.

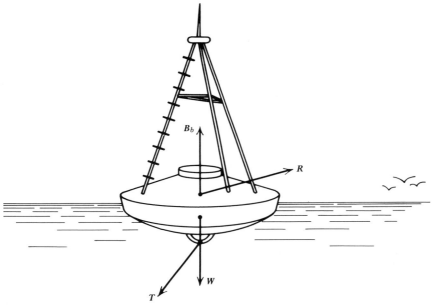

Figure 4.12.

SUBSURFACE BUOY. The buoyancy of a subsurface float is constant. The location of the buoy depends on the length of the mooring line. If the location is given, the length of the line can be approximately determined by the method outlined for the surface buoy case. Tension and inclination angles are then given by (4.34) and (4.35).

On the other hand, if the length is fixed, the location of the buoy must be found by an iteration process. (A location is assumed, and the length obtained is compared with the given length.)

Mooring Lines With Elasticity

A realistic study of deep sea mooring lines must consider the elastic properties of the mooring line components. Steady-state solutions taking in account elasticity and current variation are best obtained using computers. An approximate solution can, however, be obtained for the case of surface taut moors by the method of geometric approximation. In this approach, the final configuration of the mooring is assumed to have a simple geometric shape. The corresponding stretched length can then be easily computed and the tension derived from the known elastic response of the mooring line material. An example of this method is the circular arc approximation.

Circular Approximation

This approximation can be used to investigate the downstream excursion of the buoy and the tension in the mooring line of a surface taut moor immersed in a current which may vary with depth. Consider, for example, a surface buoy system with a mooring line made of wire rope in its upper part and of an elastic synthetic fiber rope in its lower part, and let L_1 and L_2 be the lengths the two mooring parts had just before the buoy system was deployed in the ocean.

For the mooring to be taut the initial mooring length $L_1 + L_2$ must be smaller than the water depth at the implantation site. During deployment the fiber rope, pulled by the anchor weight, stretches until the anchor hits the sea floor. Let l ($l > L_2$) be the length of the fiber rope at that time, and let T_0 be the initial tension in the fiber rope corresponding to this elongation.

Now the current pushes the anchored buoy system downstream. The fiber rope keeps on stretching until the entire mooring reaches an equilibrium position. As depicted in Figure 4.13, the equilibrium configuration is then assumed to consist of a circular arc in the fiber rope part of the mooring and of a straight line in the wire rope part.

The angle α_2 that the mooring line makes with the vertical at the anchor is given by

$$\alpha_2 = \sin^{-1} \frac{D_A}{T_A} \tag{4.38}$$

where D_A is the drag force at the anchor and T_A is the tension in the fiber rope at the anchor. The drag force D_A is the sum of all drag forces on the buoy system, namely

$$D_A = D_B + D_W + D_F \tag{4.39}$$

where D_B is the drag on the buoy, D_W is the drag on the wire rope, and D_F is the drag on the fiber rope. To compute the drag on the wire rope and on the fiber rope, the mooring line is assumed to be unstretched and normal (or nearly normal, after all this is a taut moor) to the current. With these assumptions,

$$D_W = \tfrac{1}{2}\rho \int_0^{L_1} C_{DW} d_W V_{(y)}^2 \, dy$$

$$D_F = \tfrac{1}{2}\rho \int_{L_1}^{L_2} C_{DF} d_F V_{(y)}^2 \, dy$$

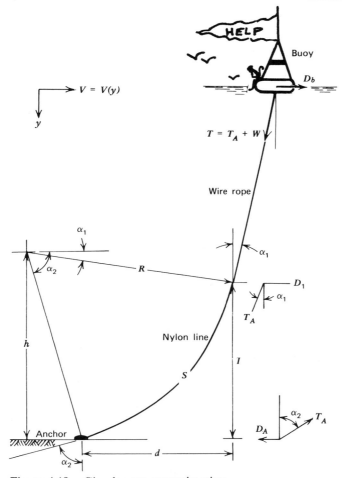

Figure 4.13.   Circular arc approximation.

where C_{DW}, C_{DF}, d_W, and d_F are the drag coefficients and the rope diameters for the wire rope and the fiber rope respectively and $V(y)$ expresses the variation of the current as a function of the depth y.

Current variations being small in the deeper part of the mooring and synthetic fiber ropes being almost neutrally buoyant, the tension T_A can be considered constant over the length of the fiber rope.

At the lower end of the wire rope, the angle α_1 between the vertical and the mooring line is given by

$$\alpha_1 = \sin^{-1} \frac{D_1}{T_A} \tag{4.40}$$

where $D_1 = D_B + D_W$ is the sum of the drag forces on the buoy and on the wire rope. Let R be the radius of the circular arc, and h be the vertical distance above the sea floor to the center of this arc. Then

$$\sin\alpha_2 = \frac{h}{R} = \frac{D_A}{T_A} \tag{4.41}$$

from which

$$h = \frac{RD_A}{T_A} \tag{4.42}$$

As can be seen from Figure 4.13, h can also be expressed in terms of l by

$$h = l + R\sin\alpha_1$$

$$h = l + \frac{RD_1}{T_A} \tag{4.43}$$

Expressions (4.42) and (4.43) can be combined to give

$$R = \frac{lT_A}{D_A - D_1} \tag{4.44}$$

The radius R and the arc length s are related by

$$s = R(\alpha_2 - \alpha_1) \tag{4.45}$$

On the other hand, if the elongation of the fiber rope is directly proportional to the tension, that is, if

$$\Delta L = k\Delta T$$

where ΔL is the change in rope length (ft), k is the rope "spring constant" (ft/lb), and $\Delta T =$ change in rope tension (lb), then the arc length s is given by

$$s = l + \frac{T_A - T_0}{k} \tag{4.46}$$

Solving for T_A,

$$T_A = k(s - l) + T_0 \tag{4.47}$$

The problem can now be solved by trial and error. An assumed value of T_A is inserted in expressions (4.38), (4.40), and (4.44). The values for the angles α_2, α_1, and the radius R thus obtained are then used in (4.45) to compute the arc length s. This computed value of s is in turn inserted in (4.47) to derive T_A. This computed value of T_A is then compared with the assumed value. The latter is corrected, and a new computation made. The process is repeated until sufficient agreement is reached between assumed and computed values of T_A.

The tension at the buoy may then be computed, to a fair approximation, using

$$T_B = T_A + W \tag{4.48}$$

where W is the immersed weight of all mooring components (wire rope, instruments, etc.). The horizontal distance d between the anchor and the junction of the two ropes is

$$d = R\left(\cos\alpha_1 - \cos\alpha_2\right) \tag{4.49}$$

Therefore the downstream excursion E of the buoy is

$$E = R\left(\cos\alpha_1 - \cos\alpha_2\right) + L_1 \sin\alpha_1 \tag{4.50}$$

Computer Techniques

Two-Dimensional Mass-Spring System. Analog Computer.   In this method (Paquette, 1965), the mooring line is represented, as shown in Figure 4.14, by a series of n straight segments each with a spring constant k_i and mass m_i.

Segment mass and forces exerted on the segment length are lumped at the segment end. The condition of static equilibrium of the entire two-dimensional mass-spring system can then be expressed by

$$m_i \ddot{x}_i = \sum_j X_{ij} = 0 \tag{4.51}$$

$$m_i \ddot{y}_i = \sum_j Y_{ij} = 0 \tag{4.52}$$

in which X_{ij} are the horizontal components of the forces applied on the mass i; Y_{ij} are the vertical components of the forces applied on the mass i; and $i = 1, 2, 3, \ldots, n$. Analog computers can be used to advantage to solve this set of $2n$ second order differential equations.

Finite Elements. Digital Computers.   This method extrapolates the conditions of equilibrium obtained for cable elements of infinitesimal length to cable segments of finite length. To this end the mooring line is first divided in a number of straight segments, the larger number the better the model. Changes of tension ΔT and cable orientation $\Delta\phi$ that take place over

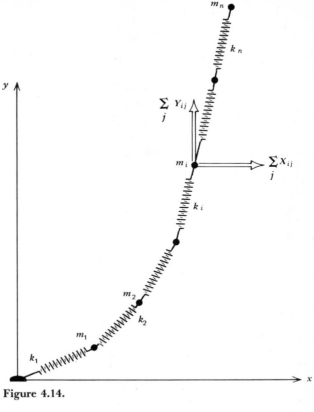

Figure 4.14.

a segment length are then given by

$$\Delta T = P \tag{4.53}$$

$$\Delta \phi = \frac{N}{T} \tag{4.54}$$

where P is the resultant of the tangential forces on the segment length, N is the resultant of the normal forces on the segment length, and T is the tension in the segment. These equations can be used, together with a constitutive equation relating tension and elongation, to compute the location of the segment ends and the tension distribution along the cable path, starting from assumed initial conditions.

For example, if T_1 is the assumed tension in the cable segment immediately below the buoy and if D_B is the drag on the buoy, then the angle of inclination of the first segment is given by

$$\Phi_1 = \cos^{-1} \frac{D_B}{T_1} \tag{4.55}$$

The stretched length L_1 of the first segment is computed using T_1 and the elongation characteristics of the segment material. The end point coordinates x_1 and y_1 of the first segment are then

$$x_1 = L_1 \cos\phi_1$$

$$y_1 = L_1 \sin\phi_1$$

The forces due to segment drag and weight are evaluated next, and the resulting changes in tension, ΔT_1, and inclination, $\Delta\phi_1$, determined using

$$\Delta T_1 = P_1$$

$$\Delta\phi_1 = \frac{N_1}{T_1}$$

where P_1 and N_1 are the tangential and normal resultants of the forces applied on the first segment. The tension in the second segment, T_2, is then given by

$$T_2 = T_1 + \Delta T_1 \tag{4.56}$$

and the inclination ϕ_2 by

$$\phi_2 = \phi_1 + \Delta\phi_1 \tag{4.57}$$

This computation is repeated for the ensemble of segments, a typical operation step being depicted in Figure 4.15.

The cable geometry resulting from this computation process is then compared against known or prescribed physical dimensions. For example, the vertical projection of all the segments used to approximate the mooring line of a surface buoy can be compared to the water depth. Similarly the computed depth of a subsurface buoy can be compared with its prescribed (design) implantation depth. A correction, proportional to the error between the computed and true value of the physical dimension, is then applied to the assumed initial condition and a new cable configuration is then computed. The iteration process is repeated as necessary until the error falls within a prescribed range.

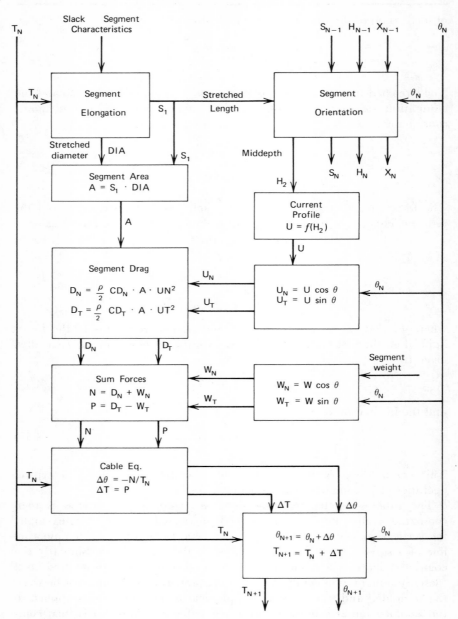

Figure 4.15. Integration procedure.

134

4.2. STATICS OF MULTILEG SYSTEMS

Two or more mooring lines may be used to constrain a floating structure. This is generally done to minimize the motion of the structure, to increase the reliability of the system, or to moor special oceanic platforms.

The principles reviewed in the analysis of single point moored systems can be applied and extended to the analysis of the geometry of, and the tension in, the different mooring lines of a multileg system. The basic approach consists in establishing the forces applied to the floats and the mooring lines and then derive the equilibrium geometry and the resulting stresses in the lines.

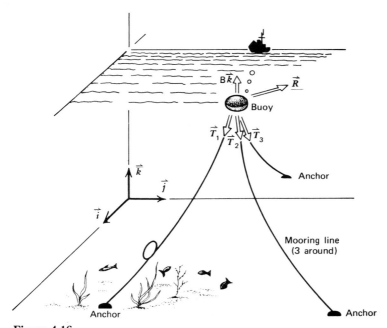

Figure 4.16.

For example, should the mooring lines of the sea spider shown in Figure 4.16 be neutrally buoyant, and should the drag on the mooring lines be much less than the drag on the buoy, then the tension in the mooring lines could be derived from the simultaneous solution of

$$\sum_{n=1}^{n=3} \vec{T}_n \cdot \vec{i} = \vec{R} \cdot \vec{i} \qquad (4.58)$$

$$\sum_{n=1}^{n=3} \vec{T}_n \cdot \vec{j} = \vec{R} \cdot \vec{j} \qquad (4.59)$$

$$\sum_{n=1}^{n=3} \vec{T}_n \cdot \vec{k} = B\vec{k} + \vec{R} \cdot \vec{k} \qquad (4.60)$$

where $\vec{T}_n$ is the tension in the mooring line, $n = 1$, 2, 3; $\vec{R}$ is the hydrodynamic resistance on the apex float; B is the net buoyancy of the float; and $\vec{i}, \vec{j}, \vec{k}$ are Cartesian unit vectors ($\vec{k}$ being vertical). The elongation $\vec{r}_n$ of each leg will be given by

$$\vec{r}_n = K_n \vec{T}_n$$

with K_n the spring constant of the nth leg. The total displacement, $\vec{S}$, of the apex will then be

$$\vec{S} = \sum_{n=1}^{n=3} \vec{r}_n \qquad (4.61)$$

Method of Imaginary Reactions

A method introducing assumed or imaginary reactions at the anchoring points has been proposed by Skop and O'Hara (1968) to perform the static analysis of complex buoy systems. To illustrate the method a simple two-dimensional case is first reviewed. Consider an elastic mooring line acted on by forces as shown in Figure 4.17.

If the horizontal and vertical components H_3 and V_3 of the reaction force at the anchor no. 2 are known, the system equilibrium conditions are then

$$\vec{H}_0 = \vec{H}_1 + \vec{H}_2 + \vec{H}_3 \qquad (4.62)$$

$$\vec{V}_0 = \vec{V}_1 + \vec{V}_2 + \vec{V}_3 \qquad (4.63)$$

The tension in the first segment is then found from

$$T_1 = \sqrt{H_0^2 + V_0^2}$$

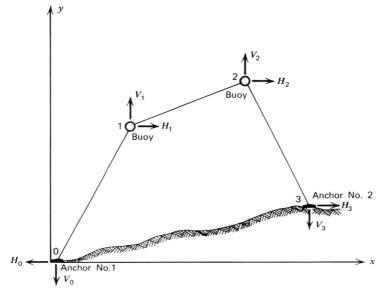

Figure 4.17.

The coordinates of the first segment end are obtained from

$$x_1 = \{ L_{0(1)} + \Delta L_{(1)} \} \cos \theta_1 \qquad (4.64)$$

$$y_1 = \{ L_{0(1)} + \Delta L_{(1)} \} \sin \theta_1 \qquad (4.65)$$

where $L_{0(1)}$ is the unstretched length of the first segment (its length when the tension is zero); $\Delta L_{(1)}$ is the elongation of the first segment due to the tension $T_{(1)}$, (if the material follows Hooke's law $\Delta L_{(1)} = k_{(1)} T_{(1)}$, $k_{(1)}$ being the spring constant for the first segment); and

$$\theta_1 = \tan^{-1} \frac{V_0}{H_0}$$

The tension in the other segments and the location of their end points are obtained in a similar way. The solution of the problem in this case is thus straightforward.

In most cases, however, H_3 and V_3 are not known and their value must be assumed. The equilibrium obtained with this "imaginary reaction" will coincide with the exact solution only if the reaction assumed value is the reaction exact value. If not, the end of the third segment will be at some

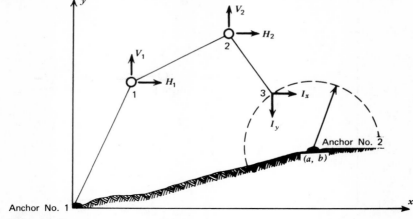

Figure 4.18.

point 3 (Figure 4.18) at a distance E from anchor no. 2 given by

$$E = \sqrt{(a - x_3)^2 + (b - y_3)^2} \tag{4.66}$$

In order to reduce this error the "imaginary" reaction I must be corrected. The correction is done by adding to the horizontal and vertical components of the reaction two forces ΔI_x and ΔI_y each respectively proportional to the amount of error in the x and in the y direction.

The expression of these corrective forces is

$$\Delta I_x = \frac{I}{2^k} \frac{(a - x_3)}{E} \tag{4.67}$$

$$\Delta I_y = \frac{I}{2^k} \frac{(b - y_3)}{E} \tag{4.68}$$

where I is the uncorrected imaginary reaction and k, the exponent of 2, assumes the values $k = 1, 2, 3 \dots$. The components of the corrected imaginary reaction I' thus become

$$I'_x = I_x + \Delta I_x \tag{4.69}$$

$$I'_y = I_y + \Delta I_y \tag{4.70}$$

A second equilibrium configuration is then computed with this corrected reaction, and a second value for the error E'

$$E' = \sqrt{(a - x'_3)^2 + (b - y'_3)^2} \tag{4.71}$$

is thus established.

If E' is smaller than E, then a successful step has been made. A new corrected imaginary reaction I'' with components

$$I_x'' = I_x' + \frac{I}{2^k}\frac{(a-x_3')}{E'}\qquad(4.72)$$

$$I_y'' = I_y' + \frac{I}{2^k}\frac{(b-y_3')}{E'}\qquad(4.73)$$

is then used to compute a third equilibrium configuration.

The process is repeated until the error E^n is found to be larger than E^{n-1}. This indicates that the correction of the preceding computation is too large. To reduce it the exponent, k, is increased to its next higher value. A new computation can then be performed.

The iteration procedure is repeated as many times as needed for sufficient agreement between the computed end point of the last segment and the location of the anchoring point $P(a,b)$. The iteration procedure is schematically represented in Figure 4.19.

The method of imaginary reactions can be easily extended to three-dimensional cases. Consider for example a three-dimensional cable divided in M equal segments as shown in Figure 4.20.

The imaginary reaction $\vec{I} = I_x\vec{i} + I_y\vec{j} + I_z\vec{k}$ is applied at the end of the last segment (point M). The components of the resultant force on this segment are

$$R_{x(M)} = I_x$$
$$R_{y(M)} = I_y$$
$$R_{z(M)} = I_z$$

Let the force $\vec{F}_{(M-1)} = F_{x(M-1)}\vec{i} + F_{y(M-1)}\vec{j} + F_{z(M-1)}\vec{k}$ be applied at the point $M-1$. The resultant on the segment before the last will then have components:

$$R_{x(M-1)} = F_{x(M-1)} + I_x = F_{x(M-1)} + R_{x(M)}$$
$$R_{y(M-1)} = F_{y(M-1)} + I_y = F_{y(M-1)} + R_{y(M)}$$
$$R_{z(M-1)} = F_{z(M-1)} + I_z = F_{z(M-1)} + R_{z(M)}$$

Similarly the components of the resultant force on any segment, n, will be expressed by

$$R_{x(n)} = F_{x(n)} + R_{x(n+1)}\qquad(4.74)$$
$$R_{y(n)} = F_{y(n)} + R_{y(n+1)}\qquad(4.75)$$
$$R_{z(n)} = F_{z(n)} + R_{z(n+1)}\qquad(4.76)$$

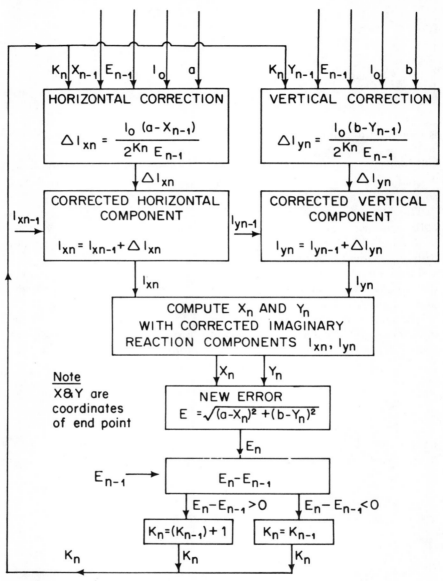

Figure 4.19. Integration loop n.

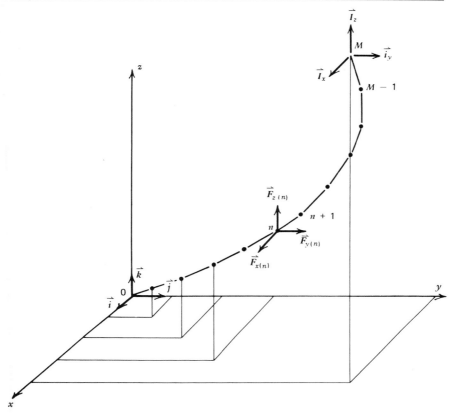

Figure 4.20.

The tension, $T_{(n)}$, in the segment, n, is then given by

$$T_{(n)} = \sqrt{R^2_{x(n)} + R^2_{y(n)} + R^2_{z(n)}} \tag{4.77}$$

The space location of the end points of this segment is obtained from

$$x_{i(n)} = x_{i(n-1)} + L_{(n)} \frac{R_{i(n)}}{T_{(n)}} \tag{4.78}$$

where $i = 1, 2, 3,$ $(x_{1(n)} = x_{(n)},\ x_{2(n)} = y_{(n)},\ x_{3(n)} = z_{(n)})$, and so on, and

$$L_{(n)} = L_{0(n)} \left\{ 1 + \frac{T_{(n)}}{B_{(n)}} \right\} \tag{4.79}$$

with $L_{0(n)}$ the unstretched length of segment n and $B_{(n)}$ the rigidity of the segment n.

Using these recurrence formulas the resultant force in each of the segment is first computed. Then, starting at the origin the tension, the elongation and the coordinates of the end of each segment are obtained.

The error

$$E = \left[\sum_{i=1}^{i=3} (x_i - a_i)^2 \right]^{1/2} \tag{4.80}$$

thus established is then used to correct the three components of the imaginary reaction. The iteration procedure for subsequent computations follows the procedure outlined for the two-dimensional case.

A generalization of the method of imaginary reactions can be used for the study of multileg buoy systems. A trimoor, for example, can be studied by varying the positions of two of the anchors. If $x_{i1}, x_{i2}, a_{i1}, a_{i2}, (i=1,2,3)$ are respectively the computed coordinates and the space locations of the two free anchors, the error E will then be given by

$$E = \left[\sum_{i=1}^{i=3} (a_{i1} - x_{i1})^2 + (a_{i2} - x_{i2})^2 \right]^{1/2}_{i=1,2,3} \tag{4.81}$$

Methods of computing the components of the hydrodynamic forces on the cable segments and iteration procedures for complex cable arrays are discussed in detail by Skop and O'Hara (1970) and Skop and Mark (1973).

Cable Equations in Three Dimensions

Another approach to obtain the equilibrium configuration of three-dimensional cable arrays is to integrate with proper boundary conditions the differential equations expressing the equilibrium conditions of a cable element immersed in a fluid velocity field. These equations are derived as follows:

Cable Coordinates.

As shown in Figure 4.21, let $\vec{u}, \vec{v}, \vec{w}$ be a set of cartesian unit vectors at any point P along the cable, and let $\vec{u}$ be in the direction of the cable at that point. Also let $\vec{i}, \vec{j}, \vec{k}$ be the set of cartesian unit vectors fixed to the earth. If, as shown in Figure 4.22, ψ is the angle between the horizontal plane and the vector $\vec{u}$ and ϕ the angle between the projection of $\vec{u}$ in the horizontal plane

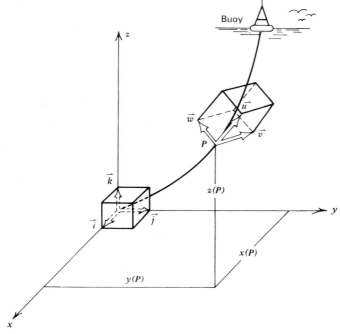

Figure 4.21. Cable attached and earth fixed reference vector sets.

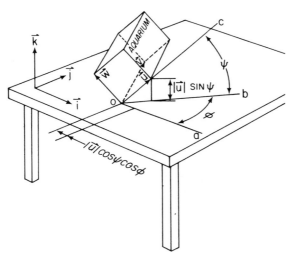

Figure 4.22 *The Box Story.* "Box" was first sitting square on the table top, vector $\vec{u}$ on line oa parallel to vector $\vec{i}$. "Box" was then rotated by an angle ϕ, vector $\vec{u}$ on line ob. "Box" was then lifted by an angle ψ, vector $\vec{u}$ along line oc, vector $\vec{v}$ still in the plane of the table top.

143

and the vector $\vec{i}$, then the relation between the cable vector set and the earth vector set is given by

$$\vec{u} = \cos\psi\cos\phi\vec{i} + \cos\psi\sin\phi\vec{j} + \sin\psi\vec{k} \qquad (4.82)$$

$$\vec{v} = -\sin\phi\vec{i} + \cos\phi\vec{j} \qquad (4.83)$$

$$\vec{w} = -\sin\psi\cos\phi\vec{i} - \sin\psi\sin\phi\vec{j} + \cos\psi\vec{k} \qquad (4.84)$$

Let $ds\,\vec{u}$ be the cable element of infinitesimal length located at P. The components of the cable element length in the $x, y,$ and z directions are then given by

$$dx = ds\,\vec{u}\cdot\vec{i} = ds\cos\psi\cos\phi \qquad (4.85)$$

$$dy = ds\,\vec{u}\cdot\vec{j} = ds\cos\psi\sin\phi \qquad (4.86)$$

$$dz = ds\,\vec{u}\cdot\vec{k} = ds\sin\psi \qquad (4.87)$$

The coordinates x, y, and z of the point P can be obtained from the integration of these relations over the variation domain of the variables ϕ and ψ.

Cable Forces.

The forces on the cable element are the cable element immersed weight, the hydrodynamic resistance on the element, and the tension forces at both ends of the element. The expression of these forces is hereafter derived.

Gravity Force.   If p is the difference between weight and buoyancy per unit of cable length, then the resultant gravity force on the cable element is given by

$$-p\,ds\,\vec{k} \qquad (4.88)$$

Tangential and Normal Components of the Hydrodynamic Resistance.   Let the three-dimensional velocity field $\vec{V}$ be given by

$$\vec{V} = V_x\vec{i} + V_y\vec{j} + V_z\vec{k} \qquad (4.89)$$

where $V_x = V_x(x,y,z)$, $V_y = V_y(x,y,z)$, $V_z = V_z(x,y,z)$. The expression of the tangential component of the resistance $\vec{F}$ is then

$$\vec{F} = F\,ds\,\vec{u} = \tfrac{1}{2}\rho C_{DT}\pi d\left(\vec{V}\cdot\vec{u}\right)^2 ds\,\vec{u} \qquad (4.90)$$

with

$$\vec{V}\cdot\vec{u} = V_x \cos\psi \cos\phi + V_y \cos\psi \sin\phi + V_z \sin\psi$$

and C_{DT} the tangential drag coefficient of the cable. Similarly, the normal components $\vec{G}$ and $\vec{H}$ of the resistance are respectively given by

$$\vec{G} = G\,ds\,\vec{v} = \tfrac{1}{2}\rho C_{DN}d\,(\vec{V}\cdot\vec{v})^2 ds\,\vec{v} \tag{4.91}$$

$$\vec{H} = H\,ds\,\vec{w} = \tfrac{1}{2}\rho C_{DN}d\,(\vec{V}\cdot\vec{w})^2 ds\,\vec{w} \tag{4.92}$$

with

$$\vec{V}\cdot\vec{v} = -V_x \sin\phi + V_y \cos\phi$$
$$\vec{V}\cdot\vec{w} = -V_x \sin\psi \cos\phi - V_y \sin\psi \sin\phi + V_z \cos\phi$$

and C_{DN} the normal drag coefficient of the cable. The quantities F, G, and H are space dependent and must be evaluated at each point P along the cable.

Tension.   At one end of the cable element the tension is $-T\vec{u}$. At the other end the tension is $(T+dT)(\vec{u}+d\vec{u})$, dT being the change in tension magnitude and $d\vec{u}$ the change in the cable orientation that takes place over the elementary length ds. As can be seen from Figure 4.23 the change in cable orientation $d\vec{u}$ is given by

$$d\vec{u} = \cos\psi\,d\phi\,\vec{v} + d\psi\,\vec{w} \tag{4.93}$$

Therefore, the expression of the tension forces are

$$-T\vec{u}$$

at one end and

$$(T+dT)(\vec{u}+\cos\psi\,d\phi\,\vec{v}+d\psi\,\vec{w}) \tag{4.94}$$

at the other end. The different forces applied to the cable element are shown on Figure 4.24.

Equations of Equilibrium.

When in static equilibrium the sum of the forces applied to the cable element is equal to zero. The condition of equilibrium is, therefore,

$$-T\vec{u}+(T+dT)(\vec{u}+d\vec{u})+F\,ds\,\vec{u}+G\,ds\,\vec{v}+H\,ds\,\vec{w}-p\,ds\,\vec{k}=0$$

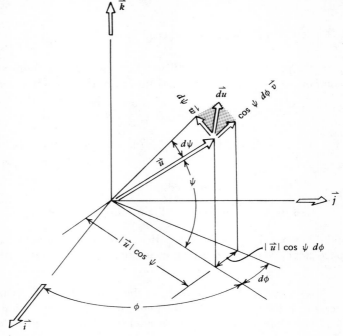

Figure 4.23.

or, neglecting higher order infinitesimals,

$$T\,d\vec{u} + dT\vec{u} + F\,ds\,\vec{u} + G\,ds\,\vec{v} + H\,ds\,\vec{w} - p\,ds\,\vec{k} = 0$$

or

$$(dT + F\,ds)\vec{u} + (T\cos\psi\,d\phi + G\,ds)\vec{v} + (T\,d\psi + H\,ds)\vec{w} - p\,ds\,\vec{k} = 0 \quad (4.95)$$

The three scalar equations of equilibrium in the directions tangential and normal to the cable element can be obtained from the scalar product of the vectorial equation (4.95) by each of the vectors of the cable attached unit vector set. Equations thus obtained are

(a) in the direction of $\vec{u}$

$$dT + F\,ds - p\sin\psi\,ds = 0$$

(b) in the direction of $\vec{v}$

$$T\cos\psi\,d\phi + G\,ds = 0$$

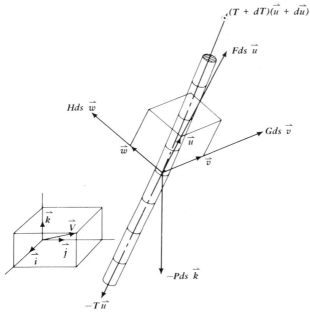

Figure 4.24.

(c) in the direction of $\vec{w}$

$$T\,d\psi + H\,ds - p\cos\psi\,ds = 0$$

The differential equations of cable equilibrium are, therefore,

$$\frac{dT}{ds} = p\sin\psi - F \qquad\qquad (4.96)$$

$$\frac{d\phi}{ds} = -\frac{G}{T\cos\psi} \qquad\qquad (4.97)$$

$$\frac{d\psi}{ds} = \frac{1}{T}(p\cos\psi - H) \qquad\qquad (4.98)$$

These equations express the change in cable tension and orientation that take place over the elementary length ds. As in previously studied two-dimensional cases, one can note that changes in tension are caused by the tangential forces whereas normal forces are responsible for changes in the cable geometry.

To summarize, Eqs. (4.85), (4.86), (4.87), (4.96), (4.97), and (4.98) express the relation between the six dependent variables, T, ϕ, ψ, x, y, and z for any point $P(s)$ along the cable path. Integration of these equations with specified boundary conditions will yield the equilibrium configuration of the cable and the steady-state distribution of tension along the cable path.

This three-dimensional analysis can be expanded to include mooring line elasticity. In that case the equations of cable equilibrium must be derived in terms of the stretched length given by

$$ds' = ds(1 + \epsilon)$$

where ds is the initial length of the cable and ϵ, the strain, is a function of the tension T in the cable element (Patton, 1972). The integration of the complex differential equations expressing the equilibrium conditions of cables subjected to three-dimensional loads is done with the help of computer techniques.

Five

DYNAMICS OF MOORING LINES

Wave action on a moored structure results in dynamic excitation of its anchoring lines. The study of the line response to wave excitation permits one to predict the amplitude and the distribution of the dynamic stresses along the line as well as to investigate conditions of resonance.

Dynamic stresses must be considered together with static stresses when selecting the type and size of mooring line components. Resonance and related large displacements may result in severe peak loads and/or line relaxation. Both effects can be very damaging for the mooring line.

Two different methods are used to investigate cable dynamics. In one approach the mooring line is considered as a continuous elastic medium, whereas in the other the mooring line is represented by a multiple degrees of freedom spring-mass system.

5.1. THE MOORING LINE AS A CONTINUOUS MEDIUM

Longitudinal Excitation

Assumptions

A closed loop solution for the response of longitudinally excited cables can be obtained if the following assumptions are made: (*a*) The mooring line, or cable, is subjected to longitudinal forces only. (*b*) Hydrodynamic resistance

149

is neglected, sometimes a fair assumption when one considers that only small tangential drag forces could occur. (*c*) The material of the line follows Hooke's law.

Cable Wave Equation

Consider a vertical and neutrally buoyant cable immersed in a perfectly still fluid. The cable lower end is fixed to the bottom. As shown in Figure 5.1(*a*), the distance *s* from the bottom to a point *P* on the line is simply given by

$$s = \int_0^P ds$$

ds being the length of an infinitesimal cable element. At some time t_0, let a time varying force $F(t)$ be applied at the cable upper end, pulling the cable upwards in a vertical direction.

Under the action of this force the cable elongates. As shown in Figure 5.1(*b*), point *P* at some time *t*, has moved to *P'* a distance ξ away from the

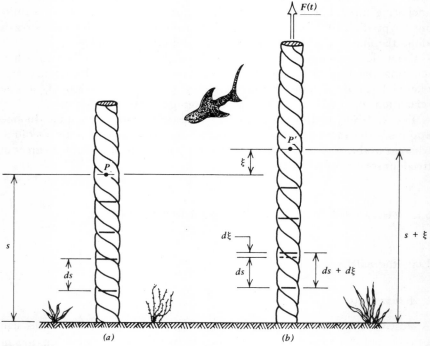

(*a*)   (*b*)

Figure 5.1.

location it had before the application of the force $F(t)$. The length of the cable elements, ds, have been increased by an amount $d\xi$ given by

$$d\xi = \frac{\partial \xi}{\partial s} ds$$

The displacement ξ of any point P along the cable is, therefore, given by

$$\xi = \int_0^P d\xi = \int_0^P \frac{\partial \xi}{\partial s} ds = \xi(s,t)$$

The strain, ϵ, or the elongation per unit of length, resulting from the application of the force $F(t)$ at the end of the cable, is in turn given by

$$\epsilon = \lim_{ds \to 0} \frac{[ds + (\partial \xi/\partial s)ds] - ds}{ds}$$

or

$$\epsilon = \frac{\partial \xi}{\partial s}$$

Assuming the cable material to follow Hooke's law, the corresponding stress σ is, thus,

$$\sigma = E\epsilon = E \frac{\partial \xi}{\partial s}$$

where E is the modulus of elasticity of the cable. If A is the cable cross-sectional area, the forces due to this stress at the lower and the upper ends of the stretched cable element are, respectively,

$$A\sigma = AE \frac{\partial \xi}{\partial s}$$

and

$$A\left(\sigma + \frac{\partial \sigma}{\partial s} ds\right) = AE\left(\frac{\partial \xi}{\partial s} + \frac{\partial}{\partial s}\left(\frac{\partial \xi}{\partial s}\right) ds\right)$$

Neglecting any fluid viscous forces, the resultant force is the difference between the forces at the two opposite ends of the cable element and is, therefore, given by

$$AE \frac{\partial^2 \xi}{\partial s^2} ds$$

The differential equation relating the resultant force and the displacement of the cable element is obtained from Newton's second law of mechanics. The result is

$$AE\frac{\partial^2 \xi}{\partial s^2} = \mu\frac{\partial^2 \xi}{\partial t^2} \tag{5.1}$$

where μ is the virtual mass, per unit of length, of the cable. Introducing

$$a^2 = \frac{AE}{\mu} \tag{5.2}$$

in expression (5.1) yields the familiar one-dimensional wave equation

$$\frac{\partial^2 \xi}{\partial s^2} = \frac{1}{a^2}\frac{\partial^2 \xi}{\partial t^2} \tag{5.3}$$

where $a = \sqrt{AE/\mu}$ is the speed of propagation of the longitudinal deformation in the immersed continuous elastic medium (see Exercise 23).

Solution of the Wave Equation

Using again the method of separation of variables, let $\xi(s,t)$ be expressed by

$$\xi(s,t) = S(s)T(t) \tag{5.4}$$

where $S(s)$ is a function of s only and $T(t)$ is a function of t only. Introducing (5.4) in (5.3), multiplying both sides by a^2 and dividing both sides by $S(s)T(t)$ yields

$$\frac{a^2}{S}\frac{d^2S}{ds^2} = \frac{1}{T}\frac{d^2T}{dt^2}$$

Let these two equal expressions be equal to a constant $-q^2$, the sign of which is selected so as to ensure harmonic solutions.
This gives

$$\frac{a^2}{S}\frac{d^2S}{ds^2} = -q^2 = \frac{1}{T}\frac{d^2T}{dt^2}$$

from which the following two differential equations in s and t are obtained:

$$\frac{d^2S}{ds^2} + \frac{q^2}{a^2}S = 0$$

$$\frac{d^2T}{dt^2} + q^2T = 0$$

The integration of these equations yields:

$$T = A \cos qt + B \sin qt$$

$$S = C \cos \frac{q}{a} s + D \sin \frac{q}{a} s$$

Introducing these values of S and T in (5.4) yields

$$\xi = (A \cos qt + B \sin qt)\left(C \cos \frac{q}{a} s + D \sin \frac{q}{a} s \right) \qquad (5.5)$$

The value of the four constants of integration is determined from the initial and boundary conditions particular to a specific situation. It should be noted here that a solution of the form

$$\xi(s_1 t) = \sum_{i=1}^{\infty} (A_i \cos q_i t + B_i \sin q_i t)\left(C_i \cos \frac{q_i}{a} s + D_i \sin \frac{q_i}{a} s \right)$$

is also a solution of the wave equation (5.3). This general solution can be used to advantage when the initial and boundary conditions are expressed in terms of Fourier series.

Cable Tension

In order to include the more frequent situation where gravity forces cannot be ignored, let us now consider a cable which is no longer neutrally buoyant. Figure 5.2 shows an elementary length of this cable located at a distance s from the fixed end. The tension T_1 at the upper face of the element is given by

$$T_1 = pds + EA\left(\frac{\partial \xi}{\partial s} + \frac{\partial}{\partial s}\left(\frac{\partial \xi}{\partial s} \right) ds \right)$$

where p is the force, per unit of length, equal to the difference between cable line weight (lb/ft) and cable line buoyancy (lb/ft) and where the second term is, as previously derived, the force at the upper face resulting from the strain caused by the application of the force $F(t)$. The tension T_2 at the lower face of the element is in turn

$$T_2 = EA \frac{\partial \xi}{\partial s}$$

The change of tension dT taking place over the length ds being the difference between the tension at both ends of the cable element is given by

$$dT = T_1 - T_2 = pds + EA \frac{\partial^2 \xi}{\partial s^2} ds$$

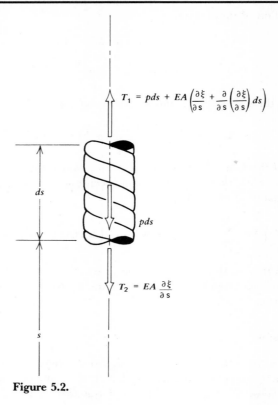

Figure 5.2.

Integrating this result yields

$$T = ps + EA \frac{\partial \xi}{\partial s} + \text{constant}$$

If T_0 is the tension when both $s = 0$ and

$$\left. \frac{\partial \xi}{\partial s} \right|_{s=0} = 0$$

then the expression of the tension $T(s,t)$ along the cable becomes

$$T = T_0 + ps + EA \frac{\partial \xi}{\partial s} \qquad (5.6)$$

The two first terms constitute the steady state, or static component of the tension; whereas, the last term accounts for the dynamic effect due to the time varying force $F(t)$.

Particular Solutions

Case I. Surface Following Buoy.   Let us consider the particular case of a surface following buoy moored, as shown in Figure 5.3, by a taut elastic line of length L. The wave surface is given by $Z = Z_0 \sin \omega t$.

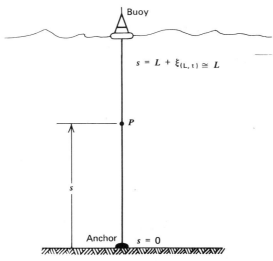

Figure 5.3.

INITIAL AND BOUNDARY CONDITIONS.   (*a*.) The initial displacement of all points in the line at time, t, is zero, that is,

$$\xi(s,0) = 0$$

(*b*.) The origin is selected at the anchor. The anchor is fixed, and, therefore,

$$\xi(0,t) = 0$$

The tension at the anchor, at time $t = 0$, is T_0.
(*c*.) The vertical displacement of the buoy and, therefore, of the displacement of the cable upper end is given by

$$\xi(L,t) = Z_0 \sin \omega t$$

SOLUTION.   The displacement $\xi(s,t)$ of any point along the line is given by (5.5) as

$$\xi(s,t) = (A \cos qt + B \sin qt)\left(C \cos \frac{q}{a}s + D \sin \frac{q}{a}s\right)$$

The initial condition $\xi(s,0)=0$ implies that $A=0$. With this in mind (5.5) reduces to

$$\xi(s,t)=\left(M\cos\frac{q}{a}s+N\sin\frac{q}{a}s\right)\sin qt$$

where $M=BC$, and $N=BD$. The boundary condition $\xi(0,t)=0$ implies that $M=0$. The expression of ξ is, thus, further reduced to

$$\xi(s,t)=N\sin\frac{q}{a}s\sin qt$$

Finally, the boundary condition

$$\xi(L,t)=Z_0\sin\omega t$$

implies that

$$q=\omega$$

and

$$N=\frac{Z_0}{\sin(\omega L/a)}$$

Thus the expression of the displacement $\xi(s,t)$ is given by

$$\xi(s,t)=\frac{Z_0}{\sin(\omega L/a)}\sin\frac{\omega}{a}s\sin\omega t$$

Differentiating this expression with respect to s and introducing the result in expression (5.6) gives the tension $T(s,t)$ as

$$T(s,t)=T_0+ps+\frac{AEZ_0}{\sin(\omega L/a)}\frac{\omega}{a}\left(\cos\frac{\omega}{a}s\right)\sin\omega t$$

The tension at the anchor is, thus,

$$T_A=T_0+\frac{AEZ_0}{\sin(\omega L/a)}\frac{\omega}{a}\sin\omega t$$

and the tension at the buoy

$$T_B=T_0+pL+(AEZ_0)\left(\frac{\omega}{a}\right)\cot\left(\frac{\omega L}{a}\right)\sin\omega t$$

It can be seen that resonance conditions will occur for

$$\sin\frac{\omega L}{a}=0$$

or

$$\omega = n \frac{\pi a}{L}$$

where

$$n = 1, 2, 3, \ldots .$$

Case II. Cable with Free Load at the Lower End.   Consider now the case of a cable supporting a load at its lower end while its upper end is forced to follow a simple harmonic displacement. Such a cable could be, for example, the mooring line of a buoy system being deployed anchor first from a ship in a regular swell.

INITIAL AND BOUNDARY CONDITIONS.   (a.) Here again, the initial displacement of all points in the line at time, t, is assumed to be zero, that is, $\xi(s,0) = 0$.
(b.) The displacement of the upper end of the line is of the form $\xi(L,t) = Z_0 \sin \omega t$.
(c.) The origin is again selected at the lower end of the line, that is, at $s = 0$. The boundary condition at that end will be obtained from the equation of motion of the suspended load.

As can be seen from Figure 5.4 the forces applied at the cable lower end are the tension $T(0,t)$ and the immersed weight given by

$$W - B$$

where $W = mg$ is the weight of the load in air, m being its mass and g the gravity acceleration, and B is the buoyancy force on the load. Neglecting the viscous damping force on the load, the equation of motion of the load, obtained with the help of Newton's law, is, therefore,

$$(W - B) - T(0,t) = m_v \frac{\partial^2 \xi}{\partial t^2}$$

where m_v is the load virtual mass, or, using (5.6),

$$W - B - \left(T_0 + EA \frac{\partial \xi}{\partial s} \bigg|_{s=0} \right) = m_v \frac{\partial^2 \xi}{\partial t^2}$$

Noting that under static conditions, $T_0 = W - B$, the equation of motion is further reduced to

$$EA \frac{\partial \xi}{\partial s} \bigg|_{s=0} + m_v \frac{\partial^2 \xi}{\partial t^2} \bigg|_{s=0} = 0$$

This is the boundary condition at the lower end of the cable.

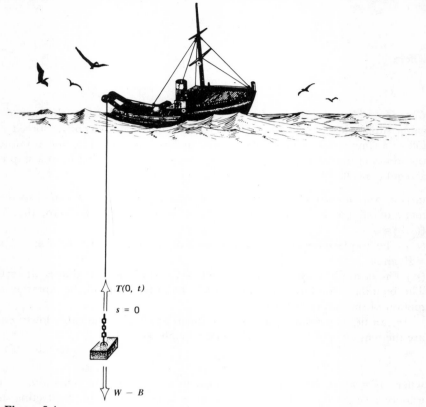

Figure 5.4.

Solution. As in Case I, the initial condition $\xi(s,0)=0$ again yields

$$\xi(s,t)=\left(M\cos\frac{q}{a}s+N\sin\frac{q}{a}s\right)\sin qt$$

Evaluating the first partial derivative with respect to displacement, s, and the second partial derivative with respect to time, t, of this expression at $s=0$ and introducing the results in the boundary condition at the cable lower end yields

$$N=Mm_v\frac{qa}{EA}$$

With this value of the constant, N, the expression of the displacement becomes

$$\xi(s,t) = M \sin qt \left\{ \cos \frac{q}{a} s + \frac{mga}{EA} \sin \frac{q}{a} s \right\}$$

Applying to this latter expression the boundary condition at the upper end of the cable yields

$$q = \omega$$

$$M = \frac{Z_0}{\cos(\omega L/a) + (m_v \omega a / EA) \sin(\omega L/a)}$$

Thus, the final expression of the steady-state displacement $\xi(s,t)$ is

$$\xi(s,t) = \frac{Z_0 \sin \omega t}{\cos(\omega L/a) + (m_v \omega a / EA) \sin(\omega L/a)} \left\{ \cos \frac{\omega}{a} s + \frac{m_v \omega a}{EA} \sin \frac{\omega}{a} s \right\}$$

This solution implies the motion is sinusoidal at $t = 0$.
   Using again (5.6) the tension $T(s,t)$ is

$$T(s,t) = ps + W - B$$

$$+ \frac{Z_0 EA \sin \omega t}{\cos(\omega L/a) + (m_v \omega / EA) \sin(\omega L/a)} \left\{ \frac{m_v \omega^2}{EA} \cos \frac{\omega s}{a} - \frac{\omega}{a} \sin \frac{\omega}{a} s \right\}$$

The tension at the surface is, thus,

$$T(L,t) = pL + W - B$$

$$+ \frac{Z_0 EA \sin \omega t}{\cos(\omega L/a) + (m_v \omega a / EA) \sin(\omega L/a)} \left\{ \frac{m_v \omega^2}{EA} \cos \frac{\omega L}{a} - \frac{\omega}{a} \sin \frac{\omega L}{a} \right\}$$

The tension at the weight, on the other hand, is given by

$$T(0,t) = W - B + \frac{Z_0 m_v \omega^2}{\cos(\omega L/a) + (m_v \omega a / EA) \sin(\omega L/a)} \sin \omega t$$

Large values of tension can be expected as the denominator of the dynamic contribution tends toward zero.

   Closed loop solutions, derived from the wave equation in continuous elastic medium, provide simple models for first approximation studies. They can serve as the basis for the frequency domain analysis of cable response to random excitation. These solutions can also be used as limit cases for comparison with results obtained from more complex models.

Vectorial Equation of Motion—All Forces Considered

Assumptions

In the derivation of the general equation of motion for an element of an elastic cable subjected to both gravity and three-dimensional hydrodynamic forces, the following assumptions are made: (*a*) No restriction is imposed on the nature of the three-dimensional velocity field $\vec{U}$ acting on the cable; (*b*) the mooring line is perfectly flexible, that is, the tension is always in the direction of a vector tangent to the cable; (*c*) the elastic behavior of the line material is characterized by a known equation of state.

Reference Spaces

In order to establish the relation between the dependent and independent variables of the problem, it is convenient to introduce two reference spaces corresponding to the unstrained and strained conditions of the cable.

As shown in Figure 5.5*a*, the arc length from the origin 0, which is selected at the point of anchoring, to point *P* along the relaxed length of the cable is denoted by *s*. In Figure 5.5*b* the cable is now strained. Under the action of the forces at play, point *P* has moved to point *P'* located at a distance *s'* from 0. The curvilinear coordinate *s'* is a function of the original

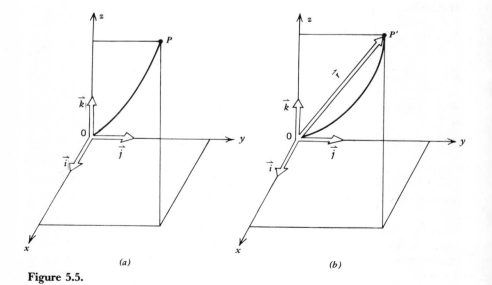

(*a*)   (*b*)

Figure 5.5.

arc length s and of the time t, that is,

$$s' = s'(s,t)$$

Point P' can also be located by a radius vector $\vec{r}$ given by

$$\vec{r} = \vec{r}(s,t) = x(s,t)\vec{i} + y(s,t)\vec{j} + z(s,t)\vec{k} \tag{5.7}$$

where $\vec{i}$, $\vec{j}$, and $\vec{k}$ constitute a set of cartesian vectors fixed to the earth. Therefore, the speed and acceleration of the material point P' can be respectively expressed by

$$\vec{V}(s,t) = \frac{\partial \vec{r}}{\partial t} \tag{5.8}$$

$$\vec{a}(s,t) = \frac{\partial \vec{v}}{\partial t} \tag{5.9}$$

Furthermore, the function $\partial s'/\partial s$ of s and t expresses the rate of change of s' as a function of s. The relation between a cable elementary length ds' in the s' space and the corresponding elementary length ds in the s space is, thus,

$$ds' = \frac{\partial s'}{\partial s} ds \tag{5.10}$$

Similarly, if m is the mass per unit of length in the s space and m' the mass per unit of length in the s' space, then conservation of mass will dictate that

$$m\,ds \equiv m'\,ds' = m' \frac{\partial s'}{\partial s} ds$$

from which

$$m = m' \frac{\partial s'}{\partial s} \tag{5.11}$$

Another useful relation between the two spaces is obtained by defining the strain ϵ, or elongation per unit of length, as

$$\epsilon \equiv \frac{ds' - ds}{ds} = \epsilon(T) \tag{5.12}$$

T being the tension. Introducing (5.10) in (5.12) yields

$$\epsilon = \frac{\partial s'}{\partial s} - 1 \tag{5.13}$$

Forces to Consider

Let us now consider a strained cable element of length ds' located at point P'. The forces that one could consider to derive the equation of motion of the cable element are shown in Figure 5.6. Their expression follows.

Weight.   The force due to gravity, $\vec{W}$, is given by

$$\vec{W} = -gm'ds'\vec{k}$$

where g is the gravity acceleration and m' the line mass per unit of length in the s' space.

Buoyancy.   The buoyancy force, $\vec{B}$, is given by

$$\vec{B} = +g\rho_w A ds'\vec{k}$$

where A is the reduced area of the cable cross section at the point P' and is a function of the tension, T, at that location, that is, $A = A(T)$, and ρ_w is the water mass density.

Normal Drag.   The normal drag, $\vec{D}$, is given by

$$\vec{D} = \tfrac{1}{2}\rho_w C_{DN} d |\vec{U}_N - \vec{V}_N|(\vec{U}_N - \vec{V}_N) ds'$$

where $\vec{U}_N$ is the component of the fluid velocity field normal to the cable,

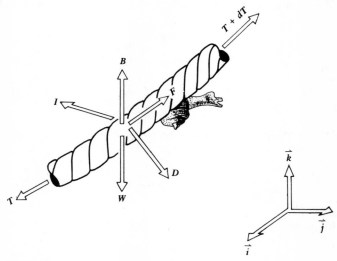

Figure 5.6.

that is,

$$\vec{U}_N = \vec{U} - (\vec{U} \cdot \vec{u})\vec{u}$$

$\vec{u}$ being a unit vector tangent to the cable at point P'. $\vec{V}_N$ is the component of the cable element velocity normal to the cable element, that is,

$$\vec{V}_N = \vec{V} - (\vec{V} \cdot \vec{u})\vec{u}$$

C_{DN} is the cable coefficient of normal drag, which could, if so required, account for strumming effects; d is the cable effective diameter at point P' and is a function of the tension, T, at that point, that is,

$$d = d(T)$$

Tangential Drag.   The tangential drag, $\vec{F}$, is given by

$$\vec{F} = \tfrac{1}{2}\rho_W C_{DT} \pi d |\vec{U}_T - \vec{V}_T|(\vec{U}_T - \vec{V}_T)ds'$$

where $\vec{U}_T$ is the component of the fluid velocity field tangential to the cable, that is,

$$\vec{U}_T = (\vec{U} \cdot \vec{u})\vec{u}$$

$\vec{V}_T$ is the component of the cable element velocity tangential to the cable element, that is,

$$\vec{V}_T = (\vec{V} \cdot \vec{u})\vec{u}$$

C_{DT} is the cable coefficient of tangential drag.

Inertial Force.   The inertial force, $\vec{I}$, due to the water added mass effect, can generally be expressed by

$$\vec{I} = m'_a \left(\frac{\partial \vec{U}}{\partial t} - \frac{\partial \vec{V}}{\partial t} \right) ds'$$

where, m'_a is the added mass per unit of length in the space s' and is given by

$$m'_a = m_a \frac{\partial s}{\partial s'} = \rho_W A C_m$$

with m_a the added mass per unit of length in the s space, and C_m the added mass coefficient of the cable.

$\partial \vec{U}/\partial t$ is the acceleration of the velocity field that would occur under unsteady flow conditions. For example, one could consider a wave velocity field superimposed to a steady-state current.

$\partial \vec{V}/\partial t$ is the acceleration of the cable element.

Tension.   The tension force at one end of the cable element is $\vec{T}(s')$ whereas at the other end the tension is $\vec{T}(s' + ds')$.

Equation of Motion

Applying Newton's law $\sum_i \vec{F}_i = m\vec{a}$ to the cable element of mass $m'ds'$ yields

$$m'ds'\frac{\partial \vec{V}}{\partial t} = -gds'(m' - \rho_\omega A)\vec{k} + \tfrac{1}{2}\rho_\omega C_{DN}d\,ds'|\vec{U}_n - \vec{V}_n|(\vec{U}_n - \vec{V}_n)$$

$$+ \tfrac{1}{2}\rho_w C_{DT}\pi d\,ds'|\vec{U}_T - \vec{V}_T|(\vec{U}_T - \vec{V}_T) + m'_a ds'\left(\frac{\partial \vec{U}}{\partial t} - \frac{\partial \vec{V}}{\partial t}\right)$$

$$+ T(s' + ds') - T(s')$$

Dividing this interesting equation by ds' and taking the limit as ds' tends to zero yields:

$$m'\frac{\partial \vec{V}}{\partial t} = -g(m' - \rho_\omega A)\vec{k} + \tfrac{1}{2}\rho_\omega C_{DN}d|\vec{U}_N - \vec{V}_N|(\vec{U}_N - \vec{V}_N)$$

$$+ \tfrac{1}{2}\rho_W C_{DT}\pi d|\vec{U}_T - \vec{V}_T|(\vec{U}_T - \vec{V}_T) + m'_a\frac{\partial \vec{U}}{\partial t}$$

$$- m'_a\frac{\partial \vec{V}}{\partial t} + \frac{\partial}{\partial s'}(\vec{T}) \tag{5.14}$$

Now let $\vec{T}$, the tension vector, be expressed by

$$\vec{T} = T\vec{u} = T\frac{\partial \vec{r}}{\partial s'}$$

where, as it will be recalled from elementary vector analysis, $\partial \vec{r}/\partial s'$ is the unit vector tangent to the cable at point P', that is,

$$\vec{u} = \frac{\partial \vec{r}}{\partial s'} \qquad \text{and} \qquad |\vec{u}| = |\frac{\partial \vec{r}}{\partial s'}| = 1$$

Using this expression for T in the quantity $\partial \vec{T}/\partial s'$ yields

$$\frac{\partial \vec{T}}{\partial s'} = \frac{\partial T}{\partial s'}\vec{u} = \frac{\partial T}{\partial s}\frac{\partial s}{\partial s'} \times \frac{\partial \vec{r}}{\partial s'}$$

Noting that

$$\frac{\partial \vec{r}}{\partial s'} = \frac{\dfrac{\partial \vec{r}}{\partial s}}{\dfrac{\partial s'}{\partial s}}$$

or, using expression (5.13)

$$\frac{\partial \vec{r}}{\partial s'} = \frac{1}{(1+\epsilon)} \frac{\partial \vec{r}}{\partial s}$$

the quantity $\partial \vec{T}/\partial s'$ can be finally written

$$\frac{\partial \vec{T}}{\partial s'} = \frac{\partial}{\partial s}\left(\frac{T}{1+\epsilon} \frac{\partial \vec{r}}{\partial s} \right) \frac{\partial s}{\partial s'}$$

This latter result can be introduced in (5.14) to yield

$$(m + m_a)\frac{\partial \vec{V}}{\partial t} = -g\left(m - \rho_w A \frac{\partial s'}{\partial s} \right)\vec{k} + \tfrac{1}{2}\rho_w C_{DN} d \frac{\partial s'}{\partial s}|\vec{U}_N - \vec{V}_N|(\vec{U}_N - \vec{V}_N)$$

$$+ \tfrac{1}{2}\rho_w C_{DT}\pi d \frac{\partial s'}{\partial s}|\vec{U}_T - \vec{V}_T|(\vec{U}_T - \vec{V}_T)$$

$$+ m_a\frac{\partial \vec{U}}{\partial t} + \frac{\partial}{\partial s}\frac{T}{(1+\epsilon)} \frac{\partial \vec{r}}{\partial s} \qquad (5.15)$$

This general equation of motion expresses the relation between the dependent variables $\vec{r}$, $\vec{V}$, T, and s' with the independent variables s and t. The dependence on s and t of the variables A, d, and ϵ is implied through the dependence of T on $\vec{r}$ and t. The dependence on s and t of the variable $\vec{U}$ is implied similarly through the prescribed functional dependence of $\vec{U}$ on $\vec{r}$ and t. Scalar equations of motion can be obtained from the projection of Eq. (5.15) in the directions of $\vec{u}$, $\vec{v}$, and $\vec{w}$, the unit vector set attached to the cable. The integration of the resulting nonlinear partial differential equations involves advanced techniques of engineering analysis, which are beyond the scope of this book, and requires the use of computers. The interested reader can find excellent descriptions of these techniques and related computer programs by Reid (1968) and Patton (1972).

5.2. THE MOORING LINE AS A SPRING MASS SYSTEM

In this approach the mooring line is represented by a finite set of discrete masses connected to each other by restoring and damping elements. (See Figure 5.7.) The value of the system parameters is determined from the

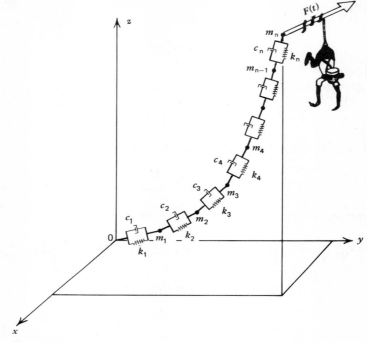

Figure 5.7.

physical characteristics of the mooring line components (weight and elasticity of the mooring line, weight and drag of inserted instrumentation or equipment, etc.).

The several degrees of freedom system obtained with this model is then excited at one end and its forced response studied for various amplitudes and frequencies of excitation.

Basic Concepts—Two Degrees of Freedom Systems

The following analysis of 2 degrees of freedom spring-mass systems will serve as an introduction to, or a review of, the basic concepts needed for the study of more complex systems.

Definitions

Degree of Freedom.   The minimum number of independent coordinates required to specify the space location of each of the masses of a vibrating system defines the degree of freedom of the system.

Free Oscillation.   When an elastic system is displaced from its static equilibrium position and then left free to move the resulting motion is called free oscillation.

Natural Frequency.   The natural frequency is the frequency of free oscillation.

Forced Oscillation is the motion resulting from cyclic forces applied to the system.

Equation of Motion.   The differential equation relating the physical parameters of the oscillating system to displacement and time derivatives of displacement is obtained from Newton's law

$$\sum_n \vec{F}_{in} = m_i \vec{a}_i$$

where $\vec{F}_{in}$ are the forces applied to the ith mass m_i with acceleration $\vec{a}_i$.

Restoring Force.   This force wants to bring the system back to its static condition (spring force). When linear, the restoring force is given by

$$F_R = kx \qquad\qquad (5.16)$$

where x is the distance from the equilibrium position and k is the spring constant. For mooring lines following Hooke's law, the spring constant k is given by

$$k = \frac{EA}{L}$$

where E is the modulus of elasticity of the mooring line, A is the cross section area of the mooring line, and L is the length of the elastic element representing the mooring line.

Damping Force.   This force slows down, or opposes, the motion (internal friction, drag, etc.). When linear, this force is proportional to the speed, that is

$$F_D = c\dot{X} \qquad\qquad (5.17)$$

where c is called the linear damping coefficient.

Exciting Force.   The exciting force is the cyclic external force applied to the system. In its simplest form it is expressed by

$$F(t) = F_0 \sin(\omega t + \phi) \qquad\qquad (5.18)$$

where F_0 is the maximum force amplitude; $\omega = 2\pi f$ is the angular frequency of the force, t is the time, and ϕ is the phase angle.

Single Degree of Freedom System.   Systems requesting only one coordinate to describe their displacement from a static equilibrium condition fall in this category. Heave and roll response of free floating buoys previously studied are examples of single degree of freedom problems.

Two Degrees of Freedom Systems Analysis

Undamped Free Oscillation.   Consider the simple spring-mass system shown in Figure 5.8. The system consists of two masses m_1 and m_2 and two springs with spring constant k_1 and k_2. The end of the first spring is attached at point 0. The two masses are constrained to move along the vertical line $0x$.

Let x_1 and x_2 represent the displacement of the masses m_1 and m_2 from their equilibrium position.

Applying Newton's law to these two masses yields

$$- k_1 x_1 + k_2(x_2 - x_1) = m_1 \ddot{x}_1$$

$$- k_2(x_2 - x_1) = m_2 \ddot{x}_2$$

or

$$m_1 \ddot{x}_1 + (k_1 + k_2)x_1 - k_2 x_2 = 0$$

$$m_2 \ddot{x}_2 - k_2 x_1 + k_2 x_2 = 0$$

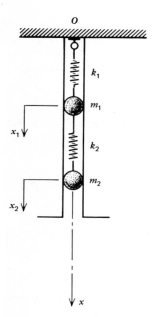

Figure 5.8.

Introducing the parameters

$$a = \frac{k_1 + k_2}{m_1}$$

$$b = \frac{k_2}{m_1}$$

$$c = \frac{k_2}{m_2}$$

the equations of motion reduce to

$$\ddot{x}_1 + ax_1 - bx_2 = 0 \tag{5.19}$$

$$\ddot{x}_2 - cx_1 + cx_2 = 0 \tag{5.20}$$

Expecting the motion of the two masses to be periodic, the tentative solutions

$$x_1 = A \sin(\omega t + \phi) \tag{5.21}$$

$$x_2 = B \sin(\omega t + \phi) \tag{5.22}$$

are introduced in the equations of motion. The result is

$$- A\omega^2 \sin(\omega t + \phi) + aA \sin(\omega t + \phi) - bB \sin(\omega t + \phi) = 0$$

$$- B\omega^2 \sin(\omega t + \phi) - cA \sin(\omega t + \phi) + cB \sin(\omega t + \phi) = 0$$

It, therefore, follows that

$$A(a - \omega^2) - Bb = 0 \tag{5.23}$$

$$- A(c) + B(c - \omega^2) = 0 \tag{5.24}$$

The condition for Eqs. (5.23) and (5.24) to be simultaneously satisfied is that the determinant of the coefficients of A and B vanishes, that is,

$$\begin{vmatrix} a - \omega^2 & -b \\ -c & c - \omega^2 \end{vmatrix} = 0$$

The expansion of the determinant yields

$$(a - \omega^2)(c - \omega^2) - bc = 0 \tag{5.25}$$

or

$$\omega^4 - \omega^2(a + c) + c(a - b) = 0 \tag{5.26}$$

The latter expression is a quadratic equation in ω^2 with solution

$$\omega^2 = \frac{a+c}{2} \pm \sqrt{\left(\frac{a+c}{2}\right)^2 - c(a-b)} \tag{5.27}$$

The two natural frequencies of the system are, therefore, given by

$$\omega_1 = \sqrt{\frac{a+c}{2} + \left[\left(\frac{a+c}{2}\right)^2 - c(a-b)\right]^{1/2}} \tag{5.28}$$

$$\omega_2 = \sqrt{\frac{a+c}{2} - \left[\left(\frac{a+c}{2}\right)^2 - c(a-b)\right]^{1/2}} \tag{5.29}$$

Either one of these two frequencies can be used in the tentative solutions (5.21) and (5.22) to satisfy the differential equations of motion (5.19) and (5.20).

The two possible solutions are, therefore,

$$x_1 = A_1 \sin(\omega_1 t + \phi_1) \tag{5.30}$$

$$x_2 = B_1 \sin(\omega_1 t + \phi_1) \tag{5.31}$$

and

$$x_1 = A_2 \sin(\omega_2 t + \phi_2) \tag{5.32}$$

$$x_2 = B_2 \sin(\omega_2 t + \phi_2) \tag{5.33}$$

Using (5.23) and (5.24), the maximum displacement of the second mass B can be expressed in terms of the maximum displacement A of the first mass as

$$B_1 = \frac{a - \omega_1^2}{b} A_1 = \frac{c}{c - \omega_1^2} A_1 = \beta_1 A_1$$

and similarly

$$B_2 = \frac{a - \omega_2^2}{b} A_2 = \frac{c}{c - \omega_2^2} A_2 = \beta_2 A_2$$

Expressions (5.30) to (5.33) can, therefore, be rewritten as

$$x_1 = A_1 \sin(\omega_1 t + \phi_1) \tag{5.34}$$

$$x_2 = \beta_1 A_1 \sin(\omega_1 t + \phi_1) \tag{5.35}$$

and

$$x_1 = A_2 \sin(\omega_2 t + \phi_2) \tag{5.36}$$

$$x_2 = \beta_2 A_2 \sin(\omega_2 t + \phi_2) \tag{5.37}$$

The sum of these two solutions being also a solution, the displacement x_1 and x_2 of the two masses can, therefore, be generally expressed by

$$x_1 = A_1 \sin(\omega_1 t + \phi_1) + A_2 \sin(\omega_2 t + \phi_2) \tag{5.38}$$

$$x_2 = \beta_1 A_1 \sin(\omega_1 t + \phi_1) + \beta_2 A_2 \sin(\omega_2 t + \phi_2) \tag{5.39}$$

The four arbitrary constants A_1, A_2, ϕ_1, and ϕ_2 are determined by the initial displacements $x_1(0)$ and $x_2(0)$ and the initial speeds $\dot{x}_1(0)$ and $\dot{x}_2(0)$ of the two masses.

If these initial conditions are such that either A_1 or A_2 are zero, then the two masses will oscillate with the same frequency and phase (ω_1 if $A_2 = 0$, ω_2 if $A_1 = 0$). In that case the system is said to oscillate in one of its principal modes.

The mode having the lowest frequency of vibration is called the first or fundamental mode. The mode with the higher frequency is called second principal mode. When the displacement of the masses is expressed as the sum of two periodic displacements of different amplitude, frequency, and phase, the resulting periodic motion is no longer simple harmonic.

It should be noted that the mode of vibration is fixed by the initial conditions; whereas, the natural frequencies of oscillation are fixed by the physical parameters—masses and spring constants—of the system.

Undamped Forced Oscillation.   As shown in Figure 5.9 let a force $F(t)$

$$F(t) = F_0 \sin pt$$

with $p = 2\pi f$ the angular frequency and F_0 the cyclic force amplitude be applied to the mass m_1 of the spring-mass system just considered.

Applying Newton's law to the two masses m_1 and m_2 yields

$$\ddot{x}_1 + \frac{k_1 + k_2}{m_1} x_1 - \frac{k_2}{m_1} x_2 = \frac{F_0}{m_1} \sin pt \tag{5.40}$$

and

$$\ddot{x}_2 - \frac{k_2}{m_2} x_1 + \frac{k_2}{m_2} x_2 = 0 \tag{5.41}$$

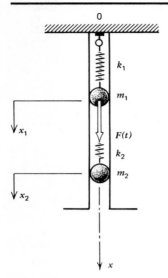

Figure 5.9.

Introducing the constants

$$a = \frac{k_1 + k_2}{m_1}, \qquad b = \frac{k_2}{m_1}, \qquad c = \frac{k_2}{m_2}, \qquad f = \frac{F_0}{m_1}$$

in (5.40) and (5.41), the equations of motion become

$$\ddot{x}_1 + ax_1 - bx_2 = f \sin pt \tag{5.42}$$

$$\ddot{x}_2 - cx_1 + cx_2 = 0 \tag{5.43}$$

The solution of (5.42) and (5.43) is the sum of the solution previously obtained for the homogeneous case (free oscillation) and of a particular solution that when placed in the left-hand side of (5.42) and (5.43) will yield the right-hand side of these two expressions. Let

$$x_1 = C \sin pt \tag{5.44}$$

$$x_2 = D \sin pt \tag{5.45}$$

where p is the frequency of the exciting force, be the particular solution. When (5.44) and (5.45) are substituted in (5.42) and (5.43) the result is

$$(a - p^2)C - bD = f$$

$$-cC + (c - p^2)D = 0$$

Solving for C and D

$$C = \frac{\begin{vmatrix} f & -b \\ D & (c-p^2) \end{vmatrix}}{\begin{vmatrix} (a-p^2) & -b \\ -c & (c-p^2) \end{vmatrix}}$$

$$D = \frac{\begin{vmatrix} a-p^2 & f \\ -c & 0 \end{vmatrix}}{\begin{vmatrix} (a-p^2) & -b \\ -c & (c-p^2) \end{vmatrix}}$$

or

$$C = \frac{f(c-p^2)}{(a-p^2)(c-p^2) - bc} \qquad (5.46)$$

and

$$D = \frac{fc}{(a-p^2)(c-p^2) - bc} \qquad (5.47)$$

The displacement of the masses m_1 and m_2, under forced oscillation are, thus, given by

$$x_1 = A_1 \sin(\omega_1 t + \phi) + A_2 \sin(\omega_2 t + \phi_2) + C\sin pt \qquad (5.48)$$

$$x_2 = \beta_1 A_1 \sin(\omega_1 t + \phi_1) + \beta_2 A_2 \sin(\omega_2 t + \phi_2) + D\sin pt \qquad (5.49)$$

where, as before, the constants A_1, A_2, ϕ_1, and ϕ_2 are determined by the initial conditions, and C and D are given by (5.46) and (5.47).

Resonance.   Equation (5.25)

$$(a-\omega^2)(c-\omega^2) - bc = 0$$

is satisfied if $\omega = \omega_1$ or $\omega = \omega_2$, ω_1 and ω_2 being the natural frequencies of the system. Therefore, at frequencies of excitation p equal to the natural frequencies, the amplitudes of the motion of the masses m_1 and m_2 are infinite. With damping the amplitudes at resonance may still be very large, and this is one of the reasons for studying the natural frequencies of systems with several degrees of freedom.

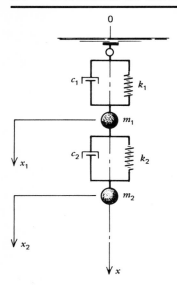

Figure 5.10.

Free Oscillation with Linear Damping. Consider the spring-mass system shown in Figure 5.10. The system consists of two masses m_1 and m_2 connected by two springs with spring constants k_1 and k_2 and two damping elements with linear damping coefficients c_1 and c_2. The motion of the two masses is again assumed to take place along the vertical line $0x$. Applying Newton's law to the two masses m_1 and m_2 yields

$$m_1\ddot{x}_1 + (c_1 + c_2)\dot{x}_1 + (k_1 + k_2)x_1 - c_2\dot{x}_2 - k_2x_2 = 0 \qquad (5.50)$$

and

$$m_2\ddot{x}_2 + c_2\dot{x}_2 + k_2x_2 - c_2\dot{x}_1 - k_2x_1 = 0 \qquad (5.51)$$

The tentative solutions,

$$x_1 = Ae^{st}$$

$$x_2 = Be^{st}$$

when placed in (5.50) and (5.51) yield

$$\{m_1s^2 + (c_1 + c_2)s + (k_1 + k_2)\}A - (c_2s + k_2)B = 0 \qquad (5.52)$$

and

$$-(c_2s + k_2)A + (m_2s^2 + c_2s + k_2)B = 0 \qquad (5.53)$$

The condition for these equations in A and B to be simultaneously satisfied is that the determinant of the coefficients of A and B vanishes, or that

$$\left(m_1 s^2 + (c_1 + c_2)s + k_1 + k_2\right)\left(m_2 s^2 + c_2 s + k_2\right) - \left(c_2 s + k_2\right)^2 = 0 \qquad (5.54)$$

The characteristic equation in s, thus obtained, has four roots, and, therefore, the complete solution for the displacements x_1 and x_2 is

$$x_1 = \sum_{i=1}^{i=4} A_i e^{s_i t}$$

$$x_2 = \sum_{i=1}^{i=4} \beta_i A_i e^{s_i t}$$

The four constants A_i are to be found from the four initial conditions of the system, namely,

$$x_1(0), \; x_2(0), \; \dot{x}_1(0), \; \dot{x}_2(0)$$

The coefficients β_i are obtained from (5.52) and are given by

$$\beta_i = \frac{B_i}{A_i} = \frac{m_1 s_i^2 + (c_1 + c_2)s_i + (k_1 + k_2)}{c_2 s_i + k_2} \qquad (5.55)$$

where $i = 1, 2, 3, 4$.

If two of the four roots are complex conjugate, that is, if

$$s_1 = -(r + id)$$

$$s_2 = -(r - id)$$

then the sum $A_1 e^{s_1 t} + A_2 e^{s_2 t}$ becomes

$$A_1 e^{s_1 t} + A_2 e^{s_2 t} = e^{-rt}\left(A_1 e^{-idt} + A_2 e^{+idt}\right)$$

$$= C e^{-rt} \sin(dt + \psi).$$

This indicates that in all cases free oscillations with linear damping exponentially decay with time.

Forced Oscillation with Linear Damping.   When a periodic force $F(t)$

$$F(t) = F_0 \sin pt$$

is applied to the mass, m_1, of the spring-mass system shown in Figure 5.10, the equations of motion of the two masses become

$$m_1 \ddot{x}_1 + (c_1 + c_2)\dot{x}_1 + (k_1 + k_2)x_1 - c_2 \dot{x}_2 - k_2 x_2 = F_0 \sin pt \qquad (5.56)$$

and

$$m_2\ddot{x}_2 + c_2\dot{x}_2 + k_2x_2 - c_2\dot{x}_1 - k_2x_1 = 0 \qquad (5.57)$$

The solution of (5.56) and (5.57) is again the sum of the transient solution previously obtained and of a particular solution satisfying these equations of motion.

After the transient, one knows that the system will move at the frequency p of the exciting force $F(t)$, and, inasmuch as damping is present, that there will be a phase difference between force and the resulting motion. The steady-state displacements will, therefore, be assumed to be of the form

$$x_1 = A \sin(pt + \phi)$$

$$= A_1 \sin pt + A_2 \cos pt \qquad (5.58)$$

where

$$A = \sqrt{A_1^2 + A_2^2}$$

and

$$\phi_1 = \tan^{-1}\frac{A_2}{A_1}$$

and

$$x_2 = B \sin(pt + \phi_2)$$

$$x_2 = A_3 \sin pt + A_4 \cos pt \qquad (5.59)$$

where

$$B = \sqrt{A_3^2 + A_4^2}$$

and

$$\phi_2 = \tan^{-1}\frac{A_4}{A_3}$$

When the values of x_1 and x_2 expressed by (5.58) and (5.59) and their time derivatives are introduced in (5.56) and (5.57), the following set of equations are obtained:

$$\left(k_1 + k_2 - m_1 p^2\right)A_1 - p\left(c_1 + c_2\right)A_2 - k_2 A_3 + c_2 pA_4 = F_0$$

$$p\left(c_1 + c_2\right)A_1 + \left(k_1 + k_2 - m_1 p^2\right)A_2 - c_2 pA_3 - k_2 A_4 = 0$$

$$-k_2 A_1 + c_2 pA_2 + \left(k_2 - m_2 p^2\right)A_3 - c_2 pA_4 = 0$$

$$-c_2 pA_1 - k_2 A_2 + c_2 pA_3 + \left(k_2 - m_2 p^2\right)A_4 = 0$$

The simultaneous solution of these four linear equations in A_i $(i = 1, 2, 3, 4)$ yields the values of the constants A_i.

The steady-state oscillation of the masses m_1 and m_2 is then given by (5.58) and (5.59).

Several Degrees of Freedom Systems—Linear Damping

System Natural Frequencies—Free Oscillation

It is often of practical importance to know if the natural frequencies of a buoy system represented by a n degrees of freedom spring-mass system are close to wave frequencies with high energy content. Furthermore when studying in detail the dynamic response of the mooring line, it may be of considerable interest to excite the model at frequencies close to resonance.

To obtain the natural frequencies of the system the equations of free undamped motion of the masses are first established. Tentative solutions of the form

$$x_i = X_i \sin\left(\omega t + \phi\right) \qquad i = 1, 2, 3, \ldots, n.$$

are then introduced in the equations of motion. The resulting set of equations in X_i is then expressed by

$$\mathcal{C} X = \lambda \mathcal{B} X$$

where $\mathcal{C}$ and $\mathcal{B}$ are square matrices of order n, X is the column matrix of the amplitudes X_i and $\lambda = m\omega^2 / k$ a dimensionless frequency parameter. The values of λ satisfying the equation

$$\left[\mathcal{C} - \lambda \mathcal{B}\right]\left[X\right] = 0$$

are obtained by solving the characteristic equation in λ resulting from the expansion of the determinant of the coefficients of the matrix

$$[\mathcal{A} - \lambda \mathcal{B}]$$

The values of λ, thus obtained, are called *eigenvalues*. To each eigenvalue corresponds a natural frequency

$$\omega_i = \sqrt{\frac{k\lambda_i}{m}}$$

and a mode of vibration defined by a set of amplitude coefficients called the *eigenvector*. The eigenvectors fix the relative ratios of amplitudes in each mode. The absolute value of the displacement amplitudes and the phase angles are derived from the $2n$ initial conditions

$$\{x_i(0)\} \qquad \text{and} \qquad \{\dot{x}_i(0)\}.$$

The following 2 degrees of freedom example illustrates the procedure.

Example. Consider the spring-mass systems shown in Figure 5.11 with initial conditions:

$$x_1(0) = 1 \text{ ft}$$

$$\dot{x}_1(0) = 0 \text{ ft/sec}$$

$$x_2(0) = 0 \text{ ft}$$

$$\dot{x}_2(0) = 0 \text{ ft/sec}$$

Solution

1. Equations of Motion

$$-2kx_1 + kx_2 = m\ddot{x}_1$$

$$kx_1 - 2kx_2 = m\ddot{x}_2$$

Dividing by k and introducing

$$x_1 = X_1 \sin(\omega t + \phi)$$

$$x_2 = X_2 \sin(\omega t + \phi)$$

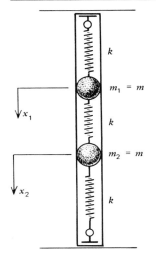

Figure 5.11.

in the equations of motion results in

$$2X_1 - X_2 = \lambda X_1$$
$$-X_1 + 2X_2 = \lambda X_2$$

2. Matrix Notation

$$\begin{bmatrix} 2 & -1 \\ -1 & 2 \end{bmatrix} \begin{bmatrix} X_1 \\ X_2 \end{bmatrix} = \lambda \begin{bmatrix} 1 & 0 \\ 0 & 1 \end{bmatrix} \begin{bmatrix} X_1 \\ X_2 \end{bmatrix}$$

or

$$[\mathcal{A}][X] = \lambda[\mathcal{B}][X]$$

3. Characteristic Equation. The determinant of the coefficients of the matrix $[\mathcal{A} - \lambda \mathcal{B}]$ is

$$\begin{vmatrix} 2-\lambda & -1 \\ -1 & 2-\lambda \end{vmatrix}$$

which when expanded gives

$$(2-\lambda)^2 - 1 = 0$$

4. Eigenvalues. The roots of the characteristic equation are

$$\lambda_1 = 1$$
$$\lambda_2 = 3$$

and the corresponding natural frequencies are

$$\omega_1 = \sqrt{k\lambda_1/m} = \sqrt{k/m}$$

$$\omega_2 = \sqrt{k\lambda_2/m} = \sqrt{3k/m}$$

5. Eigenvectors. The equation

$$[\mathcal{A} - \lambda\mathcal{B}][X] = 0$$

or

$$(2-\lambda)X_1 - X_2 = 0$$

$$-X_1 + (2-\lambda)X_2 = 0$$

must be satisfied for $\lambda_1 = 1$ or $\lambda_2 = 3$. When $\lambda = \lambda_1 = 1$, $X_1 = X_2$, therefore, the eigenvector of the first mode is

$$\begin{bmatrix} 1 \\ 1 \end{bmatrix}$$

When $\lambda = \lambda_2 = 3$, $X_1 = -X_2$, and the eigenvector of the second mode is

$$\begin{bmatrix} 1 \\ -1 \end{bmatrix}$$

In other words the displacement of the masses m_1 and m_2 is given in the first mode by

$$x_1 = X_1 \sin(\omega_1 t + \phi_1)$$

$$x_2 = X_1 \sin(\omega_1 t + \phi_1)$$

and in the second mode by

$$x_1 = X_1 \sin(\omega_2 t + \phi_2)$$

$$x_2 = -X_1 \sin(\omega_2 t + \phi_2)$$

6. Absolute Value of Displacement Amplitudes. The four initial conditions applied to the general solution

$$x_1 = X_1 \sin(\omega_1 t + \phi_1) + X_1 \sin(\omega_2 t + \phi_2)$$

$$x_2 = X_1 \sin(\omega_1 t + \phi_1) - X_1 \sin(\omega_2 t + \phi_2)$$

yield

$$1 = X_1 \sin\phi_1 + X_1 \sin\phi_2$$

$$0 = X_1 \sin\phi_1 - X_1 \sin\phi_2$$

$$0 = \omega_1 X_1 \cos\phi_1 + \omega_2 X_1 \cos\phi_2$$

$$0 = \omega_1 X_1 \cos\phi_1 - \omega_2 X_1 \cos\phi_2$$

The sum of the two last equations yields

$$2\omega_1 X_1 \cos\phi_1 = 0$$

therefore, $\phi_1 = \pi/2$. The difference of the two last equations yields

$$2\omega_2 X_1 \cos\phi_2 = 0$$

therefore, $\phi_2 = \pi/2$.
Introducing these values of ϕ_1 and ϕ_2 in the first equation yields

$$X_1 = \tfrac{1}{2}$$

The exact solution is, thus, finally

$$x_1 = \frac{1}{2}\sin\left(\sqrt{\frac{k}{m}}\ t + \frac{\pi}{2}\right) + \frac{1}{2}\sin\left(\sqrt{\frac{3k}{m}}\ t + \frac{\pi}{2}\right)$$

or

$$x_1 = \frac{1}{2}\cos\sqrt{\frac{k}{m}}\ t + \frac{1}{2}\cos\sqrt{\frac{3k}{m}}\ t$$

and

$$x_2 = \frac{1}{2}\cos\sqrt{\frac{k}{m}}\ t - \frac{1}{2}\cos\sqrt{\frac{3k}{m}}\ t$$

Steady-State Response

The method previously described to establish the steady-state response of a 2 degrees of freedom system with linear damping can be expanded to investigate the response of a system with n degrees of freedom when periodically excited by forces of the form

$$F(t) = F_0 \sin pt$$

The displacement x_i of each mass m_i is first assumed to be given by

$$x_i = A_{i1} \sin pt + A_{i2} \cos pt$$

Next the displacements and their time derivatives are introduced in the equations of motion. The resulting set of $2n$ linear simultaneous equations in A_{ij} ($i = 1, 2, 3, \ldots, n; j = 1, 2$) is then solved. The set of A_{ij} displacement coefficients, thus obtained, entirely describe the response of the system.

When the degree of freedom is larger than three there is considerable work involved in expanding the determinant of the coefficients of the matrix $[\mathcal{C} - \lambda \mathcal{B}]$, in solving for the n roots λ and in establishing the n eigenvectors or the $2n$ A_{ij} coefficients describing the steady-state response.

The analysis of the dynamic response of the systems with a large number of degrees of freedom requires special algorithms and computation techniques usually designed to be performed with the help of digital computers.

Nonlinear Damping

When damping terms of the form

$$F_{Di} = c|\dot{x}_i|\dot{x}_i$$

are introduced to account for the hydrodynamic resistance on the set of masses $\{m_i\}$, the resulting equations of motion are no longer explicitly integrable.

As previously outlined, one approach to overcome this difficulty is to replace the nonlinear damping force by a linear force of the form

$$F'_{Di} = c'|\dot{x}_i|$$

where the coefficient of linearization c' is such that the total energy per cycle dissipated by the equivalent force F'_{Di} is the same as for the actual damping force F_{Di}.

If the quadratic form is retained, the equation of motion of the ith mass m_i is given by

$$k_i(x_{i-1} - x_i) - k_{i+1}(x_i - x_{i+1}) - c_i|\dot{x}_1|\dot{x}_i = m_i\ddot{x}_i \qquad (5.60)$$

The solution of a set of n such equations can be directly obtained with the help of analog computers, provided n is not too large, or indirectly with the help of digital computers. In the latter approach the nonlinear equation of motion (5.60) is replaced by a pair of two linear first order differential equations. These equations are obtained by defining a variable

$$y_i = \frac{dx_i}{dt} = \dot{x}_i$$

and substituting this variable in the equation of motion. The resulting pair
of equations is, thus,

$$y_i = \dot{x}_i$$

$$k_i(x_{i-1} - x_i) - k_{i+1}(x_i - x_{i-1}) - c_i|y_i|y_i = m_i \dot{y}_i$$

The computer program then integrates the set of $2n$ equations in small time
increments starting from known initial conditions at time zero and ending at
a fixed time limit.

The methods of spring-mass systems analysis just reviewed can be expanded to three dimensions when modeling the dynamic response of three-
dimensional mooring lines.

The subject of mooring dynamics has received considerable attention in
recent years. Advanced methods of cable dynamic analysis are described in a
number of references cited in Part II.

PART II
EXERCISES

EXERCISE 18

A subsurface buoy is moored with a wire rope weighing 0.25 lb/ft. The depth of the water is 800 ft, and the drag on the buoy is estimated to be 125 lb. What should be the buoyancy of the float if:

    1. (a) The float is to be 200 ft above the sea bottom? (b) The wire rope should pull horizontally on the anchor?

    2. What is then the length of the wire rope? What would happen if the buoyancy is doubled, but the length of the wire remains unchanged?

EXERCISE 19

A subsurface buoy with 400 lb of net buoyancy is to be set 100 m above the sea floor. The mooring line to be used is a 0.5 in. diameter neutrally buoyant rope. A 2 knots uniform current is used as a first approximation of the prevailing tide current profile. The drag on the buoy is then 300 lb.

1. Using the explicit solution of the cable equations obtained for neutrally buoyant and short cables, compute the minimum length of rope required to moor the buoy.

2. If one were to assume that the mooring line follows the tension vector at the buoy, all the way to the anchor, the length of the rope would then be 125 m. Using, again, the explicit solution for neutrally buoyant cables find the location of the buoy above the sea floor when the mooring line is 125 m long, and the percent error introduced by the "straight line" approximation.

EXERCISE 20

1. Find the angle of inclination with the horizontal of a 0.5 in. diameter free ended tow cable towed at 4 knots. The line density of the cable is 0.5 lb/ft. How much cable must be paid out to reach the bottom if the water depth is 2000 m? (Assume stranded cable. Use Figure 4.3 to obtain value of normal drag coefficient.)

2. How much cable must be paid out in order to tow, at 4 knots, a "fish" with an immersed weight of 6000 lb and a drag of 2400 lb, 1000 m above the sea floor? What is then the tension on the cable at the ship? ($F/R = 0.01$.)

EXERCISE 21

A surface buoy is moored in 1000 m of water. The tension at the buoy is 858 lb, and the angle of inclination of the line with the horizontal is 89°. The cable characteristics are

Diameter	5/16 in.
Immersed line density	0.41 lb/m
Normal drag coefficient	$C_{DN} = 1.8$, $F/R = 0.02$

Using Pode's tables find the length of the cable and the tension at the anchor. What is the buoy excursion downstream? (The uniform water speed is 50 cm/sec.)

EXERCISE 22

Use the circular arc approximation to investigate the mooring line tension at the buoy, at the anchor, and the buoy downstream excursion of a compound surface mooring as depicted in Figure II.1. Use a current profile given by

$$V = 150 \text{ cm/sec}, \quad y < 10m$$

$$V = (2.52)(150)y^{-0.4}\text{cm/sec}, \quad y \geqslant 10m$$

The drag on the buoy is estimated to be 250 lb.

EXERCISE 23

1. Prove that the units of $a = (AE/\mu)^{1/2}$ are units of speed, where A is the cable cross sectional area, E is the cable modulus of elasticity, and μ is the virtual mass per unit of length of the cable.
2. Evaluate the speed of propagation of longitudinal deformation in a cable with the following parameters:

$$A = 0.785 \text{ in.}^2$$
$$E = 14 \times 10^6$$
Weight per unit of length $W = 1.25 \text{ lb/ft}$

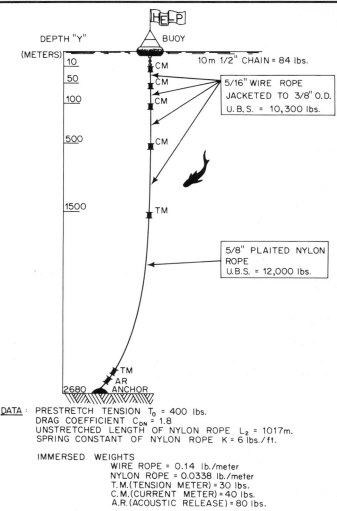

DEPTH "Y"
(METERS)

BUOY

10m 1/2" CHAIN = 84 lbs.

5/16" WIRE ROPE
JACKETED TO 3/8" O.D.
U.B.S. = 10,300 lbs.

5/8" PLAITED NYLON
ROPE
U.B.S. = 12,000 lbs.

DATA : PRESTRETCH TENSION T_0 = 400 lbs.
DRAG COEFFICIENT C_{DN} = 1.8
UNSTRETCHED LENGTH OF NYLON ROPE L_2 = 1017m.
SPRING CONSTANT OF NYLON ROPE K = 6 lbs./ft.

IMMERSED WEIGHTS
WIRE ROPE = 0.14 lb./meter
NYLON ROPE = 0.0338 lb./meter
T.M.(TENSION METER) = 30 lbs.
C.M.(CURRENT METER) = 40 lbs.
A.R.(ACOUSTIC RELEASE) = 80 lbs.

Figure II.1.

EXERCISE 24

1.   A vertical mooring line is excited at one end by a force $F(t)$. Considering the mooring line to be a continuous elastic medium, with a modulus of elasticity, E, a constant cross section, A, and a virtual mass per unit of length, μ, derive the expressions for the line elongation $\xi(s,t)$ and the line tension $T(s,t)$ as functions of s the distance from the origin (undisturbed end of the line) and of t the time.

2. Use these expressions to solve the following boundary value problem: A spar buoy is moored in a regular swell. (See Figure II.2.) It is perfectly decoupled from wave excitation and therefore has no heave motion. Neglecting the damping and inertial forces on the buoy, find an expression for the tension $T(s,t)$ in the mooring line.

Hint: The boundary condition at $s = L$ is

$$T(L,t) = F_0 \sin \omega t$$

where F_0 can be found from the pressure force on the buoy.

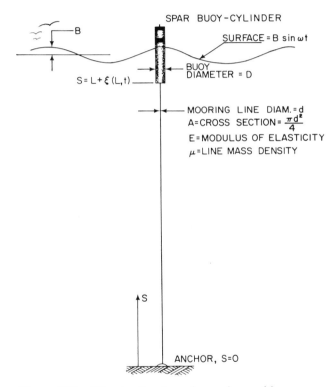

SPAR BUOY-CYLINDER

SURFACE = B sin ωt

B

$S = L + \xi (L,t)$

BUOY DIAMETER = D

MOORING LINE DIAM. = d
A = CROSS SECTION = $\frac{\pi d^2}{4}$
E = MODULUS OF ELASTICITY
μ = LINE MASS DENSITY

S

ANCHOR, S=0

Figure II.2. Mooring line boundary value problem.

EXERCISE 25

Consider a taut moor consisting of a cylindrical surface buoy of constant cross section A and weight W and an elastic mooring line with modulus of elasticity, E, diameter, d, and line virtual mass density, μ.

1. Derive the equation of heave motion of the buoy when excited by a
    simple harmonic wave of the form

    $$y = Z_0 \sin \omega t$$

    Assume the damping force on the buoy to be linear and take the buoy
    added mass into consideration.
2. Derive the expression of the tension $T(s,t)$ in the mooring line, assuming
    the line to be a continuous elastic medium. What is then the tension
    response amplitude operator?
3. Obtain the frequency of resonance of this simple system.

EXERCISE 26

A spherical instrument package is attached to a free drifting spar buoy of
constant cross section A by a relatively long, elastic, and neutrally buoyant
pennant line (Figure II.3).

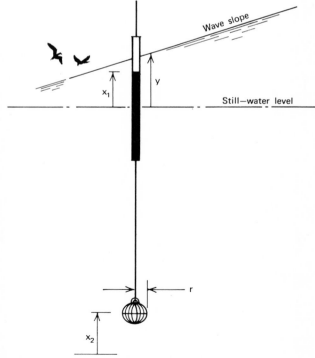

Figure II.3.

1. Obtain the static equilibrium conditions (in the absence of wave excitation). Assume the unstretched length of pennant line to be L_0.

2. Derive the differential equations of heave motion of the buoy and of the instrument package when excited by a harmonic wave of the form

$$y = Z_0 \cos \omega t$$

Assume that the pennant line behaves like a linear spring with a spring constant $K = AE/L_0$ where A is the cross-sectional area of the line and E is the modulus of elasticity of the line, and that the damping forces on the buoy and on the sphere due to water viscosity are linear. Neglect the viscous damping and the mass of the line, but consider the added mass effects for the buoy and the sphere.

3. Draw a sketch of the equivalent 2 degrees of freedom spring-mass system.

4. Obtain the expression of the natural frequencies of heave of the system.

EXERCISE 27

A bottom buoy system consisting of one buoy, a short and neutrally buoyant mooring line, and one anchor is lowered overboard and then left free to fall to the bottom (Figure II.4). Let $t = 0$ be the instant when the buoy system starts its trip to the bottom; $t = t_1$ be the time when it reaches terminal

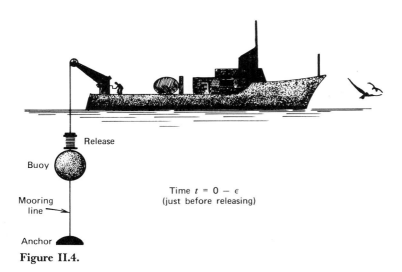

Figure II.4.

velocity; and $t = t_2$ be the time when the anchor hits the bottom. Given the following:

m_A	= virtual mass of the anchor	= 120 slugs
m_B	= virtual mass of the buoy	= 10 slugs
W	= immersed weight of the anchor	= 3000 lb
B	= net buoyancy of the buoy	= 1700 lb
D_B	= buoy drag over the time interval	$t_1 \leqslant t < t_2 = 1000$ lb
D_A	= anchor drag over the time interval	$t_1 \leqslant t < t_2 = 300$ lb

Compute the tension in the mooring line at the following times:

$t = 0 - \epsilon$	just before releasing
$t = 0 + \epsilon$	just after releasing
$t = t_1$	
$t_1 \leqslant t < t_2$	
$t \gg t_2$	(neglect bottom currents)

Draw a sketch of the tension versus time.

EXERCISE 28

A bottom buoy system consisting of a syntactic foam float, a nylon line with sensor/release package, and one anchor is launched buoy first. [See Figure II.5(A).] As it freely sinks faster and faster, the anchor acquires a certain amount of kinetic energy. At the end of its free fall, the anchor, held back by the rope and the buoy, slows down. A certain amount of energy is thus absorbed by the rope, and one wonders if the rope is strong enough to take the transient load. Obtain, in terms of the parameters shown in the sketch, an expression for the maximum load in the cable when the following conservative assumptions are made:

1. The anchor falls vertically.
2. The anchor reaches terminal velocity V_T before it starts to stretch the mooring line [Figure II.5(B)].
3. The buoy starts to sink only when the anchor free fall speed is reduced to zero [Figure II.5(C)]. In other words, the rope absorbs all of the anchor energy.
4. The mooring line follows Hooke's law.

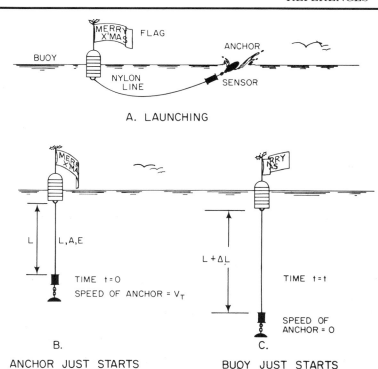

A. LAUNCHING

B.
ANCHOR JUST STARTS
TO PULL LINE

TIME t = 0
SPEED OF ANCHOR = V_T

C.
BUOY JUST STARTS
TO SINK

TIME t = t
SPEED OF
ANCHOR = 0

PARAMETERS: A = CROSS SECTION OF LINE
E = MODULUS OF ELASTICITY
L = LINE LENGTH
ΔL = LINE ELASTIC ELONGATION
V_T = TERMINAL ANCHOR VELOCITY
M = MASS OF ANCHOR AND SENSOR

Figure II.5.

REFERENCES

Adamchak, J., and J. H. Evans. *Ocean Engineering Structures*, The M.I.T. Press, Cambridge, 1969.

Albertsen, N. D. "A Survey of Techniques for the Analysis and Design of Submerged Mooring Systems," U. S. Navy Civil Engineering Laboratory, Technical Report R-815, Port Hueneme, California, August 1974.

Berteaux, H. O., and N. K. Chhabra. "Computer Programs for the Static Analysis of Single Point Moored Surface and Subsurface Buoy Systems," Woods Hole Oceanographic Institution, *W.H.O.I. Ref. No. 73-22* (unpublished manuscript), Woods Hole, Massachusetts, March 1973.

Boulot, M. "Effort et Deformation Dans un Cable Soumis a un Courant Permanent et Excite Par Le Mouvement d'un Flotteur dans la Houle," Proceedings 12th Congress of the International Association for Hydraulic Research, Volume 4, pp. 220–224, 1967.

Brainard, J. P. "Dynamic Analysis of a Single Point, Taut, Compound Mooring," Woods Hole Oceanographic Institution, *W.H.O.I. Ref. No. 71-42*, (unpublished manuscript), Woods Hole, Massachusetts, June 1971.

Broome, G. W., Jr. "Excursion Analysis of Mooring Systems with Three or More Legs," Department of Naval Architecture and Marine Engineering, Massachusetts Institute of Technology, Thesis for Master of Science Degree (unpublished manuscript), August 24, 1970.

Casarella, M. J., and M. Parsons. "A Survey of Investigations on the Configuration and Motion of Cable Systems Under Hydrodynamic Loading," Department of Mechanical Engineering and Institute of Ocean Science and Engineering, The Catholic University of America, Washington, D.C., *MTS Journal*, Vol. 4, No. 4, July–August, 1970.

Casarella, M. J., and Y.-I. Choo. "A Survey of Analytical Methods for Dynamic Simulation of Cable-Body Systems," *Journal of Hydronautics*, Vol. 7, No. 4, pp. 137–144, October 1973.

Choo, Y.-I., and M. J. Casarella. "Hydrodynamic Resistance of Towed Cables," The Catholic University of America, Washington, D.C., *Journal of Hydronautics*, Vol. 6, No. 4, pp. 126–131, October 1971.

Crandall, S. H. *Engineering Analysis*, McGraw-Hill, New York, 1956.

Dale, J. R. "A Force Balance Analog for Determining Characteristics of Ocean Cable Systems," U. S. Naval Air Development Center, Johnsville, Pennsylvania, Report No. NADC-AE-6517, November 1965.

Darling, R. C. "Cable Length Determinations for Deep-Sea Oceanographic Operations," U. S. Department of Commerce, Environmental Science Services Administration, Oast and Geodetic Survey, United States Printing Office, Washington, D.C., Technical Bulletin No. 30, June 1966.

Dillon, D. B. "An Inventory of Current Mathematical Models of Scientific Data-Gathering Moors," Hydrospace-Challenger, Inc., Technical Report 4450 0001, Rockville, Maryland, February 1973.

Dominguez, R. F., J. H. Nath, S. Neshyba, and D. A. Young. "Analysis of a Two Point Mooring for a Spar Buoy," Oregon State University, Department of Oceanography, Corvallis, Oregon, Data Report No. 38, Reference 69-34, December 1969.

Firebaugh, M. S. "An Analysis of the Dynamics of Towing Cables," Massachusetts Institute of Technology, Department of Ocean Engineering, Doctor of Science Thesis (unpublished manuscript), January 14, 1972.

Fofonoff, N. P. "Current Measurement from Moored Buoys," Woods Hole Oceanographic Institution, Woods Hole, Massachusetts, *W.H.O.I. Reference No. 68-30*, (unpublished manuscript), May 1968.

Goodman, T. R., P. Kaplan, T. P. Sargent, and J. Bentson. "Static and Dynamic Analysis of a Moored Buoy System," Oceanics, Incorporated, Prepared for National Data Buoy Center, Contract Number NAS8-26879, April 1972.

Griffin, G. T. "Nondimensional Steady-State Cable Configurations," Naval Underwater Systems Center, Technical Report 4379, New London, Connecticut, August 1972.

Harleman, D. R. F., and W. C. Shapiro. "Investigations on the Dynamics of Moored Structures in Waves," Massachusetts Institute of Technology, Hydrodynamics Laboratory, Cambridge, Massachusetts, Technical Report No. 28, July 1958.

Holmes. "Mechanics of Raising and Lowering Heavy Loads in Deep Oceans —Cable and Pay-Load Dynamics," U.S.N.C.E.L., Port Hueneme, California, Technical Report R-433, 1966.

Hong, S. T. "Frequency Domain Analysis for the Tension in a Taut Mooring Line," University of Washington, Department of Civil Engineering, Technical Report No. SM 72-1, Seattle, Washington, July 1972.

Kaplan, P., A. I. Raff, and T. P. Sargent. "Experimental and Analytical Studies of Buoy Hull Motions in Waves," Oceanics, Incorporated, Prepared for National Data Buoy Center, Contract NAS8-26879, April 1972.

Marks, W. "The Application of Spectral Analysis and Statistics to Seakeeping," The Society of Naval Architects and Marine Engineers, New York, Technical and Research Bulletin No. 1-24, September 1963.

Martin, W. "Tension and Geometry of Single Point Moored Surface Buoy System: A Computer Program Study," Woods Hole Oceanographic Institution, Woods Hole, Massachusetts, *W.H.O.I. Ref. No. 68-79*, (unpublished manuscript), December 1968.

Morrow, B. W. "Determination of the Optimum Scope of a Moored Buoy," *Journal of Ocean Technology*, Vol. 2, 1967.

Morrow, B. W. "A Method of Determining the Shape and Tension of Towing Cables," University of Miami, 1966.

Nath, J. H. "Analysis of Deep Water Single Point Moorings," Oregon State University, Department of Oceanography, Corvallis, Oregon, Technical Report for Office of Naval Research, CER70-71JHN4, August 1970.

Nath, J. H. "Dynamics of Single Point Ocean Moorings of a Buoy—A Numerical Model for Solution by Computer," Oregon State University, Department of Oceanography, Corvallis, Oregon, Reference 69-10, July 1969.

Paquette, R. G., and B. E. Henderson. "The Dynamics of Simple Deep Sea Buoy Moorings," GM Defense Research Laboratories, Santa Barbara, California, TR65-79, November 1965.

Patton, K. T. "The Response of Cable Moored Axisymmetric Buoys to Ocean Wave Excitation," NUSC Technical Report 4331, Naval Underwater System Center, New London, Connecticut, June 1972.

Pode, L. "An Experimental Investigation of the Hydrodynamic Forces on Stranded Cables," *David Taylor Model Basin* Report 713, Department of the Navy, May 1950.

Pode, L. "Tables of Computing the Equilibrium Configuration of a Flexible Cable in a Uniform Stream," *David Taylor Model Basin* Report 687, Department of the Navy, March 1951.

Pode, L. "The Configuration and Tension of a Light Flexible Cable in a Uniform Stream," David Taylor Model Basin, Report 717, Department of the Navy, April 1950.

Pode, L. "A Method of Determining Optimum Lengths of Towing Cables," *David Taylor Model Basin Report 717*, Department of the Navy, April 1950.

Polachek, H., T. S. Walton, R. Meijia, and C. Dawson. "Transient Motion of an Elastic Cable Immersed in a Fluid," *Mathematics of Computation*, Vol. 17, No. 81, January 1963.

Reber, R. K. "The Configuration and Towing Tension of Towed Sweep Cables Supported by Floats," BuSHIPS Report 75, 1944.

Reid, R. O. "Dynamics of Deep-Sea Mooring Lines," Texas A & M University, College of Geosciences, Department of Oceanography, College Station, Texas, Project 204, Reference 68-11F, July 1968.

Richardson, W. et al. "Current Measurements from Moored Buoys," Woods Hole Oceanographic Institution, Woods Hole, Massachusetts, *W.H.O.I. Ref. No. 63-1* (unpublished manuscript), 1963.

Sargent, T. P., A. I. Raff, and J. Bentson. "Computer Program Documentation Report—Buoy–Cable Dynamics Program," Oceanics, Incorporated, Prepared for National Data Buoy Center, Contract NAS8-26879, April 1972.

Skop, R. A., and G. J. O'Hara. "The Static Equilibrium Configuration of Cable Arrays by Use of the Method of Imaginary Reactions," Naval Research Laboratory Report 6819, Washington D.C., February 1969.

Skop, R. A., and R. E. Kaplan. "The Static Configuration of a Tri-Moored Subsurface Buoy Cable Array Acted on by Current Induced Forces," Naval Research Laboratory Report 6894, Washington D. C., May 1969.

Skop, R. A., and G. J. O'Hara. "The Method of Imaginary Reactions," *MTS Journal*, Vol. 4, No. 1, January–February 1970.

Skop, R. A., and G. J. O'Hara. "A Method for the Analysis of Internally Redundant Structural Cable Arrays," Naval Research Laboratory Report, *MTS Journal*, Vol. 6, No. 1, January–February 1972.

Skop, R. A., and J. Mark. "A Fortran IV Program for Computing the Static Deflections of Structural Cable Arrays," Naval Research Laboratory Report 7640, Washington D. C., August 1973.

Thorne, C. J., et al. *Steady State Motion of Cables in Fluids*, Part I, "Tables of Neutrally Buoyant Cable Functions," U. S. Naval Ordnance Test Station, 1962.

Thorne, C. J., et al. *Steady State Motion of Cables in Fluids*, Part 2, "Tables of Cable Functions for Vertical Plane Motion," PMR TM 63-9, U. S. Naval Test Station, 1963.

Vandiver, J. K. "Dynamic Analysis of a Launch and Recovery System for a Deep Submersible," Woods Hole Oceanographic Institution, Woods Hole, Massachusetts, *W.H.O.I. Reference No. 69–88* (unpublished manuscript), December 1969.

Wang, H. T., and T. L. Moran. "Analysis of the Two-Dimensional Steady-State Behavior of Extensible Free-Floating Cable Systems," Department of the Navy, Naval Ship Research and Development Center, Bethesda, Maryland, Report 3721, October 1971.

Wang, H. T. "A Two-Degree-of-Freedom Model for the Two-Dimensional Dynamic Motions of Suspended Extensible Cable Systems," Department of the Navy, Naval Ship Research and Development Center, Bethesda, Maryland, Report 3663, October 1971.

Whicker, L. F. "Theoretical Analysis of the Effect of Ship Motion on Mooring Cables in Deep Water," *David Taylor Model Basin Report 1221*, Department of the Navy, Hydromechanics Laboratory Research and Development Report, March 1958.

Wilson, B. W. "Characteristics of Anchor Cables in Uniform Ocean Currents," A & M College of Texas, Department of Oceanography and Meteorology, Technical Report No. 204-1, April 1960.

Wilson, B. W. "Characteristics of Deep Sea Anchor Cables in Strong Ocean Currents," A & M College of Texas, Department of Oceanography and Meteorology, Technical Report Nos. 204-3 and 204-3A, March 1961.

Yamamoto, T., C. E. Smith, and J. Nath. "Longitudinal Vibration in Taut Line Moorings," *MTS Journal*, Vol. 8, No. 5, June 1974.

Zarnick, E. E., and M. J. Casarella. "The Dynamics of a Ship Moored by a Cable System Under Sea State Excitation," The Catholic University of America, Institute of Ocean Science and Engineering, Washington D.C., Report 72-5, July 1972.

OCEANOGRAPHIC BUOY SYSTEMS

Chapter

Six

OCEANOGRAPHIC BUOY SYSTEMS, CLASSES, DESIGN, AND COMPONENTS

An oceanographic buoy system can be defined as a floating structure deployed in the ocean for the purpose of measuring environmental data. The word "buoy" is often loosely used to describe both the float and its anchoring line. When referring to a system made of several structural components supporting a number of instruments, the expression "buoy system" should be preferred, and the use of the word "buoy" should be restricted to the floating hull or buoyant components of the system.

6.1. CLASSES AND DESCRIPTION OF OCEANOGRAPHIC BUOY SYSTEMS

Because of their inherent capacity of efficiently providing long-term series measurements of meteorological and oceanographic parameters, a relatively large number of buoy systems are each year deployed in the world's oceans. These systems can be divided into moored and free drifting systems. These, in turn, can be classified into surface and subsurface buoy systems.

199

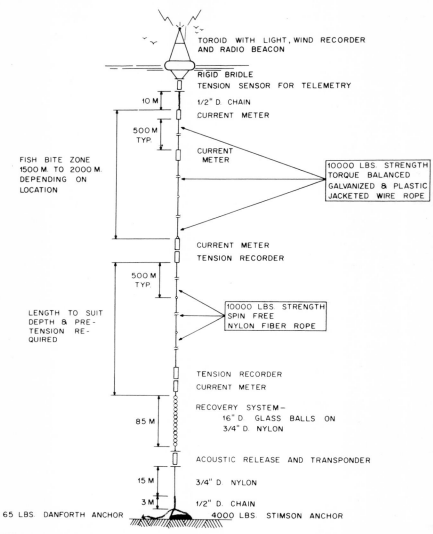

Figure 6.1. Single point moored surface buoy system W.H.O.I. taut moor.

Moored Systems

Long-term series measurements and synoptic coverage of large oceanic areas can be obtained by the systematic deployment of moored and instrumented buoy systems. Such arrays constitute a three-dimensional pattern capable of monitoring the spatial and temporal distribution of environmental variables.

Surface Buoy Systems

Surface buoy systems are necessary when monitoring parameters at the air–sea interface, in the upper part of the water column, and whenever a surface expression for radio telemetry is required. A great variety of surface buoy systems have been designed and implanted; the shape and dimension of the float and the type of anchoring depend in each case on the system purpose and the design constraints.

Single Point Moored Surface Buoy Systems.   These systems have only one anchoring point. The scope of the mooring line, that is, the ratio of the mooring line length to the water depth, can be small or large. A small scope results in a taut moor (Figure 6.1), a large scope in a slack moor (Figure 6.2). The advantages of a taut moor are reduced buoy watch circle and sensor motion, simplicity, and ease of deployment. The disadvantages are high dynamic loading due to wave action and high static tension under severe current conditions. These high stresses, often resulting in mooring losses, are reduced when the scope of the mooring line is increased. The motion of the float and of the sensors will then, however, become considerable, thus introducing an undesirable error in the measurements of velocity fields and other oceanic variables. The lower part of a slack moor must be supported or self-supporting so as to avoid piling up and chafing of the line on the bottom.

Surface buoys can be surface following (disks or skiffs) or surface decoupled (spars). Surface following buoys have the advantage of a large buoyancy to drag ratio. However, the heave and roll motion of these buoys imparts severe dynamic stresses to the line, reduces the efficiency of radio transmission, and may severely limit the threshold of scientific measurements made from the moving platform.

Spar buoys have a small buoyancy to drag ratio and are not as effective in providing the buoyancy required to support long mooring lines. However, when motion due to wave action must be suppressed, spar buoys are used to advantage. Spar buoys are often moored from an auxiliary subsurface buoy which supports the bulk of the mooring line (Figure 6.3). Spar buoys of large dimensions can provide heave and roll stability in most sea conditions. Such buoys can be used as manned sea laboratories (Figure 6.4).

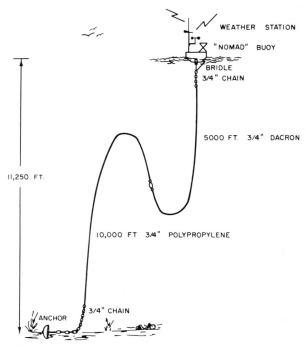

Figure 6.2. Single point moored surface buoy system "Nomad" slack moor.

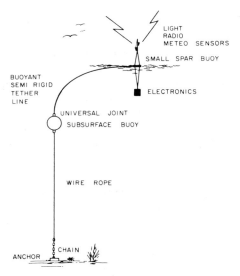

Figure 6.3. Two buoys—single point moored buoy system (C.O.B. France).

202

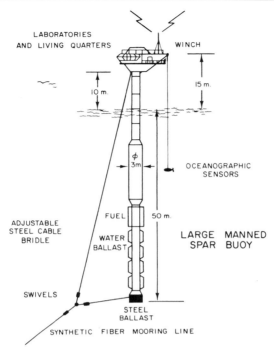

LABORATORIES
AND LIVING QUARTERS

WINCH

10 m.

15 m.

φ
3m

OCEANOGRAPHIC
SENSORS

ADJUSTABLE
STEEL CABLE
BRIDLE

FUEL

WATER
BALLAST

50 m.

LARGE   MANNED
SPAR   BUOY

SWIVELS

STEEL
BALLAST

SYNTHETIC FIBER MOORING LINE

Figure 6.4.   Single point moored French Bouée Laboratoire I.

Multileg Surface Buoy Systems.   These systems have several anchoring points. They are usually installed when station-keeping and system long-life are prime objectives. Their advantages are: (*a*) reduced horizontal motion of surface buoy and instrumentation; (*b*) ample clear space below the surface buoy to deploy instrumentation; (*c*) use of the mooring legs for close spacing of oceanic sensors and study of small scale phenomena; (*d*) reduction of the possibility of kinking and fouling, which exists in the mooring line of single point mooring systems; (*e*) increased life expectancy; and (*f*) increased probability of system recovery. On the other hand, multileg systems are expensive and difficult to deploy.

The surface buoy can be connected by slack and compliant mooring lines to a number of single point moored subsurface buoys. An example of this configuration is the Oregon State University TOTEM buoy (Figure 6.5). In another configuration, the surface buoy is connected by a single mooring line to a single subsurface buoy at the apex of a rigid tripod. This arrangement provides a stable structure for near surface measurements (Figure 6.6). The large multibuoy multileg ship anchorage system depicted in Figure 6.7 illustrates the magnitude of complex moored systems which can be deployed in the oceans.

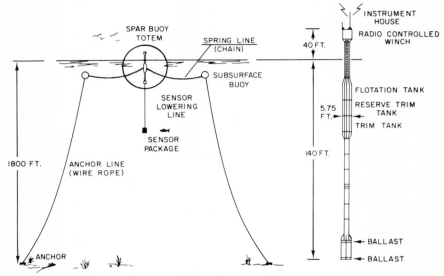

Figure 6.5. Multileg surface buoy system. O.S.U. "Totem" spar buoy.

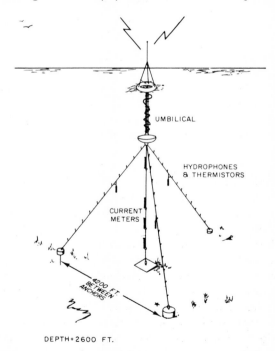

Figure 6.6. Multileg subsurface buoy system. W.H.O.I. "Sea Spider."

204

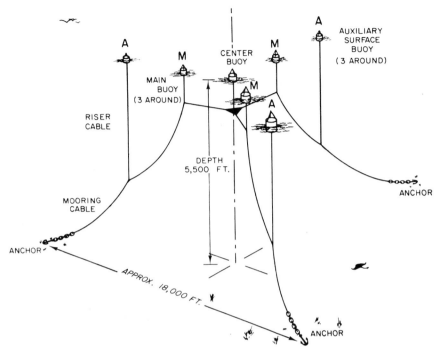

Figure 6.7. Multileg surface buoy system—"Toto II"—anchorage.

Subsurface Buoy Systems

Subsurface buoy systems are used when measurements at or near the surface are not required. Buoys set at 100 m or more below the sea surface are no longer subjected to surface excitation. Dynamic loads and sensor motion due to wave action are, therefore, suppressed. Endurance of the mooring line components is increased and the noise level of the scientific data reduced. Subsurface moorings are usually recovered by disconnecting the line from its anchor, thus allowing the float to surface. Dependable anchor releases are critical to the successful use of submerged buoy systems.

Single Point Moored Subsurface Buoy Systems.   The great majority of oceanographic subsurface buoy systems have a single anchoring point. Cost efficiency and ease of implantation result from their simple configuration. Their compliance to oceanic currents and the resulting vertical motion of

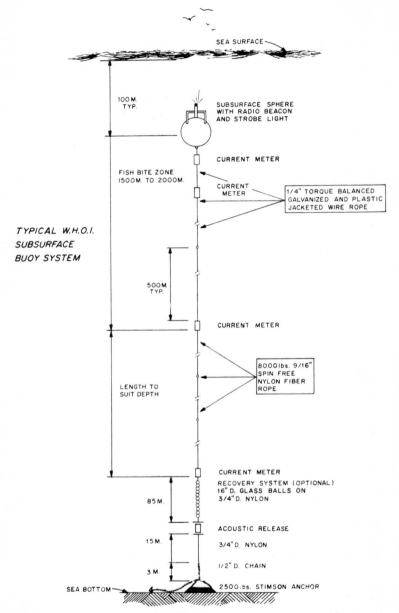

SEA SURFACE

100 M.
TYP.

SUBSURFACE SPHERE
WITH RADIO BEACON
AND STROBE LIGHT

CURRENT METER

FISH BITE ZONE
1500M. TO 2000M.

CURRENT
METER

1/4" TORQUE BALANCED
GALVANIZED AND PLASTIC
JACKETED WIRE ROPE

TYPICAL W.H.O.I.
SUBSURFACE
BUOY SYSTEM

500M.
TYP.

CURRENT METER

8000lbs. 9/16"
SPIN FREE
NYLON FIBER
ROPE

LENGTH TO
SUIT DEPTH

CURRENT METER

RECOVERY SYSTEM (OPTIONAL)
16" D, GLASS BALLS ON
3/4" D. NYLON

85 M.

ACOUSTIC RELEASE

15 M.

3/4" D. NYLON

3 M.

1/2" D. CHAIN

SEA BOTTOM

2500.lbs. STIMSON ANCHOR

Figure 6.8. Single point moored subsurface buoy system.

buoy and sensors are the drawback of a number of these systems. The size, shape, and material of the buoy vary with the mooring rigidity requirements and the implantation depth.

Typical subsurface and near bottom buoy systems are depicted in Figures 6.8 and 6.9.

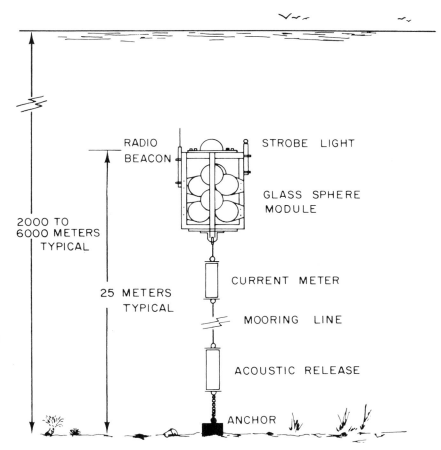

Figure 6.9.   Typical W.H.O.I. bottom buoy system.

Multileg Subsurface Buoy Systems.   Subsurface buoy systems with several anchoring points have essentially the same advantages and drawbacks as the surface multileg systems, that is, stability and reliability gained at the cost of increased complexity. A good example of this type of system is the IWEX

(Internal Wave Experiment) trimoor (Figure 6.10). This system consists of three equally spaced and neutrally buoyant mooring lines inclined at an angle of 54° from the horizontal and attached at the apex to a single subsurface buoy.

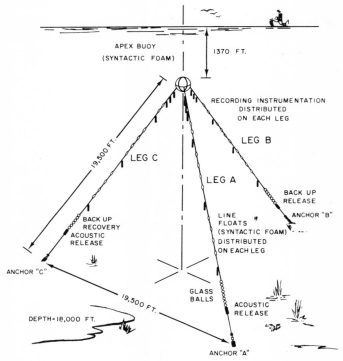

Figure 6.10.   Multileg subsurface buoy sytstem W.H.O.I. "IWEX" trimoor.

Instrumentation can be suspended from a central line below the buoy and from the legs. Auxiliary lines and floats attached to the legs of a trimoor can be used to build sophisticated moored cable structures.

Free Drifting Systems

Systems deployed without anchoring are free to move as wind and currents push them along. Simultaneous measurements of oceanic parameters and system position provide a record of the time and space variation of the parameters measured. When locked to the surrounding waters, these systems are used for Lagrangian measurements of surface or deep sea currents.

Surface Free Drifting Systems

These systems are used to provide surface and near surface measurements. Uncertainty of recovery generally restricts their size and sophistication. Their location is established by radio direction finding or satellite interrogation. Free drifting systems used to monitor near surface currents usually consist of a surface buoy with its radio transmitter, a pennant line, and a drogue of such shape and size as to insure motion of the system at the speed of the surrounding water (Figure 6.11).

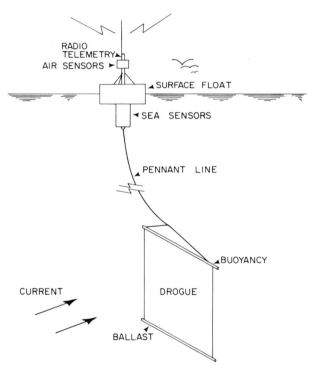

Figure 6.11. Conceptual sketch of free drifting surface buoy.

Subsurface Free Drifting Systems

A body immersed at a given depth will remain at this depth if its density, ρ, equals the density of the water, ρ_W, at that depth, and if its rate of change of density is smaller than the rate of change in the density of the water at that level; that is, if

$$\left.\frac{d\rho}{dz}\right|_{z=z_0} < \left.\frac{d\rho_W}{dz}\right|_{z=z_0} \tag{6.1}$$

This interesting result has been used to develop subsurface buoys free to move with the water mass at predetermined depths. Acoustic telemetry is used for position tracking and transmission of oceanographic data. A sophisticated deep sea free drifting system is shown in Figure 6.12.

Figure 6.12.   Ocean mid-depth free drifting sound source (W.H.O.I. 1973 O.E. Instrumentation Department).

6.2.   BUOY SYSTEM DESIGN

System Design Logic

The structural design of a buoy system can be defined as the rational specification of the system configuration and system components. This specification is usually a function of the buoy system purpose and the design constraints. The system purpose states the mission: what to do, where, when, for how long and for what reasons. The system requirements (stability, payload, life) and environmental constraints (sea states, pressure, corrosion, etc.) can then be formulated. The system requirements will define the type of structure to use; the environmental constraints will define the mechanical loads on the structure components. A preliminary design can then be made, and its cost and requirements for logistics (deployment, servicing, and recovery) evaluated against the budget limits and available support. When an acceptable compromise is achieved, the design is finalized, and a prototype is then built. Figure 6.13 is a schematic representation of these phases usually followed in the design of a buoy system.

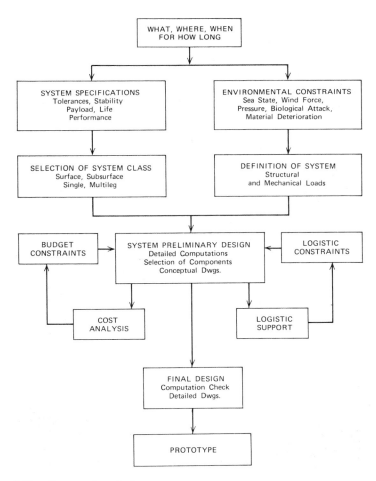

Figure 6.13.   Buoy system design.

Buoy Hulls and Floats

Classes of Buoys

Buoys and floats provide the buoyancy necessary to adequately support the anchoring lines and the buoy system instrumentation and ancillary equipment. The many types of surface and subsurface buoys that have been designed and built to suit a large variety of oceanic applications can be classified in one of the following three classes of buoys.

Surface Following Buoys.   As the name implies, the buoys in this category have a tendency to closely follow the waves. Disk shapes, boat hull shapes, and toroids are examples of surface following buoys. These buoys are subjected to strong heave and roll motion, and unless of large dimension, they may well capsize in breaking seas. These buoys, however, have certain advantages: They can provide ample reserve buoyancy when strong currents

Figure 6.14.   Twelve ft diameter discus buoy.

increase the mooring line tension. Their contribution to the total system drag is relatively small. Being of simple shape, their fabrication is easy and their cost is relatively low. Examples of these types of buoys are shown in Figures 6.14, 6.15, and 6.16.

Surface Decoupled Buoys.   Reduced heave and roll motion of surface buoys is often desirable. A buoy of large mass and small cross section at the water level will experience small vertical acceleration as the water level changes with passing waves. As a result, the buoy heave motion will be small. Furthermore, if the buoy mass is distributed to provide a strong righting moment, roll will be reduced to a minimum. A floating slender cylinder with a counterweight at its lower end is a familiar example of surface decoupled buoys. However, it will be found that the length of a spar of constant cross section must be large to still be effective at large wave periods.

Improved versions of the elementary spar are often made of a series of watertight and water-filled tanks supporting a mast or a tower at the upper

Figure 6.15.   Eight ft diameter toroid buoy (W.H.O.I.).

Figure 6.16.   40 ft diameter discus buoy (N.O.A.A.). EB-10 is a 40 ft discus shaped buoy having a hull depth of 7.5 ft that is designed to survive in severe environments and withstand severe currents, 155 knot winds, and 60 ft waves. The buoy is equipped with meteorological sensors attached to its four ft circular mast and hull-mounted oceanographic sensors. Environmental measurement capability include air temperature and pressure, wind velocity, dewpoint, precipitation rate, global and infrared radiation, water temperature, and salinity. The 100 tons buoy can be moored in depths up to 20,000 ft.

end and a damping plate at the lower end. A typical spar buoy is shown in Figure 6.17.

To be efficient, spar buoys cannot have much reserve buoyancy. Furthermore, their draft is usually large, and, therefore, their hydrodynamic resistance is relatively high. These two limiting factors must be seriously considered when the spar buoy is to be moored in deep water. It may then be of advantage to connect the spar buoy to an auxiliary surface or subsurface buoy.

Subsurface Buoys.   Buoys placed below the water surface are commonly referred to as subsurface buoys. The size, shape, and materials of subsurface buoys vary with the intended buoy implantation depth. In the upper part of the water column, large amounts of buoyancy can be provided by conven-

Figure 6.17.   53 ft long spar buoy (W.H.O.I.).

tional pressure resistant shells or the use of pressure resistant solids of relatively low density. As the depth increases, the shell thickness or the floating material density must increase to resist the hydrostatic pressure. The weight of the buoy increases, and its efficiency decreases rapidly. Buoys deployed in large oceanic depths are usually made of a number of small buoyant elements—like thick wall glass balls or high density syntactic foam modules—structurally held together.

Materials and methods used in the fabrication of surface and subsurface buoys are further reviewed in the section on materials and fabrications.

External Forces To Consider in Buoy Design

When moored in the oceanic environment, surface buoys are subjected to wind action, wave action, oceanic currents, and sometimes icing. Subsurface buoys must resist considerable hydrostatic pressure. In addition, buoys are submitted to severe loads during deployment and retrieval. A brief review of these environmental and operational constraints and of their incidence on the design of buoy hulls and floats follows.

Wind Action.   Wind causes additional drag on the buoy. The wind resistance force results in stresses on the buoy superstructure (mast, tower, etc). It also introduces a capsizing moment.

Wave Action.   Wave action results in roll and heave. Avoiding capsizing of the buoy in severe seaways is of practical importance. Often the amount of allowable roll and heave that the buoy can experience when excited by a particular wave (significant wave, for example) of a given sea spectrum is specified as a design criterion. Natural periods of roll and heave, damping elements, and mass distribution must then be adjusted to match the design specifications.

Wave action also introduces, as previously discussed, drag and inertial forces due to water particle velocities and acceleration. These forces must be considered when designing the buoy hull and the mooring point of attachment. The buoy structural design must allow for stresses due to waves crashing on the buoy deck. It must also consider the inertial forces resulting from angular acceleration, especially on components far from the center of roll. Finally, fatigue and corrosion due to wave motion and water splash should be taken into account in the buoy design.

Oceanic Currents.   The hydrodynamic resistance force due to currents passing the buoy and its resulting moment must be considered when designing the buoy hulls and the mooring attachment.

Icing.   Ice covering the deck and the superstructure of a surface buoy will cause an upward shift of the buoy center of gravity. This will diminish the righting moment and change the buoy response in roll and heave. Increased structure area will result in larger wind drag force and capsizing moment. Icing is another design consideration that should not be overlooked.

Hydrostatic Pressure.   Structural stresses due to hydrostatic pressure must be evaluated when designing spar buoys of large draft and, of course, are a prime consideration in the design of subsurface and bottom floats.

Launching and Retrieval Loads.   Careful consideration must be given at the design stage to the transient loads resulting from launching and retrieval operations. During deployment, buoys may have to sustain the weight of the anchor and of the entire mooring line prior to anchor bottoming. When retrieving, the load at the point of lift may be the sum of the buoy weight in air, the weight of the mooring line still attached to the buoy (including sometimes the anchor), plus dynamic loading due to ship motion.

The analysis of the stresses resulting from the forces in the buoy structural frame and/or in the buoy shell is beyond the scope of this book.

Materials and Fabrication

Materials commonly used in the fabrication of buoys and floats, and certain considerations regarding their construction are hereafter reviewed.

Surface Buoys.   A large number of surface buoys are made of watertight hulls of simple geometry. Light density foams externally protected by shells of hard plastic are also often used for the fabrication of surface buoys.

Buoy hulls can be made of steel, aluminum, or fiberglass. Steel offers many advantages: Fabrication and welding follow standard practices, points of lift and mooring attachment can be made very strong, corrosion and fouling protection can be readily obtained from standard marine procedures, and cost of material is low. Weight of steel structural members and plates might, however, be a drawback. If weight is not a major concern, steel remains an excellent material to build resistant, long-lasting, and economic buoys.

Aluminum, a popular material among buoy designers because of its lighter density, offers many disadvantages. Aluminum alloys for marine use (AL 5083, AL 6061, AL 6063, for example) must be carefully selected. Good welding is delicate, and the heat generated during the welding process considerably reduces the strength of the aluminum alloy at and close to the weld. Welds often open up. Aluminum being anodic to steel will corrode around all steel fasteners. Points of buoy pickup and mooring attachment must be reinforced to avoid failure and chafing. Aluminum coating and painting require special processes.

Fiberglass hulls are somewhat heavier than aluminum hulls, their strength and resistance to the environment are excellent. Cost, however, is still a drawback, except when produced in relatively large quantities.

Plastic foam floats can be easily made by mixing and pouring foam components (polyurethane, for example) into a mold of given shape. When expanded and solid, the light density foam can then be covered by layers of resin impregnated fiberglass cloth that will harden into a solid shell. Small to medium size surface buoys (15 ft diameter or less) can be made with this technique. Larger size buoys are usually of metallic construction.

Subsurface Buoys.   Subsurface buoys can be made of the following materials.

METALLIC PRESSURE RESISTANT SHELLS.   The shell shape that best resists external pressure is the sphere. Therefore, most hollow containers used as subsurface buoys are spherical. Examples of high compressive strength metals used for the fabrication of pressure resistant shells are steel (A285–Grade C), high strength steel (HY 80), aluminum (6061-T6, 7075-T6), and titanium (6Al-2Cb-1Ta-8 Mo).

Metallic spherical shells can be made to resist the deepest ocean depths. However, at large depths, these spheres will no longer float. An estimation of the depth that spheres of given metals can reach before they start to either sink or yield can be obtained as follows:

The buoyant force, B, on a spherical shell of radius R, shell thickness t, and weight density ρ_M is approximately given by

$$B = \rho_W \frac{4}{3}\pi R^3 - \rho_M 4\pi R^2 t \qquad (6.2)$$

ρ_W being the sea water weight density. When the sphere starts to sink, B is equal to zero. From (6.2) the shell thickness is then

$$t = \frac{R}{3}\frac{\rho_W}{\rho_M}$$

and the thickness to radius ratio t/R is then

$$\frac{t}{R} = \frac{1}{3}\frac{\rho_W}{\rho_M} \qquad (6.3)$$

The stress in the shell due to hydrostatic pressure, assuming the stress to be uniaxial (thin shell theory), can be readily obtained by considering the forces necessary to maintain one half sphere in equilibrium (see free body diagram Figure 6.18). For equilibrium, the external force equals the internal force, that is,

$$\int p\,dA = p2\pi R^2 \int_0^{\pi/2} \cos\theta \sin\theta\, d\theta = p\pi R^2 = 2\pi Rt\sigma.$$

Solving for the compression stress, σ,

$$\sigma = \frac{pR}{2t} \qquad (6.4)$$

From this expression of the stress, the pressure resulting in yielding is given by

$$p = \frac{2t\sigma_y}{R} \qquad (6.5)$$

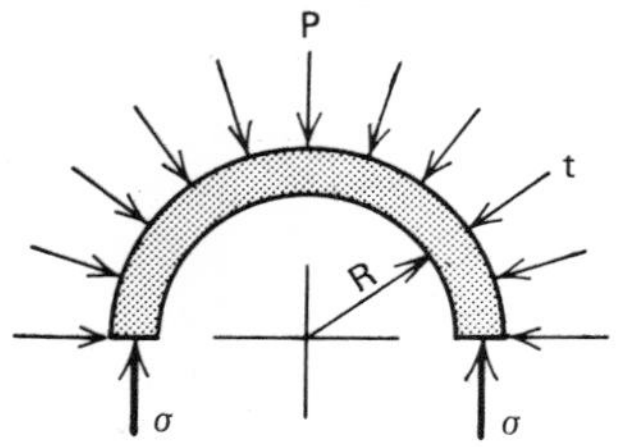

Figure 6.18.

This pressure is directly proportional, for a given material, to the thickness to radius ratio t/R. The maximum, t/R, available before the sphere becomes too heavy to float, is given by (6.3) as

$$\left(\frac{t}{R}\right)_{\text{max}} = \frac{1}{3}\frac{\rho_W}{\rho_M}$$

This value of t/R introduced in (6.5) gives the pressure beyond which it becomes impossible to build a floating sphere:

$$p_{\text{max}} = \frac{2}{3}\sigma_y\frac{\rho_W}{\rho_M} \qquad (6.6)$$

Pressure and depth limits, thus obtained, are tabulated in Table 6.1 for different materials.

TABLE 6.1.   DEPTH LIMIT FOR CERTAIN METALLIC SPHERICAL SHELLS BUOYANCY

Material	Weight Density (lb/ft^3)	Compressive Yield Stress (psi)	Pressure at Yield (psi)	Water Depth	
				ft	m
Steel A285—Grade C	489.0	30,000	2,620	5,890	1,796
HY 80 Steel	495.0	90,000	7,750	17,420	5,330
Aluminum 6061-T6	169.3	35,000	8,750	19,700	6,030
Aluminum 7075-T6	174.5	68,000	16,450	37,000	11,300
Titanium 6211	279.9	105,000	16,000	35,950	10,980

How to select the radius and wall thickness of a subsurface spherical buoy with given specification and material is illustrated in the following example.

Example. Determine the wall thickness, t, and the radius, R, of a spherical buoy with the following specifications:

Material—HY 80 Steel with compressive yield stress of 90,000 psi.
Working depth—600 m
Buoyancy required—$B = 25,000$ lb
Safety factor at yield $= 1.5$

Solution.

1. Working pressure at 600 m is 874.5 psi
2. Yield pressure—$P_y = (1.5)$ Working pressure $= (1.5)(874.5) = 1312$ psi
3. Using (6.5) the t/R ratio is then given by

$$\frac{t}{R} = \frac{P_y}{2\sigma_y}$$

and, therefore,

$$t = \frac{P_y R}{2\sigma_y} = \frac{1312R}{(2)(90,000)} = 7.28 \times 10^{-3} R$$

4. Using this value of t in 6.2 yields

$$B = \rho_W \frac{4}{3}\pi R^3 - \rho_M 4\pi R^2 (7.28 \times 10^{-3})R$$

from which

$$B = 222.6 R^3$$

5. Using the required buoyancy and solving for R

$$R = \sqrt[3]{25,000/222.6} = \sqrt[3]{112.3} = 4.825 \text{ ft}$$

6. The wall thickness t is then given by

$$t = (7.28)10^{-3}(4.825) = 0.035 \text{ ft} = 0.420 \text{ in.}$$

7. The weight of the buoy in air will then be

$$W = 4\pi R^2 t \rho_M$$

$$= (4\pi)(4.825)^2(0.035)(495)$$

$$= 5065 \text{ lb}$$

Hollow buoys are sometimes filled with compressed air to help reduce the pressure differential across the shell. The compressed air will add to the buoy weight, however. Furthermore, the buoy may have to resist the internal pressure when on deck and, therefore, must be carefully designed and built following industrial pressure vessel standard fabrication practices.

NONMETALLIC PRESSURE RESISTANT SHELLS.   Materials other than metals have been used, mostly on an experimental basis, for the construction of pressure resistant shells. Such materials are concrete, certain plastics, glass, and wound fiberglass filaments. Among these, only polysterene and glass have been used extensively in the fabrication of small spheres for shallow and medium depths applications.

THIN SHELLS FILLED WITH FLUIDS LIGHTER THAN WATER.   Another way to provide buoyancy while submerged is to fill thin shells with fluids—gases or liquids—that are lighter than water. Large quantities of fluids can be stored in metallic or nonmetallic (rubber) thin wall containers that can be hydrodynamically shaped. At depth, the pressure differential across the shell can be maintained to a very small value by applying through convenient means (diaphragm, for example) the sea ambient pressure to the fluid stored in the buoy.

Examples of compressed gases that can be used for the purpose of providing buoyancy are air, nitrogen, hydrogen, helium, and hydrazine (N_2H_4). Gas density increases with pressure. As the pressure increases, the density difference between air and water becomes less and less. Table 6.2 shows how the efficiency of compressed air-filled buoys decreases with depth.

TABLE 6.2. BUOYANCY PROVIDED BY ONE CUBIC FOOT OF AIR AT INCREASING DEPTH. (ASSUMING TEMPERATURE TO BE CONSTANT AND EQUAL TO 0°C.)

Depth (ft)	Pressure (psi)	Weight of 1 ft³ of Air (lb)	Buoyancy Provided (lb)
Surface	0	Neglect	64.0
1000	444	2.3	61.7
5000	2220	11.3	52.7
10,000	4440	20.3	43.7
20,000	8880	31.6	32.4

Only light density gases like helium and hydrogen can still provide buoyancy at great oceanic depths. However, the difficulties of storing and handling compressed and potentially explosive (hydrogen) gases severely restrict their usefulness.

Hydrocarbon liquids have often been used to provide buoyancy at all ocean depths. The specific gravity of hydrocarbon liquids is rather high, ranging from approximately 0.7 for lighter gasolines to 0.9 for diesel fuel, and their handling can be problematic. Their cost efficiency, however, is good when large amounts of buoyancy are to be provided at considerable depths. The deep sea research submersibles *Trieste* (U.S.) and *Archimede* (French) use tons of gasoline as their principal source of buoyancy.

SOLIDS LIGHTER THAN WATER. Solids lighter than water that can resist the extreme pressure of the ocean depths are few indeed. Certain plastics like polyethylene (specific gravity = 0.92 to 0.96) polypropylene (specific gravity ≅ 0.91) are lighter than water. However, due to their intrinsic weight, the efficiency of these plastics as buoyancy materials is rather poor.

Composite materials made of pressure resistant hollow spheres embedded in a resin matrix (Figure 6.19) are also used as buoyant "solids." These materials differ markedly in density, working depth, quality and cost. Table 6.3 summarizes the properties of certain composite materials. Syntactic foam is made of glass microspheres (diameters ranging from 10 to 200 microns) embedded in a resin matrix. Syntactic foam is at the present the best material for the fabrication of deep sea buoys. It will resist the highest pressures of the ocean, and at these pressures will provide more buoyancy than any other material. Syntactic foam is rugged and easy to machine and assemble. Water absorption due to implosion of microspheres is small unless the foam is of poor quality. It may amount to 2% or less of the foam weight at the first immersion, becoming negligible in subsequent uses. The main drawback of syntactic foam remains its very high cost. An all ocean depths buoy made of syntactic foam is shown in Figure 6.20.

Cluster of Small Floats. High pressure resistant glass spheres are easier to mass produce when of small diameter (18 in. or less). The heat curing of syntactic foams also sets limits on the size of blocks or slabs that can be manufactured. Small buoyant elements can be attached to frames (Figure 6.21) or inserted into profiled shapes to build efficient deep sea buoys.

In some cases, inserting a series of floats in a mooring line is the simplest and most practical way to provide the buoyancy required.

The small but finite probability of implosion must be considered when using glass spheres in critical applications. An imploding sphere may cut a mooring line, damage an instrument, or cause the implosion of other glass spheres in its immediate vicinity. Keeping glass spheres separate by at least

Figure 6.19. Buoyancy composite material. (Emerson & Cuming Inc. Eccofloat EG-23). A lightweight composite buoyancy material made of 2 in. diameter glass-reinforced plastic eccospheres HS, 0.38 in. diameter epoxy eccospheres EP, and an epoxy/glass microballoon® syntactic foam.

TABLE 6.3. PROPERTIES OF CERTAIN FLOATING COMPOSITE MATERIALS

Material	Weight Density (lb/ft³)	Working Depth Range (ft)	Buoyancy per Cubic Foot (lb)
EG-30 Composite Material	32	0–6000	32
Syntactic Foam	34	5000–7500	30
Syntactic Foam Scotchply XP-241-42H	42	20,000–36,000	22

Figure 6.20. Syntactic foam bottom buoy.

one sphere diameter will considerably reduce the possibility of sympathetic implosion. Spheres prone to implosion can be eliminated by systematically testing all the spheres of a given lot to the rated working pressure.

Practical Design Considerations

Good buoy designs should always incorporate features that will add to the buoy reliability, seaworthiness, and ease of handling. Years of experience have shown the following considerations to be particularly important and useful.

Compartmentation of Buoy Hull.   It is often advantageous to divide the hull of surface buoys into a number of leak tight compartments. This will prevent total flooding in case of a leak (welds opening up, or puncture by firearms of passing sportsmen). Separate compartments (or wells) can be used to store batteries, electronics, and recording equipment.

Foam Filling of Buoy Hull.   Compartments not used for storage or the entire hull can be filled with light density (2 lb/ft^3) foam. This will add to the buoy cost and weight. It is, however, a simple and effective way to prevent flooding by leakage.

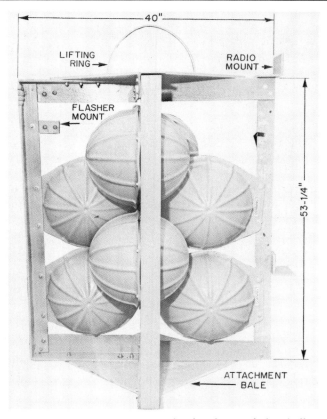

Figure 6.21. Bottom buoy made of a cluster of glass balls.

Anticapsizing Features.   A rigid bridle can be used to lower the point of attachment of the mooring line, thus increasing the righting moment. An elegant way to prevent complete capsizing (bottom up) is to provide a small amount of flotation at the highest point of the surface buoy structure (Sphere or prism of foam on top of tower as shown in Figure 6.15). A breaking wave can still tip the buoy over on its side, but the small float attached to the tower (or mast) will prevent complete rotation. The tension in the mooring line will eventually right up the buoy.

Lifting.   As mentioned before, high transient loads, several times the weight of the buoy, can be experienced during launching and retrieving. It is of prime importance to insure that points of lift have ample strength, that they will not deteriorate after months of environmental exposure (like a wire rope loop that may corrode), and that they are clearly marked as lifting points. The strength of new buoys should be tested before their setting. Lifting the buoy with a test load (an anchor, for example) attached to it is a simple way to test the strength of the buoy and of its points of lift. Failure at sea of the lift point during deployment or retrieval is always extremely dangerous and can well be catastrophic.

Storing.   Buoys must be stored on decks of ships that will eventually roll and pitch. Therefore, the buoy must be tied down before sailing. Lugs or rings placed at the periphery of the buoy can be very helpful for that purpose.

Three equally spaced lugs on the bottom of a buoy can serve a dual purpose: provide feet for the buoy to rest on when stored and provide strong points of attachment for a three part bridle for mooring line connections when deployed. Special cradles may have to be made to store buoys of particular shapes.

Grabbing.   Securing a line from the recovering ship to a floating buoy is relatively straightforward if grabbing and taking hold of the buoy is easy. On the other hand, it takes time and talent to lasso or net from a rolling ship a bare spherical buoy without a single pick up bail. The designer should try to combine grabbing and lifting in one single ring, bail, or lug. If not feasible, the grabbing points should clearly be marked "do not lift." Catching with a grapnel hook a short line stretched between the main buoy and a small auxiliary float can be of great help when trying to grab hold of the buoy (Figure 6.22).

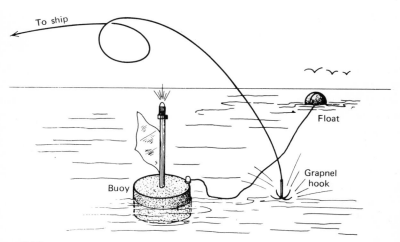

Figure 6.22.

Means of Location.   Buoys may have to be recovered in fog, at night, or in bad weather. Even in good weather, it is always difficult to spot a small object on the ocean surface. Buoys should, therefore, be equipped with proper means for facilitating their location. These could include: bright and fluorescent painting, flags (orange or yellow), radar reflectors, strobe lights, radio beacon, and acoustic pingers. The design of subsurface buoys should be checked to make sure that they remain stable upright after surfacing. A capsized buoy, with its light, radio antenna, and flag down in the sea is hard to find.

Identification and Markings.   It is good practice to clearly and permanently identify the owner of the buoy. It is the only way the owner will have a chance to see it again, or hear from it, should the mooring line fail. To prevent well intentioned seamen from cutting a surface buoy from its mooring in a recovery attempt, it might help to display the geographical coordinates of the buoy site. On the other hand, no captain in his right mind will try to pick up an unidentified spherical object with protruding antennas and sensors. Markings like "No Danger" or "Oceanographic Research Buoy" might, just might, make the difference between eventual recovery or abandonment at sea.

Anchoring Lines

Metallic Mooring Lines

Wire Ropes.   Ropes made of metallic wires are extensively used as mooring line components. These ropes have excellent strength to drag ratio. They are easy to handle, and their cost is relatively low. In many instances, wire ropes must be used to resist fish bites. A good understanding of their properties and limitations is necessary for their efficient use in deep sea mooring applications.

TERMINOLOGY.   A knowledge of the principal terms of wire rope terminology is important for intelligent communication in the field (engineering specifications, purchase orders, scientific papers, etc.).

Wire. The elementary unit of any wire rope is the wire. Wires are obtained by drawing through reducing dies, to the desired size, rods of the metal selected for the rope. The specified strength and ductility of the wires is obtained by a combination of drawing and annealing operations. Wires are spooled on bobbins which fit into stranding machines.

Strand. A number of wires twisted together or laid around a central wire (king wire) constitutes a strand. For example, six wires of equal size can be twisted around a central wire of the same size. The resulting strand is then a 1×7 strand (one strand made of seven wires). Twelve additional wires could fit around this layer of six, and the resulting strand would have 19 wires (1×19). If all the wires are laid in the same direction, they are stranded in one operation, and the strand is called a "one operation strand." The number of layers and operations varies with the anticipated uses of the strand. Furthermore, the majority of strands are made of wires of different sizes and therefore, have different configurations.

Strand constructions. When using wires of different sizes, smaller wires may be inserted between larger wires in the same layer, or layers of smaller wires may be inserted between layers of larger wires. When the alternation of wire sizes is in the outer layer, the configuration is called a *Warrington* construction. When the alternation of wire sizes takes place in an inner layer, the configuration is called a *Filler Wire* construction. Finally, the alternation of layers made of small and large wires is called a *Seale* construction. Most complex strands are made of a combination of these basic types (see Figure 6.23).

A number of mechanical characteristics depend in the long run on the strand configurations.

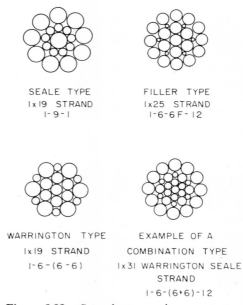

SEALE TYPE
1x19 STRAND
1-9-1

FILLER TYPE
1x25 STRAND
1-6-6 F-12

WARRINGTON TYPE
1x19 STRAND
1-6-(6-6)

EXAMPLE OF A
COMBINATION TYPE
1x31 WARRINGTON SEALE
STRAND
1-6-(6+6)-12

Figure 6.23. Strand constructions.

Wire Ropes. Several strands of wires twisted around a central member constitute a wire rope.

Core. The central member of a wire rope is called the core. It may be a strand, a fiber core, or a smaller wire rope (Independent Wire Rope Core, I.W.R.C.). Either natural (sisal) or synthetic (polypropylene) fibers are used in the fiber cores. Fiber cores are normally saturated with lubricant. The core is the foundation of the wire rope supporting the other strands and maintaining them in position when the rope is in use and under load. Independent wire rope cores that better resist the lateral pressure of the strands and have lesser stretch are more frequently used.

Preforming. Wires and strands can be formed to the spiral shape that they will assume in the strands and in the ropes in a preforming operation. The definite advantage of this operation is to reduce the tendency for the wire rope elements to open up at a cut end, to reduce the initial torsional stresses in the wire, and to insure uniform distribution of stresses when under load. All this results in longer life and preforming is most of the time a standard process.

Lay. Wires in the strands can be laid in one of two possible directions: to the left or to the right of the central wire. Strands of the rope can also be laid either way, there being four possible ways of constructing standard wire ropes.

When the strands are laid in a clockwise direction around the core, the wire rope construction is defined as right lay. If the strands are laid in a counterclockwise direction, the rope is called left lay.

If the wires in the strands are laid around the central wire in the same direction as the strands of the rope are laid around the core, the resulting construction is called *Lang* lay. In the opposite case, the resulting construction is called regular lay. The four possible constructions therefore are:

Left lay	Regular lay
Right lay	Regular lay
Left lay	*Lang* lay
Right lay	*Lang* lay

The right lay regular lay and the right lay *Lang* lay are the most extensively produced types of wire rope construction. The *Lang* lay is more flexible and has better abrasion resistance. The regular lay has better torque balance and kink resistance.

Length of lay. The length of lay is the pitch of the helix formed by the wires in a strand or by the strands in a rope. Ropes with shorter lay are more flexible.

Size. The size of a rope is equal to the diameter of the circle that will just contain the rope.

Wire rope designation. In order to fully and properly describe a wire rope, the following eight parameters must be specified in the indicated order:

1. Length;
2. Size;
3. Wire rope construction, that is, number of strands in the rope and the number of wires in the strand;
4. Strand construction, that is, Warrington, Seale, or standard;
5. Material;
6. Direction of lay (left or right);
7. Type of lay (regular or *Lang*);
8. Type of rope core.

Example. 3281 ft 1 in. 6×19 Seale Preformed Galvanized Improved Plow Steel right lay *Lang* lay I.W.R.C.

Kinks. Kinks are the mortal enemy of wire ropes. They start as a loop of the rope winding on itself, (Figure 6.24), and when the loop is pulled tight, wires and strands are permanently bent, ruining the rope at the point of kink (Figure 6.25). There are two kinds of kinks—tightening kinks and loosening kinks. The first tightens the lay of the wire rope, while the second tends to open the rope. Loosening kinks are more damaging and easier to form. Most of the kinks originate in torsional energy stored in the rope and slack conditions. Proper choice of wire rope construction and handling techniques can minimize the danger of kinks. In particular, in free hanging operations (cargo handling, lowering of mooring anchors, etc.), ropes should be torque balanced and not allowed to twist or become slack.

Jackets. Plastic materials (polyurethane, polyethylene) can be extruded over the finished wire rope. The resulting "jacket" provides additional protection against abrasion and corrosion.

These few definitions constitute a brief introduction to the terminology used in wire rope engineering. A much more detailed terminology has been established by the Association of American Wire Rope Engineers to properly describe the amazingly large number of different wire rope characteristics and types.

MATERIALS. The large majority of wire ropes are made of carbon steel, but stainless steels and various alloys have also been used in oceanographic applications. High strength to weight ratio is a desirable characteristic of mooring line components, and, therefore, ropes made of higher strength

$\frac{1}{4}$" 1 x 19 JACKETED WIRE ROPE

Figure 6.24.   Example of wire rope twisted on itself.

steels are generally preferred. Typical grades of carbon steel used are improved and extra improved plow steel with breaking stress ranging from 250,000 to 275,000 psi, and ultrahigh strength steels with breaking stress in excess of 275,000 psi.

Stainless steels are used for higher corrosion resistance and for certain nonmagnetic applications. Standard stainless steel wire ropes are made from the 18-8 stainless steel series (18% chrome, 8% nickel), type 316 having the better corrosion resistance. Stainless steel ropes have from 15 to 20% less strength than improved plow steels and are also less resistant to fatigue. The use of stainless steel ropes introduces the possibility of galvanic corrosion at the termination points. This may be a difficult problem to solve in a practical way. Stainless steel ropes are considerably more expensive than carbon steel ropes.

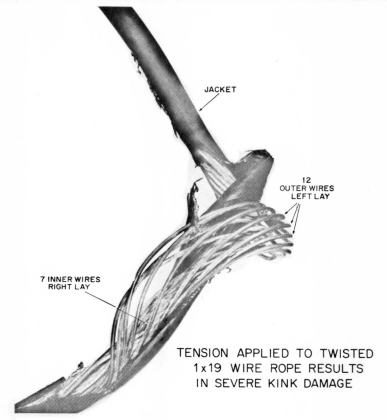

JACKET

12
OUTER WIRES
LEFT LAY

7 INNER WIRES
RIGHT LAY

TENSION APPLIED TO TWISTED
1×19 WIRE ROPE RESULTS
IN SEVERE KINK DAMAGE

Figure 6.25. Loosening kink on 1×19 wire rope.

Nonferrous metals have been used to a very limited extent. Mooring lines made of copper alloys (phosphor bronze, copper nickel), nickel alloys (Inconel, Monel), and titanium have been made for experimental and evaluation purposes. These special ropes offer good corrosion resistance, but their mechanical properties (strength, endurance) are less than steel and their cost is high.

MECHANICAL CHARACTERISTICS. The mechanical characteristics of importance for the design of metallic mooring lines follow.

Strength. For equal size and equal line density, the better rope for mooring line use is the stronger rope. The strength of a rope depends on the strength of the wires and on the construction of the rope (stranding factor). The actual ultimate breaking strength (UBS) of a wire rope ranges from 80 to 90% of the strength obtained by summing the strength of the individual wires. The rated breaking strength (RBS) listed in the manufacturers' catalogs is generally less (as much as 10%) than the actual or ultimate breaking strength. Very high tensile strength steels may be brittle and not suited for applications where cyclic loading due to wave action is present. Table 6.4 shows a set of weight and strength versus size data for a widely used oceanographic wire rope. The yield strength of wire ropes varies considerably with rope configurations and materials and is generally difficult to obtain. In some cases, the elastic limit is an important design factor and, if not known, must be experimentally established.

TABLE 6.4   SIZE, WEIGHT, AND STRENGTH OF 3 × 19 TORQUE-BALANCED ROPE. *

Size (in.)	Weight In Air (lb/ft)	Weight in Water (lb/ft)	Approx. Elastic Limit	Breaking Load (lb)	Thick- ness (in.)	OD (in.)	Jacket Weight (lb/ft)	Weight in Air (lb/ft)	Weight in Water (lb/ft)
	Bright or AMGAL MONITOR AA Torque-Balanced Rope				Jacket Dimensions		Polyethylene Jacketed Rope		
3/16	0.0586	0.0509	3000	4000	0.032	0.269	0.014	0.073	0.047
1/4	0.0997	0.0867	5063	6750	0.032	0.329	0.019	0.119	0.081
5/16	0.153	0.133	7725	10,300	0.032	0.392	0.026	0.179	0.125
3/8	0.220	0.191	11,100	14,800	0.032	0.456	0.033	0.253	0.181
7/16	0.304	0.264	15,000	20,000	0.032	0.524	0.042	0.346	0.250
1/2	0.392	0.341	19,275	25,700	0.080	0.682	0.090	0.482	0.319
9/16	0.492	0.428	24,375	32,500	0.080	0.746	0.104	0.596	0.402
5/8	0.602	0.523	30,225	40,300	0.080	0.807	0.118	0.720	0.493
3/4	0.879	0.764	43,350	57,800	0.080	0.941	0.152	1.03	0.722
7/8	1.21	1.05	58,500	78,000	0.080	1.077	0.190	1.40	0.995
1	1.56	1.36	75,450	100,600	0.080	1.201	0.228	1.79	1.28
1-1/8	1.96	1.70	93,000	124,000	0.080	1.326	0.270	2.23	1.62

*Data by United States Steel Corporation

Weight. Metallic ropes are heavy. This is the main disadvantage of their use as oceanic mooring lines. The line density depends on construction and materials and varies as the square of the diameter. The weight of a mooring line can be an important fraction of its breaking strength. In great depths, lines of size decreasing with depth (tapered or stepped down) can be used to advantage. In many moorings, distributed buoyancy must be provided along the line to support its weight.

Size. The size of a mooring line should be kept as small as possible for ease of handling and storage. Drag is also a function of size, and a decrease in diameter results in a reduction of the component of tension due to hydrodynamic forces.

Elongation and rotation properties. The elongation of a wire rope depends on the construction of the rope, on the material of the wires, on the magnitude of the load, and on the end conditions of the wire rope. If one or both ends are free to turn (free hanging load or swivels in the line), the strands of the rope or the wires of the strand will unlay and the rope will elongate accordingly. This elongation is not recoverable for the most part, and may amount to as much as 4% of original length. If both ends are restrained, the elongation is then made of two parts: the nonrecoverable construction stretch, which follows the first application of the load, and the elastic stretch, which follows Hooke's Law up to the elastic limit. The elastic stretch is expressed by

$$\Delta L = \frac{PL}{AE} \tag{6.7}$$

where ΔL is the elongation in inches, L is the original length in inches, P is the load in pounds, A is the metallic area in square inches, and E is the modulus of elasticity of the rope in pounds per square inch. The metallic area is the total area of the wires, and due to the voids in the rope construction, A is less than the area of the circle of same diameter as the rope. The modulus of elasticity, E, of the rope is much less than the modulus of elasticity of the wires. Values of A and E are usually available from the rope manufacturer.

Generally, metallic ropes have little ductility, and, therefore, elongation due to sustained loading (cold flow) is small and occurs only at a very high percentage of the breaking strength. At these very high load levels, steel ropes may break in relatively short times. All causes of elongation must be seriously considered in applications where mooring scope and placement of instrumentation are critical.

Single-point moored buoy systems are essentially one-free end systems. During deployment, the heavy anchor is free to turn, causing the wires or the strands to rotate and the strand or the rope to unlay and open up. This action can be very detrimental to the line, and may result in the split of the jacket material, in the reduction of the strength, and in the formation of kinks (Figure 6.26).

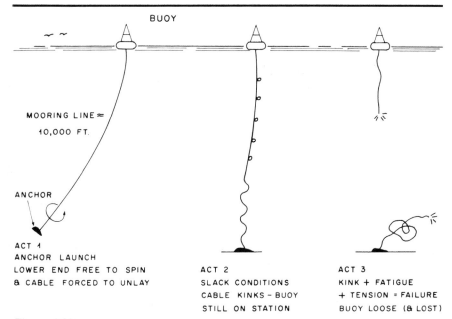

BUOY

MOORING LINE ≈
10,000 FT.

ANCHOR

ACT 1
ANCHOR LAUNCH
LOWER END FREE TO SPIN
& CABLE FORCED TO UNLAY

ACT 2
SLACK CONDITIONS
CABLE KINKS – BUOY
STILL ON STATION

ACT 3
KINK + FATIGUE
+ TENSION = FAILURE
BUOY LOOSE (& LOST)

Figure 6.26.

Nonrotating ropes can be designed in such a way that the tendency for the strands to rotate in one way is balanced by the tendency for the wires in the strands to rotate the other way (3×19). A certain amount of torque balance can be achieved in one strand mooring lines by varying the wire diameters and the pitch angles of different layers (1×43, 1×51).

Exact rotation characteristics of wire ropes must be established experimentally. Wire ropes with strong rotation tendencies (6×19, 7×25) are doomed to failure when used as deep-sea mooring lines. The application of an external torque to a nonrotating rope can also cause severe damage to the rope.

Flexibility. Flexibility may be used to advantage for better resistance to repeated loading and ease of handling especially in the larger sizes of ropes (above 0.5 in. diameter). Mooring line flexibility, however, is not as important as in the case of running lines. The larger number of wires in a flexible rope results in higher corrosion rates. When using stiffer ropes, attention must be paid to the selection of the size of drums and sheaves over which the line may pass when in use. Small sized sheaves may overstress the wires and permanently damage the rope during paying out operations. A conservative relation between wire size and sheave size is given by

$$\sigma = \frac{Ed}{D} \tag{6.8}$$

where σ is the allowable stress of the wire (lb/in.^{2}), E is the modulus of elasticity of the *rope* (lb/in.^{2}), d is the diameter of the wire (in.), and D is the diameter of the sheave (in.).

Endurance. Wave action results in low frequency cyclic longitudinal loading of mooring lines. Vortex shedding may create a strumming situation in a taut line with high frequency lateral loading. The number of cycles over relatively short periods may be surprisingly high, and fatigue of the wires particularly at the wire rope terminations can be a cause of failure. The endurance limit of mooring lines under longitudinal loading is difficult to ascertain. Cyclic load tests can, however, be very useful in determining the relative performance of candidate rope specimen. The resistance to fatigue will be greatly increased if the cyclic loads are kept below 20% of the breaking strength of the rope.

Construction. When evaluating the construction of different wire ropes for mooring line application, the following aspects should be considered:

1.   The larger the number of wires, the more flexible the rope, but also the less resistant to abrasion and corrosion.
2.   Large wires on the outside protect from abrasion. Small wires in the inside corrode fast, and the corrosion cannot be detected.
3.   Under tension, all wire ropes have a tendency to spin and open up. Mooring lines should be as spin free as practical.
4.   The more complex the construction, the higher the price. However, the reliability of the mooring depends on the performance of the wire rope.

Safety factor. The safety factor is the ratio of the wire rope strength (lb) to the design or anticipated working load (lb). The strength used in establishing the safety factor can be either ultimate or yield strength. Type of application, life expectancy and allowance for the approximations made in the evaluation of the line stresses must be considered when selecting the safety factor. Whenever possible, high values of safety factor (6 to 8 based on UBS) should be used to insure mooring reliability.

WIRE ROPE TERMINATION.   Lengths of mooring line must be terminated at their points of attachment to each other or points of instrument insertion. Stress concentration and incompatibility of materials introduced at the termination point can and often have been the cause of rapid deterioration and catastrophic failure of the line. The design of wire rope termination for underwater use should incorporate the following characteristics.

Strength. The termination should not constitute a "weak" point in the line, and should be capable of developing as a bare minimum the rated breaking strength of the rope itself.

Dimensions. To resist shock loads and deterioration due to fatigue, chafing, and corrosion, good practice recommends to use mooring line fittings of a higher strength and larger dimensions than the fittings normally used in land applications. Mass transition between wire rope and fitting should be considered for vibration damping.

Material. To avoid accelerated corrosion, the material of the fitting should be the same as the material of the wires. Never use fitting materials that will make the rope anodic with respect to the fitting (copper clamps on steel wire ropes, for example, should be systematically avoided).

Ease of fabrication and handling. Terminations should be easy to apply to the rope. Their configuration should be flexible to accommodate different field uses or conditions. Good types of wire rope termination for underwater uses are:

1. Wire rope splices over wire rope thimble.
2. Epoxy filled sockets.
3. Swaged fittings. In a swaging process, a hollow fitting is first placed over the wire rope end. The fitting is then pressed over the rope with the help of a hydraulic press. Figure 6.27 shows a swaged termination that has been used with success on a great number of deep-sea moorings.

Successful terminations are highly dependent on quality control.

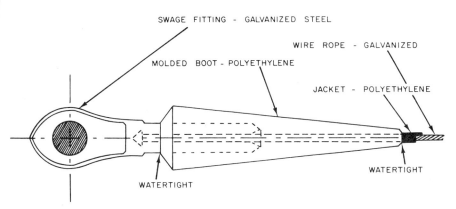

Figure 6.27. Typical W.H.O.I. wire rope termination for mooring line application.

Electromechanical Cables.   Electromechanical cables are used to transmit electrical signals between different points of a mooring line. Transmission to a surface buoy of signals from distributed sensors for recording and/or telemetry purposes is an example of electromechanical cable use. Most underwater standard conducting cables have been developed for towing uses or bottom applications. Mooring lines with conductors must be specially engineered to provide adequate electrical and mechanical characteristics.

Electromechanical cables essentially consist of low resistance conductors with their insulation and of steel wires acting as strength members (armor). Conductors can be independent or coaxial. The armor is generally made of several layers with a high degree of torque balance. As a group, electromechanical cables have a lesser strength to size ratio than plain wire ropes and, therefore, larger diameter cables must be used.

Electromechanical termination must provide continuity of signal transmission, water tightness, and strength integrity. Their design and fabrication are difficult and critical. Figure 6.28 shows the details of a termination design which has been used with success in a number of deep-sea buoy systems.

To summarize, metallic mooring lines have good strength to size ratio, but poor strength to weight ratio. They are susceptible to corrosion, fatigue, and kinks. Proper protection and judicious selection of rope size and construction will markedly increase their reliability.

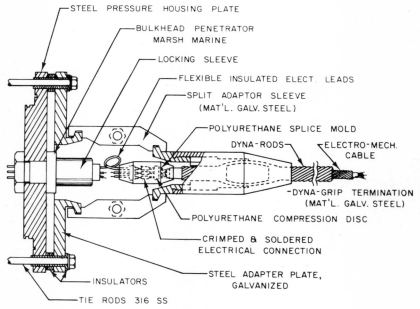

Figure 6.28.   Electromechanical termination assembly.

Nonmetallic Mooring Lines

Ropes made of synthetic fiber (nylon, dacron, etc.) are often used as buoy system anchoring lines. These ropes do not corrode nor deteriorate appreciably in sea water. Their strength to immersed weight ratio is excellent. They are easy to handle and terminate.

Fiber ropes, however, are relatively easy to cut, especially when under tension. The use of small size fiber ropes in geographic locations and oceanic depths where fish attacks are likely to occur has often resulted in mooring losses.

Construction of Synthetic Fiber Ropes.   The building unit of fiber ropes is the filament. Filaments are produced by extruding controlled quantities of molten plastic materials through fine holes. Fineness of filaments is expressed in deniers. A 1 denier filament has a weight of 1 g and a length of 9000 m.

An arrangement of parallel continuous filaments is called a bundle. A number of twisted filaments constitute a yarn. Bundles or yarns twisted together form a multiply. Several multiplies are used to make a strand, and, finally, several strands are used to make a rope. The four basic constructions of fiber ropes are:

1. Stranded. Most common construction, rope generally made of three strands running in the same direction (left or right).
2. Plaited. Made generally of an even number of strands, plaited or twisted, in pairs of opposite direction.
3. Braided. Made of a great number of equally distributed left- and right-hand yarns.
4. Parallel Yarns. (Nolaro®, Uniline®) Made of a large number of bundles or yarns held together by a minimum of twist and enclosed in a protective plastic jacket or external braid.

A combination of these basic types is sometimes used (cable laid rope, double braided, etc.). The stranded construction has a strong tendency to unlay under free end conditions and, therefore, should not be used in mooring lines. These different configurations are shown in Figure 6.29.

Materials.   Materials commonly used in the fabrication of synthetic fiber ropes are: Nylon (polyamide), Dacron® (polyester), Polypropylene, and Polyethylene. New synthetic fibers (Kevlar® 29, Kevlar® 49) with great potential for mooring line applications have been recently introduced. A brief review of the general properties of these common and newer materials follows.

NYLON.   A large percentage of synthetic fiber ropes are made of nylon. Nylon ropes have a bright appearance and are soft and somewhat slippery. The nominal strength of nylon ropes is the largest of the common synthetic

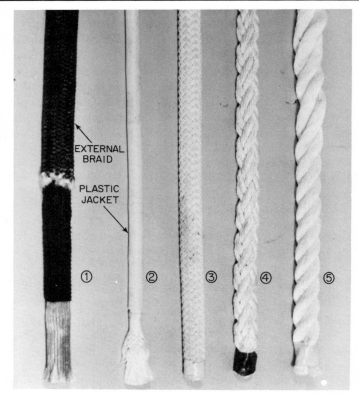

Figure 6.29. Typical synthetic fiber rope configurations. 1. Parallel yarns (Uni-line®). 2. Parallel yarns (Nolaro®). 3. Braided. 4. Plaited. 5. Stranded.

fiber ropes. When wet, nylon shrinks and loses approximately 10% of its strength. The specific gravity of nylon is 1.14. Nylon ropes are highly elastic, have excellent endurance under repeated loadings, and have excellent energy absorption capacity. Abrasion resistance of nylon is good, and its resistance to chemicals is fair. Nylon ropes should be recommended whenever high strength and high shock absorption are required. Large stretch under load may be a drawback.

DACRON (POLYESTER).   Dacron ropes have a dull white appearance, are hard and smooth, but not slippery. Their strength is somewhat less (10% or less) than the strength of nylon when dry. Dacron strength does not change appreciably when wet, and, therefore, dacron ropes are as strong as nylon ropes when immersed. The specific gravity of dacron is 1.38. Dacron ropes are less elastic than nylon ropes and will absorb less energy. Their endurance is very good, and their resistance to abrasion and chemicals are excellent.

Dacron ropes should be used when high strength must be combined with low and predictable long term stretch. Dacron ropes should not be used for shock absorption.

POLYPROPYLENE.   Polypropylene ropes have a shiny appearance. They are hard and stiff to the touch. The average nominal strength of dry polypropylene ropes is only 60% the dry strength of nylon ropes, but is slightly larger wet than dry. With a specific gravity of 0.91, polypropylene is the lightest of the synthetic fibers used in ropes. Polypropylene ropes elongate less than nylon, but more than dacron ropes. They are good for energy absorption and have an excellent endurance and abrasion resistance. Their resistance to chemicals is good. Attention must be paid when using polypropylene ropes to friction heat and creep. The use of polypropylene ropes should be recommended in applications where strength and long term stretch are not critical and when rope floatability is desired.

POLYETHYLENE.   Polyethylene ropes are not extensively used in mooring applications. They are smooth in appearance and very slippery. Their average nominal strength is about 50% the strength of nylon and does not change when wet. Polyethylene is slightly buoyant with a specific gravity of 0.95. The initial and elastic stretch characteristics of polyethylene ropes are approximately the same as the characteristics of polypropylene; however, polyethylene creeps at a much faster rate than any other synthetic. It has comparatively little energy absorption characteristics and does not perform well under repeated loading. Its resistance to abrasion is good. Polyethylene ropes should be used only in a limited number of uncritical applications.

HIGH MODULUS ORGANIC FIBERS (KEVLAR®).   Very high tensile strength, high modulus of elasticity fibers, made from organic polymers, have been recently developed and commercially produced under the Dupont trade name of Kevlar®. Ropes manufactured with this material have excellent characteristics. Kevlar® ropes are light (specific gravity is 1.4), and their strength can nearly equal the strength of steel cables of the same diameter. Filament elongation at break is low (2 to 3%), and rope resistance to creep is high. Kevlar® main drawback remains its relatively elevated cost.

Table 6.5 compares the average properties of 1 in. diameter ropes made of nylon, dacron, polypropylene, and polyethylene.

Mechanical Characteristics

STRENGTH.   Synthetic fiber ropes, with the exception of Kevlar® ropes, have a much lesser "strength" than wire ropes of equal size, and, consequently, larger diameter ropes must be used to sustain a given load. The resulting increase in hydrodynamic resistance must be considered when making trade

TABLE 6.5. COMPARATIVE TABLE OF AVERAGE SYNTHETIC ROPE CHARACTERISTICS (1 IN. DIAMETER ROPE).*

Type of Material	Nylon	Dacron	Polyethyelene	Polypropylene
Ultimate Tensile Strength (lb)	25,000	22,000	12,500	14,000
Wet Strength Compared to Dry Strength	90%	100%	100%	105%
Breaking Strength (ft)	96,000	72,000	66,000	78,000
Energy Absorption (ft-lb/ft)	15,000	7000	4600	9000
Endurance to Cyclic Loading	Good	Excellent	Fair	Excellent
Dry Weight of 100 ft of Rope (lb)	26	30.5	18.5	18.5
Specific Gravity of Fiber	1.14	1.38	0.95	0.91
Buoyancy	Negative	Negative	Positive	Positive
Elasticity—Elongation** at 20% of Ultimate Strength	17%	7%	6%	10%
Water Absorption in % of Rope Dry Weight	9%	1%	0%	0%
Recommended Safety Factor (Industrial Application)	9	9	6	6
Resistance to Plastic Flow	Good	Excellent	Poor	Fair

*Average of data supplied by manufacturers.
**After first loading to 50% of tensile strength.

off studies of wire versus synthetic fiber ropes for mooring line applications. To a first approximation, the breaking strength (UBS) of all ropes can be expressed by:

$$\text{UBS} = C_s d^2 \qquad (6.9)$$

where C_s is a strength constant varying with rope construction and material (lb/in.²) and d is the rope diameter (in.). Values of C_s for 1 in. diameter ropes of various types are tabulated in Table 6.6. The table also expresses the strength of these ropes as a percentage of 1 in. diameter 3×19 high strength steel wire rope with a breaking strength of 100,600 lb.

The strength listed in manufacturers' catalogues is generally the average strength at break. Strength depends on the material, on the size, and to an extent, on the construction of the rope (parallel fibers have much higher strength). Dacron and nylon have approximately the same strength, and polypropylene and polyethylene have about half the strength of nylon.

TABLE 6.6.   STRENGTH OF VARIOUS ONE INCH DIAMETER SYNTHETIC FIBER ROPES.

Rope Material	Rope Construction	C_s Strength Constant (lb/in.²)	Strength as a percent of 1 in. 3×19 Wire Rope Strength
High Strength Steel	3×19	100,600	100
Nylon	Three strands, stranded	25,000	25
	Eight strands, plaited	25,000	25
	Double braid	31,300	31
Dacron	Three strands, stranded	22,000	22
	Eight strands, plaited	22,000	22
	Double braid	28,400	29
	Nolaro	40,000	40
Polypropylene	Three strands, stranded	14,000	14
Polyethylene	Three strands, stranded	12,600	12
Kevlar®	Eight strands, plaited	69,000	69
	Nolaro	84,000	84

TABLE 6.7. SYNTHETIC FIBER ROPE TECHNICAL DATA.*

Rope Size in inches		Nylon			Dacron			Polypro		
Diameter	Circumference	Pounds per 100 Feet	Feet per Pound	Breaking Test (lbs)	Pounds per 100 Feet	Feet per Pound	Breaking Test (lbs)	Pounds per 100 feet	Feet per Pound	Breaking Test (lb)
3/16	5/8	1.0	100.0	1000	1.2	83.4	1000	.70	143.0	800
1/4	3/4	1.5	66.7	1650	2.0	50.0	1650	1.2	83.4	1250
5/16	1	2.5	40.0	2550	3.1	32.2	2550	1.8	55.6	1900
3/8	1-1/8	3.5	28.5	3700	4.5	22.2	3700	2.8	35.7	2700
7/16	1-1/4	5.0	20.0	5000	6.2	16.1	5000	3.8	26.3	3500
1/2	1-1/2	6.5	15.4	6400	8.0	12.5	6400	4.7	21.3	4200
9/16	1-3/4	8.3	12.3	8000	10.2	9.8	8000	6.1	16.4	5100
5/8	2	10.5	9.5	10,400	13.0	7.7	10,000	7.5	13.3	6200
3/4	2-1/4	14.5	6.9	14,200	17.5	5.7	12,500	10.7	9.3	8500
13/16	2-1/2	17.0	5.9	17,000	21.0	4.8	15,500	12.7	7.9	9900
7/8	2-3/4	20.0	5.0	20,000	25.0	4.0	18,000	15.0	6.7	11,500
1	3	26.0	3.8	25,000	30.5	3.3	22,000	18.0	5.5	14,000
1-1/16	3-1/4	29.0	3.4	28,800	34.5	2.9	25,500	20.4	4.9	16,000
1-1/8	3-1/2	34.0	2.9	33,000	40.0	2.5	29,500	23.7	4.2	18,300

1-1/4	3-3/4	40.0	2.5	37,500	46.3	2.2	33,200	27.0	3.7	21,000
1-5/16	4	45.0	2.2	43,000	52.5	1.9	37,500	30.5	3.3	23,500
1-1/4	4-1/2	55.0	1.8	53,000	66.8	1.5	46,800	38.5	2.6	29,700
1-5/8	5	68.0	1.5	65,000	82.0	1.2	57,000	47.5	2.1	36,000
1-3/4	5-1/2	83.0	1.2	78,000	98.0	1.02	67,800	57.0	1.7	43,000
2	6	95.0	1.05	92,000	118.0	0.85	80,000	69.0	1.4	52,000
2-1/8	6-1/2	109.0	0.92	106,000	135.0	0.74	92,000	80.0	1.2	61,000
2-1/4	7	129.0	0.77	125,000	157.0	0.64	107,000	92.0	1.1	69,000
2-1/2	7-1/2	149.0	0.67	140,000	181.0	0.55	122,000	107.0	0.93	80,000
2-5/8	8	168.0	0.59	162,000	205.0	0.49	137,000	120.0	0.83	90,000
2-7/8	8-1/2	189.0	0.53	180,000	230.0	0.43	154,000	137.0	0.73	101,000
3	9	210.0	0.47	200,000	258.0	0.39	174,000	153.0	0.65	114,000
3-1/4	10	263.0	-0.38	250,000	318.0	0.31	210,000	190.0	0.53	137,000
3-1/2	11	316.0	0.32	300,000	384.0	0.26	254,000	232.0	0.43	162,000
4	12	379.0	0.26	360,000	460.0	0.22	300,000	275.0	0.36	190,000

*Data by Columbian Rope, Auburn, New York

WEIGHT.   As a group, synthetic fiber ropes weigh much less than wire ropes of equal strength. Furthermore, the specific gravity of synthetic fibers is close to unity, and, therefore, the immersed weight of synthetic fiber ropes is but a fraction of their weight in air. Ropes made of polypropylene and polyethylene are even slightly buoyant.

Weights of synthetic fiber ropes of different constructions and materials are part of the mechanical characteristics usually provided by rope manufacturers. Table 6.7 shows a typical set of available data.

Fiber specific gravity and rope immersed weight as a percentage of rope weight in air are presented in Table 6.8. This table can be used, as illustrated in the following example, to obtain the immersed weight of a given rope by simple multiplication of its weight in air by the immersed weight percent shown in Table 6.8.

Example. Find the immersed weight of 100 ft of: (1)   5/8 in. nylon rope and (2)   13/16 in. polypropylene rope.

Solution. From the technical data by Columbian Rope (Table 6.7), the weight in air of 100 ft of 5/8 in. nylon rope is 10.5 lb and of 100 ft of 13/16 in. polypropylene rope is 12.7 lb.

Using Table 6.8, the immersed weight of the nylon is given by

$$\frac{(10.5)(12.6)}{100} = 1.32 \text{ lb}$$

and of the polypropylene

$$\frac{(12.7)(-8.7)}{100} = -1.10 \text{ (buoyant)}$$

STRETCH.   Knowing the elastic response of the mooring line to specific loadings is of prime importance to the mooring line designer. The stretch or amount of elongation of the rope will determine the shape of the mooring line, the location of the buoy and of the instruments inserted in the line. Furthermore, under sustained high loading, the rope may creep, and as its diameter reduces, the stress in the fibers increases. Failure may then occur in relatively short times (days). In addition, the dynamic response of the mooring lines depends on the stress-strain characteristics of the particular rope used.

The elastic behavior of synthetic fiber ropes is difficult to ascertain and has not yet been fully evaluated and described. It is a function of rope construction, rope material, type of load, load history, time, and environmental conditions. In many cases, the elongation characteristics of specific ropes must be experimentally established prior to their implementation as mooring line components.

**TABLE 6.8.   SPECIFIC GRAVITY AND
IMMERSED WEIGHT PERCENT OF
VARIOUS ROPE MATERIALS.**

Rope Material	Specific Gravity	Immersed Weight as a Percent of Weight in Air
Steel	7.85	87
Nylon	1.14	12.6
Dacron	1.38	27.6
Polypropylene	0.92	− 8.7
Polyethylene	0.95	− 5.3
Kevlar ®	1.41	29.1

It is useful to separately investigate the elastic response of synthetic fiber ropes to static loading and to cyclic loading.

Stretch under sustained loading. When a load is applied for the first time to a rope, the total stretch will be the sum of three different modes of elongation: the construction stretch, the elastic stretch, and the elongation due to cold flow. The construction stretch occurs when initial loading places the fibers and the strands in paths different from their original helical construction. The elastic stretch is a function of the elastic characteristics of the fibers and is an important fraction of the total elongation. These two modes occur simultaneously and almost instantaneously. They are usually nonlinear, and they interfere with each other. Typical elongation curves of fiber ropes used in oceanographic moorings are shown in Figure 6.30.

If the high loads are maintained, cold flow due to the plasticity of the fibers takes place. The rope further elongates with time until it eventually breaks.

Stretch under cyclic loading. Launching transient, wave action, and varying currents result in mooring line loads that vary with time. A study of the stress-strain behavior of synthetic fiber ropes under cyclic loads is helpful in formulating a realistic model of the mooring line response to these time varying loads.

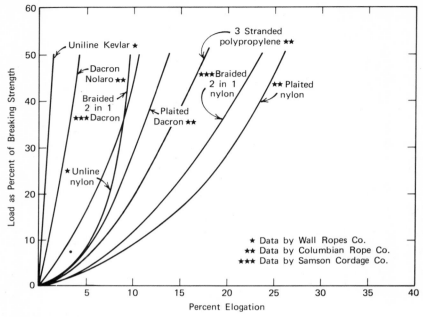

Figure 6.30. Typical elongation curves of various ropes.

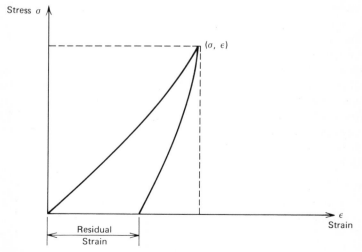

Figure 6.31. Synthetic fiber rope first loading cycle.

248

When stressing a new sample of synthetic fiber rope from a zero stress condition to a certain maximum stress, σ, and then down again to a zero stress condition, a stress-strain curve of the type shown in Figure 6.31 is obtained. This curve shows a certain amount of residual strain at the end of this first cycle. If the same rope sample is stressed through the same cycle a number of times, several hysteresis loops will be obtained (Figure 6.32). The residual strain increases with each cycle, the increase, however, becoming less and less as the number of cycles grows. Furthermore, the last hysteresis loops have a tendency to superimpose each other. This suggests the possibility of approximating the elastic response of the rope after a large number of these cycles by a "permanent" residual strain and a "stable" hysteresis loop.

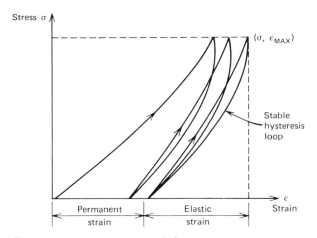

Figure 6.32.   Stable hysteresis loop.

Should a second sample of the same rope be loaded to a larger maximum stress, and the loading cycle to that stress be repeated a number of times, then a new value of the "permanent" strain and a new stable hysteresis loop will be obtained.

This process can be repeated a number of times yielding a set of permanent strain values and stable hysteresis loops. The set of permanent strain values is used to establish the permanent strain as a function of applied stress (Figure 6.33). The center lines (axes) of the stable hysteresis loops are of identical shape and thus a single function can be used to uniquely describe them. This function is the average elastic response of the rope (Figure 6.34).

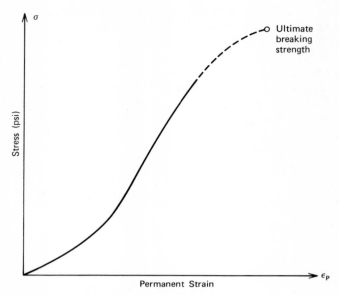

Figure 6.33. Typical curve of permanent strain.

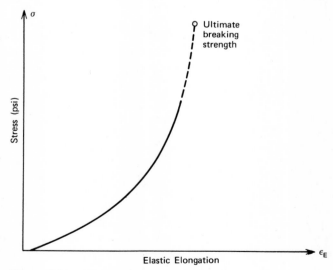

Figure 6.34. Typical curve of elastic strain.

The total strain for a particular load history will be the sum of the permanent strain and the elastic strain. It will be given by

$$\epsilon_i = f_1(\sigma_{max}) + f_2(\sigma_i) \tag{6.10}$$

where $f_1(\sigma)$ and $f_2(\sigma)$ are the analytical expressions respectively approximating the empirical curves of permanent and elastic strain; σ_{max} is the highest stress experienced during the load history; and σ_i is the stress at the time the particular strain ϵ_i is computed.

The elastic behavior under cyclic loads of certain synthetic fiber ropes has been experimentally established (Wilson, 1967; Berteaux, 1973). An example of the results thus obtained is presented in Figure 6.35, which shows the permanent and elastic elongation curves obtained for eight strand nylon plaited ropes.

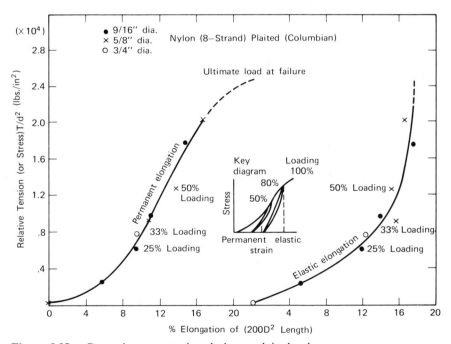

Figure 6.35. General stress—strain relations—plaited nylon.

In this particular case, the empirical expression relating rope stress to permanent and elastic elongation were found to be, respectively,

$$\frac{T - T_0}{D^2} = 88\epsilon_P^{1.94} \tag{6.11}$$

$$\frac{T-T_0}{D^2} = 74.8\epsilon_E^{1.87}$$ (6.12)

The different parameters in expressions (6.11) and (6.12) have the following signification: T is the tension in the rope (lb), T_0 is the tension originally applied to the rope to establish its standard length (lb)

$$T_0 = 200D^2$$

D is the diameter of the rope (in.), ϵ_P is the permanent elongation percent, given by

$$\epsilon_P = 100\frac{\Delta L_P}{L_0}$$ (6.13)

where ΔL_P is the permanent elongation of the rope; L_0 is the length at 200 D^2, experimentally found to be $L_0 = 1.04L_F$, L_F being the free (slack) length of this particular type of nylon rope; ϵ_E is the elastic elongation percent, given by

$$\epsilon_E = 100\frac{\Delta L_E}{L_0}$$ (6.14)

ΔL_E being the elastic elongation of the rope.

The following example illustrates the use of these relations.

Example. Establish the stretched length of a mooring line made of 3000 ft of 1 in. diameter eight strand plaited nylon rope when submitted to a tension of 5200 lb, knowing that at some previous time, a tension of 10,200 lb has been applied to the rope.

Solution.

(1)   Length at 200 D^2 tension

$$L_0 = (1.04)3000 = 3120 \text{ ft}$$

(2)   Permanent elongation due to the 10,200 lb tension,

$$T_0 = 200D^2 = 200 \text{ lb}$$

Using expression (6.11)

$$(\epsilon_P)^{1.94} = \frac{10,000}{88}$$

from which

$$\Delta L_\mathrm{P} = (0.115)(3120) = 359 \text{ ft}$$

(3)   Elastic elongation due to the 5200 lb tension. Using expression (6.12)

$$(\epsilon_\mathrm{E})^{1.87} = \frac{5000}{74.8}$$

from which

$$\Delta L_\mathrm{E} = (0.095)(3120) = 296 \text{ ft}$$

(4)   The stretched length of the rope is the sum of its length at $200\,D^2$, plus the permanent elongation, plus the elastic elongation:

$$L_\mathrm{s} = 3120 + 359 + 296 = 3775 \text{ ft}$$

ENDURANCE.   Lengths of synthetic fiber ropes inserted in a mooring line are, like other components, repeatedly loaded by wave and current action. Synthetic fibers may break under fatigue and ropes with the best endurance and elastic properties should be selected (nylon, dacron). The endurance limit of synthetic ropes longitudinally loaded is not well known and fatigue data are yet to be established.

RESISTANCE TO ABRASION AND CUTS.   All synthetic fiber ropes have little abrasion and cut resistance when compared to steel ropes. They will chafe easily, and no moving metallic parts should come in contact with the rope when in use (clips, clamps, attachments, etc.).

Length Measurements.   Prediction of the total length that a rope will have when subjected to a known tension is both difficult and important. Such prediction can be attempted by extrapolating experimental results obtained from short samples to long lengths of rope. For the extrapolation to be valid, measurements of rope samples and total rope length should follow the same method.

Rope measurements can be made either by length or by weight. In the first approach, the initial length of the sample is submitted to a small tension. The standard proposed by the Cordage Industry for this initial tension is the "$200\,D^2$ tension," that is, a tension equal in pounds to 200 times the square of the rope diameter expressed in inches. Amount of elongation that the samples undergo when subjected to tensile loads are then expressed as a percentage of the initial standardized $200\,D^2$ length. To predict the stretched length that a particular quantity of rope will have when submitted to identical loadings, the entire rope must be first measured under a $200\,D^2$ tension. The stretched length can then be computed by extrapolating the results obtained from the sample to this 200 D^2 initial length.

In the other approach, the sample is first carefully weighted. It is then submitted to the anticipated load history, and its length at the load of interest carefully measured. The stretched length per unit of weight of the rope can then be established, and this result used to predict either the stretched length of a given amount of rope or the weight of rope needed to reach a given length.

The following examples illustrate the use of these two methods.

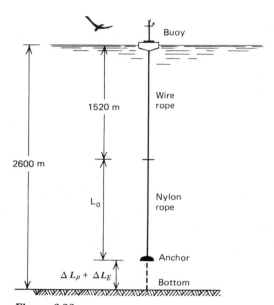

Figure 6.36.

Example. A taut mooring (Figure 6.36) is to be set in 2600 m of ocean depth. The length of the wire rope and metallic components (chain, instruments) is 1520 m.

Compute the 200 D^2 length of 5/8 in. nylon plaited rope needed to assure a minimum tension of 400 lb in the mooring line. Neglect the elongation of the wire rope, and assume that the rope experiences an average peak tension of 2000 lb during launching operations.

Solution.

1. The stretched length of the nylon rope is the sum of the length L_0 at 200 D^2, plus the permanent elongation, ΔL_P, plus the elastic elongation, ΔL_E, that is,

$$L_0 + \Delta L_P + \Delta L_E = 2600 - 1520$$

$$= 1080 \text{ m}$$

2. Expression (6.11)

$$\frac{T - T_0}{D^2} = 88 \left(\frac{100 \Delta L_P}{L_0} \right)^{1.94}$$

with a tension $T = 2000$ lb, is used to find the permanent elongation $\Delta L_P = 0.08 \, L_0$.

3. Expression (6.12)

$$\frac{T - T_0}{D^2} = 74.8 \left(\frac{100 \Delta L_E}{L_0} \right)^{1.87}$$

with tension, T, equal to 400 lb, is used to find the elastic elongation

$$\Delta L_E = 0.036 \, L_0$$

4. The 200 D^2 length L_0 is found by solving

$$L_0 (1 + 0.08 + 0.036) = 1080$$

or

$$L_0 = \frac{1080}{1.116} = 968 \text{ m}$$

Example. A subsurface buoy must be set 2715 m above the sea floor. A 0.5 in. dacron mooring line is to be used to moor the buoy. A sample of the rope when stretched to the tension that the mooring line will experience is found to measure 117 cm and to weigh 0.325 lb. How many pounds of rope should be ordered to satisfy the design requirement?

Solution. The sample after experiencing the same load history as the mooring line will experience, has a weight to length ratio of

$$\frac{0.325 \text{ lb}}{1.17 \text{ m}}$$

The amount of line x that will stretch to a length of 2715 m is, therefore,

given by

$$x = (2715)\,\frac{0.325}{1.17}$$

$$x = 754 \text{ lb}$$

Safety Factor.   The tensile loads of moorings deployed at sea for several months will vary from high values at the time of deployment (and possibly recovery) and, when submitted to strong environmental constraints, to low values in periods of calm weather and weak currents.

The designer has, therefore, the difficult task of selecting a rope that will resist both the transient peak loads (hours), as well as loads that might be much less in magnitude, but are applied over much longer periods of time (months). Synthetic fiber ropes are susceptible to creep, and the safety factor should be chosen so as to not only accommodate the short duration high loads, but also assure that creep will not be a cause of concern at the anticipated lower load levels and longer periods of application.

Terminations.   Ends of synthetic fiber ropes are terminated by either eye splicing (Figure 6.37) or socketing (Figure 6.38).

When terminating a rope with an eye splice, the rope should be supported by a thimble, as shown in Figure 6.37. The thimble should be of the proper size for the rope diameter and of such material and construction as to resist deformation, abrasion, and corrosion. In addition, the splice should be seized to prevent the eye from opening and the thimble to fall off when the rope is submitted to high tension.

Ropes that cannot be easily spliced (Nolaro, Uniline) are generally terminated by socketing. The splayed end of the rope is introduced in the receptacle of the steel socket, and epoxy is poured over it. The epoxy flows in

Figure 6.37.   Synthetic fiber rope termination—eye splice.

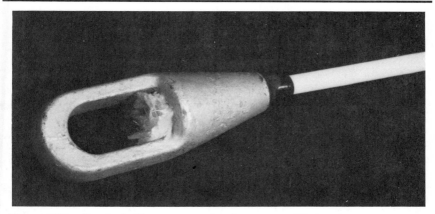

Figure 6.38. Synthetic fiber rope termination—epoxy filled socket.

all interstices to fill all cavities and is then left free to cure. Epoxy filled terminations that are as strong as the rope itself are difficult to produce.

Chain—Connecting Hardware—Ancillary Equipment

Chain.   Aid to navigation buoys and other shallow water buoy systems often use chain for their moorings. As the depth increases, the weight of the chain required becomes prohibitive, and lighter mooring lines must be used.

Lengths of chain are, however, often inserted in deep-sea mooring lines to provide additional reliability at points where higher strength and abrasion resistance are necessary. For example, chain is used to advantage immediately below the buoy and above the anchor and on both sides of instrument casings attached in the line. A length of chain placed above the anchor will reduce the tension seen by the anchor and can prevent the lower end of the mooring line from chafing on the ocean floor.

Characteristics of two types of chain often encountered in mooring line applications are summarized in Figures 6.39 and 6.40.

To ensure protection against corrosion, steel welded chains of smaller size should be galvanized.

Connecting Hardware.   Metallic fittings are used to connect lengths of mooring line to the buoy, to the anchor, to instrument casings, or to each other. Fittings used for this purpose are shackles, links, rings, and swivels. The design and selection of these fittings is of critical importance for the reliable performance of the entire mooring. Strength required to resist the

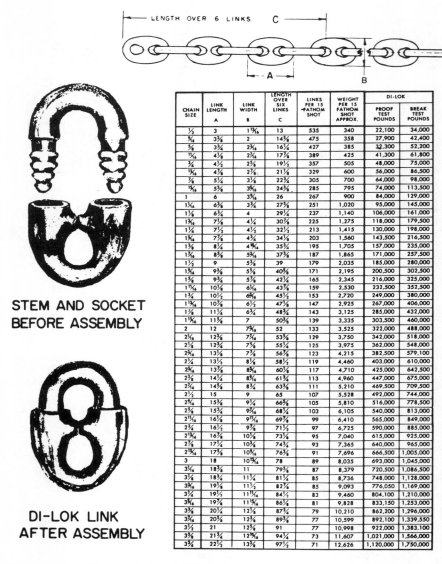

STEM AND SOCKET
BEFORE ASSEMBLY

DI-LOK LINK
AFTER ASSEMBLY

CHAIN SIZE	LINK LENGTH A	LINK WIDTH B	LENGTH OVER SIX LINKS C	LINKS PER 15 FATHOM SHOT	WEIGHT PER 15 FATHOM SHOT APPROX.	DI-LOK PROOF TEST POUNDS	DI-LOK BREAK TEST POUNDS
½	3	1 13/16	13	535	340	22,100	34,000
9/16	3 3/8	2	14 5/8	475	358	27,900	42,400
5/8	3 3/4	2 3/16	16 1/4	427	385	32,300	52,200
11/16	4 1/8	2 3/16	17 7/8	389	425	41,300	61,800
3/4	4 1/2	2 5/8	19 1/2	357	505	48,000	75,000
13/16	4 7/8	2 7/8	21 1/8	329	600	56,000	86,500
7/8	5 1/4	3 1/8	22 3/4	305	700	64,000	98,000
15/16	5 5/8	3 5/16	24 3/8	285	795	74,000	113,500
1	6	3 9/16	26	267	900	84,000	129,000
1 1/16	6 3/8	3 3/4	27 5/8	251	1,020	95,000	145,000
1 1/8	6 3/4	4	29 1/4	237	1,140	106,000	161,000
1 3/16	7 1/8	4 1/4	30 7/8	225	1,275	118,000	179,500
1 1/4	7 1/2	4 1/2	32 1/2	213	1,415	130,000	198,000
1 5/16	7 7/8	4 3/4	34 1/8	203	1,560	143,500	216,500
1 3/8	8 1/4	4 15/16	35 3/4	195	1,705	157,000	235,000
1 7/16	8 5/8	5 3/16	37 3/8	187	1,865	171,000	257,500
1 1/2	9	5 3/8	39	179	2,035	185,000	280,000
1 9/16	9 3/8	5 5/8	40 5/8	171	2,195	200,500	302,500
1 5/8	9 3/4	5 7/8	42 1/4	165	2,345	216,000	325,000
1 11/16	10 1/8	6 1/16	43 7/8	159	2,530	232,500	352,500
1 3/4	10 1/2	6 5/16	45 1/2	153	2,720	249,000	380,000
1 13/16	10 7/8	6 1/2	47 1/8	147	2,925	267,000	406,000
1 7/8	11 1/4	6 3/4	48 3/4	143	3,125	285,000	432,000
1 15/16	11 5/8	7	50 3/8	139	3,335	303,500	460,000
2	12	7 3/16	52	133	3,525	322,000	488,000
2 1/16	12 3/8	7 7/16	53 5/8	129	3,750	342,000	518,000
2 1/8	12 3/4	7 5/8	55 1/4	125	3,975	362,000	548,000
2 3/16	13 1/8	7 7/8	56 7/8	123	4,215	382,500	579,100
2 1/4	13 1/2	8 1/8	58 1/2	119	4,460	403,000	610,000
2 5/16	13 7/8	8 5/16	60 1/8	117	4,710	425,000	642,500
2 3/8	14 1/4	8 9/16	61 3/4	113	4,960	447,000	675,000
2 7/16	14 5/8	8 3/4	63 3/8	111	5,210	469,500	709,500
2 1/2	15	9	65	107	5,528	492,000	744,000
2 9/16	15 3/8	9 1/4	66 5/8	105	5,810	516,000	778,500
2 5/8	15 3/4	9 3/16	68 1/4	103	6,105	540,000	813,000
2 11/16	16 1/8	9 11/16	69 7/8	99	6,410	565,000	849,000
2 3/4	16 1/2	9 7/8	71 1/2	97	6,725	590,000	885,000
2 13/16	16 7/8	10 1/8	73 1/8	95	7,040	615,000	925,000
2 7/8	17 1/4	10 3/8	74 3/4	93	7,365	640,000	965,000
2 15/16	17 5/8	10 9/16	76 3/8	91	7,696	666,500	1,005,000
3	18	10 13/16	78	89	8,035	693,000	1,045,000
3 1/16	18 3/8	11	79 5/8	87	8,379	720,500	1,086,500
3 1/8	18 3/4	11 1/4	81 1/4	85	8,736	748,000	1,128,000
3 3/16	19 1/8	11 1/2	82 7/8	85	9,093	776,050	1,169,000
3 1/4	19 1/2	11 11/16	84 1/2	83	9,460	804,100	1,210,000
3 5/16	19 7/8	11 15/16	86 1/8	81	9,828	833,150	1,253,000
3 3/8	20 1/4	12 1/8	87 3/4	79	10,210	862,200	1,296,000
3 7/16	20 5/8	12 3/8	89 3/8	77	10,599	892,100	1,339,550
3 1/2	21	12 5/8	91	77	10,998	922,100	1,383,100
3 9/16	21 3/4	12 13/16	94 1/4	73	11,607	1,021,000	1,566,000
3 3/4	22 1/2	13 3/8	97 1/2	71	12,626	1,120,000	1,750,000

Figure 6.39. Characteristics of di-lock drop forged chain. Data by Baldt Anchors.

258

Trade Size, Inches	Material Size, Inches	Inside Length Link, Inches	Inside Width Link, Inches	Links Per Foot, Number	Weight Per 100 Feet, Pounds	Working Load Limit, Pounds
3/16	7/32	.95	.40	12 1/2	40	750
1/4	9/32	1.00	.50	12	71	1250
5/16	11/32	1.10	.50	10 3/4	108	1875
3/8	13/32	1.23	.62	9 3/4	156	2625
7/16	15/32	1.37	.75	8 3/4	211	3450
1/2	17/32	1.50	.81	8	275	4500
5/8	21/32	1.87	1.00	6 3/8	410	6800
3/4	49/64	2.12	1.12	5 5/8	595	9500
7/8	29/32	2.50	1.37	4 3/4	780	11375
1	1 1/32	2.75	1.50	4 3/8	1000	13950

Figure 6.40. Characteristic of proof coil welded chain. Data by McKay Chain Co.

Figure 6.41. Sling link and safety anchor shackles.

mooring line tension should not be the only design criterion. Abrasion due to fittings relative motion will always be present to some extent, and so will be the corrosive action of the sea water. Selecting a fitting of a size larger than seems necessary is often a small price to pay to gain a considerable increase in mooring reliability.

Shackles should preferably be of the safety type illustrated in Figure 6.41.

Drop forged galvanized steel fittings are most commonly used in oceanographic moorings. Typical fitting sizes and strengths are presented in Figures 6.42 and 6.43.

Safe Working Load—Tons	Size Inches	Inside Length		Inside Width at Pin	Diameter		Tolerance Plus or Minus		Weight Pounds Each	
		2130	2150		Pin	Outside of Eye	Length	Width	ANCHOR	CHAIN
2	1/2	1 7/8	1 5/8	13/16	5/8	1 5/16	1/16	1/16	.82	.76
3 1/4	5/8	2 3/8	2	1 1/16	3/4	1 9/16	1/8	1/16	1.58	1.56
4 3/4	3/4	2 13/16	2 3/8	1 1/4	7/8	1 7/8	1/4	1/16	2.82	2.62
6 1/2	7/8	3 5/16	2 13/16	1 7/16	1	2 1/8	1/4	1/16	3.95	3.65
8 1/2	1	3 3/4	3 3/16	1 11/16	1 1/8	2 3/8	1/4	1/16	5.6	5.35
9 1/2	1 1/8	4 1/4	3 9/16	1 13/16	1 1/4	2 5/8	1/4	1/16	7.85	7.27
12	1 1/4	4 11/16	3 15/16	2 1/32	1 3/8	3	1/4	1/16	11.2	10.2
13 1/2	1 3/8	5 1/4	4 7/16	2 1/4	1 1/2	3 5/16	1/4	1/8	15.2	13.35
17	1 1/2	5 3/4	4 7/8	2 3/8	1 5/8	3 5/8	1/4	1/8	19.5	18.5
25	1 3/4	7	5 3/4	2 7/8	2	4 5/16	1/4	1/8	31.3	28.5
35	2	7 3/4	6 3/4	3 1/4	2 1/4	5	1/4	1/8	46.3	41.1
50	2 1/2	10 1/2	8	4 1/8	2 3/4	6	3/4	1/8	94	84.5
75	3	13	9	5	3 1/4	6 1/2	3/4	1/8	145	123
100	3 1/2	15	10 1/2	5 3/4	3 3/4	8	1	1/4	250	218
130	4	17	12 1/2	6 1/2	4 1/4	9	1	1/4	358	310

DIMENSIONS IN INCHES

SAFETY CHAIN SHACKLE

SAFETY ANCHOR SHACKLE

Figure 6.42. Characteristics of safety anchor and chain shackles. Data by Crosby-Laughlin Co.

WELDLESS SLING LINKS

Diam. Stock Inches	Inside Length Inches	Inside Width Small End	Inside Width Large End	Weight Pounds Each	Safe Load Single Pull Pounds
⅜	2¼	¾	1½	.23	1800
½	3	1	2	.53	2900
⅝	3¾	1¼	2½	1.1	4200
¾	4½	1½	3	1.9	6000
⅞	5¼	1¾	3½	2.9	8300
1	6	2	4	4.3	10800
1¼	7¾	2½	5	8.5	16750
1⅜	8¼	2¾	5½	11.3	20500

WELDLESS RINGS

DIMENSIONS		Weight Pounds Each	Safe Load Single Pull Pounds
Diam. Stock Inches	Inside Diam. Inches		
⅞	4	2.75	7200
⅞	5½	3.5	5600
1	4	3.68	10800
1⅛	6	6.5	10400
1¼	5	7	17000
1⅜	6	10	19000

Figure 6.43. Characteristics of drop forged steel links and rings. Data by Crosby-Laughlin Co.

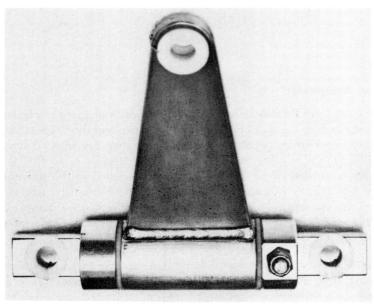

Figure 6.44. Orthogonal swivel.

Swivels are sometimes inserted in mooring lines to permit the preferential rotation of one of the two components they connect. For example, a swivel placed below a surface buoy would help prevent the transmissions of any buoy rotational motion to the mooring line and, thus, would help reduce the torsional stresses in the line. As another example, instruments suspended from the legs of a trimoor remain free to hang vertically when connected by orthogonal swivels (Figure 6.44) that isolate the instruments from possible mooring line torque.

Swivels must be free to rotate under high mooring tension and after long periods of immersion. Oil filled, galvanized steel, thrust bearing swivels of the type shown in Figure 6.45 have worked adequately in a number of cases.

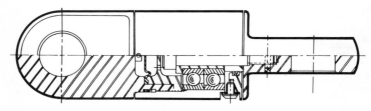

Figure 6.45.   Oil filled thrust bearing swivel. Preformed Line Products Co.

Ancillary Equipment

LINE FLOATS.   Additional buoyancy is often required to help support the weight of mooring lines and of the attached instrumentation. This buoyancy is usually provided by pressure resistant glass spheres of small diameter or small floats made of syntactic foam.

Glass spheres can be held in nets and the nets tied to the mooring line (Figure 6.46). They can also be housed in plastic containers that, in turn, can be bolted to sections of chain (Figure 6.47), or to special clamps (Figure 6.48). Figure 6.49 shows a syntactic foam float of simple and efficient design made of two identical halves straddling the mooring line.

RELEASE DEVICES.   Release devices are often incorporated in the design of anchoring lines to provide separation at some convenient point in the mooring. These devices are used to permit or facilitate the recovery of buoy systems or to protect certain components from excessive tension.

Figure 6.46. Glass balls in nets.

Figure 6.47. Glass balls in plastic containers bolted to a length of chain.

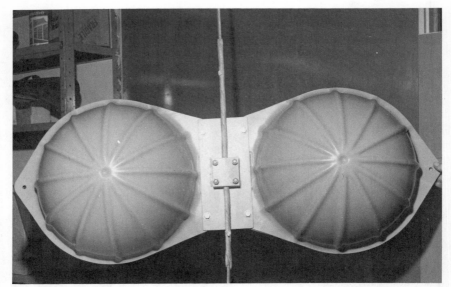

Figure 6.48. Glass spheres in plastic containers clamped on mooring cable.

Figure 6.49. Syntactic foam float straddling mooring cable.

264

Release devices can be passive or active. Passive devices consist of weak links that break when large forces are exerted on them.

Examples of weak links are short lengths of wire rope or fiber rope of smaller diameter or strength. than the rest of the mooring, shear pin arrangements, hydrostatic releases that are held together by ambient pressure, and so on. Weak links are simple and inexpensive, but the reduction in mooring strength resulting from their insertion severely limits their usefulness.

Active devices, on the other hand, can be made as strong as required. These releases incorporate a separation mechanism operating at a preset time or on command. Time delay releases are actuated either by clock work or controlled corrosion or dissolution rates. Command releases are actuated by electrical or acoustic pulses. Explosives are often used to either break a structural component (cable cutter, explosive bolt) or provide sufficient gas pressure to move a piston and free a locking mechanism.

Anchors

Anchors are used to maintain moored buoy systems on station. Anchor selection is a critical part of buoy system design. The anchor must provide enough holding power, and yet the anchor size and weight must be kept within reason. Predominant factors in the design and/or selection of anchors are the direction and intensity of mooring line tension at the anchor and the type of bottom (level, inclined, muddy, sandy, etc.). Anchors are commonly divided into three categories—deadweight anchors, embedment anchors, and special anchors.

Deadweight Anchors

Cast iron clumps, concrete casting of simple shape, old railroad car wheels, bundles of surplus anchor chain, and almost anything that is compact and heavy can make a deadweight anchor. This type of anchor is simple and inexpensive. It provides excellent resistance to vertical pull and is often used on subsurface buoys set in small or moderate currents or whenever the horizontal pull at the anchor is expected to be small.

The anchor weight necessary to resist a predicted mooring tension, T, when placed on a bottom of known slope θ and coefficient of friction μ, can be estimated from a free body diagram of the anchor. Figure 6.50 shows the forces at play for the case where the tension is pulling "downwards" (worst case). Summing the forces in the vertical and horizontal direction yield

$$W = B + T_V + \mu N \sin\theta + N \cos\theta \tag{6.15}$$

$$\mu N \cos\theta = T_H + N \sin\theta \tag{6.16}$$

where W is the weight of the anchor; B is the weight of water displaced by the anchor; T_V is the vertical component of tension and is equal to $T\sin\phi$; T_H is the horizontal component of tension and is equal to $T\cos\phi$; N is the normal reaction of bottom; and μN is the bottom friction. Combining expressions (6.15) and (6.16), the anchor weight is found to be

$$W = B + T\sin\phi + T\cos\phi \left[\frac{\mu\sin\theta + \cos\theta}{\mu\cos\theta - \sin\theta} \right] \tag{6.17}$$

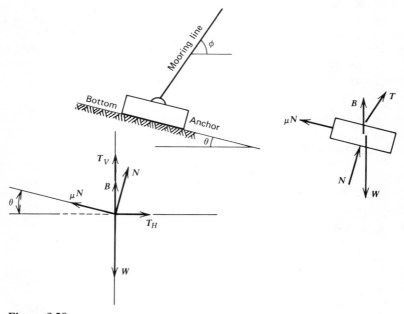

Figure 6.50.

As the slope increases, the weight necessary to resist the tension increases. In the limiting case, $\theta = \tan^{-1}\mu$, the anchor is sliding down the slope. The weight becomes infinitely large, and the anchoring problem cannot be solved with a deadweight type anchor.

When the bottom is horizontal, the weight is given by

$$\lim_{\theta \to 0} W = B + T\sin\phi + \frac{T}{\mu}\cos\phi \qquad (6.18)$$

For a given tension, the weight is inversely proportional to the friction coefficient. If this coefficient is small, the weight needed to resist the horizontal component of the tension may become prohibitively large.

To summarize, deadweight anchors are easy to fabricate, inexpensive, and expendable. They are, however, susceptible to lateral displacement when subjected to horizontal pulling. Their holding power is further reduced by sloping and unstable bottoms. Their use should be restricted to applications where the tension is expected to be essentially vertical.

Embedment Anchors

Embedment anchors are designed to dig into the sea floor as they are pulled along by a horizontal force until they embed themselves deeply and firmly in the bottom material (Figure 6.51).

The principal parts of a typical embedment anchor are shown in Figure 6.52. The flukes are the plates that plow into the bottom and create the resistance to lateral pull. The crown trips and maintains the flukes at the

HORIZONTAL PULL RESULTS IN ANCHOR DRAG.   AS   THE ANCHOR DRAGS, THE FLUKES DIG IN, EMBEDDING THE ANCHOR DEEPLY IN THE BOTTOM MATERIAL.

Figure 6.51.   Embedment anchor working principle.

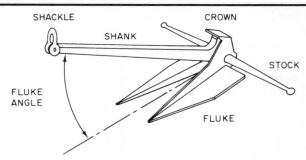

Figure 6.52.   Anchor parts.

proper fluke angle (angle between the flukes and the shank). The shank transmits the pull of the mooring line to the anchor. The stock prevents the anchor from rotating on itself.

Proper selection of the fluke angle is critical for rapid and complete anchor embedment. Typical values of fluke angles are 30° to 35° for sand bottoms and up to 50° for mud bottoms. Figure 6.53 shows six types of embedment anchors. The rugged stockless anchor is a good anchor for a variety of sea bottoms. Its design combines weight for holding in hard bottoms with ability of biting and digging in softer sea floors. The Lightweight, the Danforth, the Stato, and the Boss anchors are different versions of light weight anchors with large flukes. These anchors perform well in sand, clay, and mud as long as the pull is horizontal. A length of chain is usually placed ahead of the anchor to help keep the shank horizontal. The mushroom anchor is used for permanent moorings in muddy bottoms. As the anchor oscillates under strain, mud fills the inverted cup of the "mushroom" and the anchor buries itself deeper.

A measure of the efficiency of embedment anchors is expressed by the ratio of the horizontal force which will break away the anchor to the anchor's own weight. This ratio is commonly called the holding power. It is experimentally established, and its value is highly dependent on anchor type, bottom type, and fluke angle. Average holding power of typical embedment anchors are tabulated for sand and mud bottoms in Table 6.9.

The advantage of embedment anchors is to combine lightweight and large resistance to lateral pull. The disadvantages are the necessity for dragging the anchor along the bottom before it can dig and hold, and the tendency for the anchor to pull out of the bottom if a vertical force is applied at the end of the shank.

NAVY STOCKLESS ANCHOR

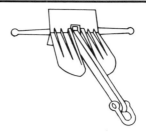

STATO ANCHOR

DANFORTH ANCHOR

LIGHT WEIGHT (LWT) ANCHOR

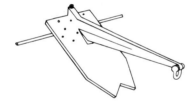

BOSS ANCHOR

MUSHROOM ANCHOR

Figure 6.53.   Embedment anchors.

TABLE 6.9.   AVERAGE ANCHOR HOLDING POWER

	Bottom Type	
Anchor Type	Sand	Mud
Stockless*	6	2 or less
Lightweight*	16	9
Stato*	20	15
Boss**		35

*Smith, 1965.
**Beck, 1972.

Special Anchors

Frequently, mooring lines are forced by strong currents or buoy system configuration to exert their pull at a large angle from the bottom. The anchor must then resist both the vertical and the horizontal components of the tension. To this end, the anchor design must combine deadweight and lateral pull resistance. A clump placed ahead of an embedment anchor, heavy anchors equipped with flukes (porcupine design), heavy anchors that

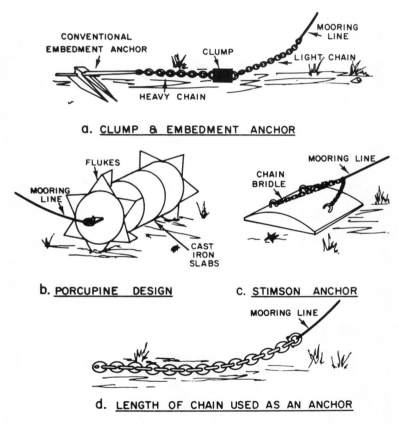

Figure 6.54.   Anchoring schemes combining embedment and dead weight.

tilt and dig when pulled by horizontal forces (Stimson anchors), and lengths of heavy chain have been used to provide vertical and horizontal pull resistance. These anchoring schemes are depicted in Figure 6.54.

The horizontal holding power of stud link anchor chains has been experimentally established to be between 0.3 and 0.5 in mud bottoms and between 1.0 and 1.5 in sand. The following example illustrates a simple anchoring design using chain only.

Example. The horizontal and vertical components of tension at the bottom end of a buoy system mooring line are expected to be 2000 lb each. The bottom is known to be a mixture of sand and clay. What length of chain with an immersed line density of 40 lb/ft should be recommended to anchor the mooring? (See Figure 6.55.)

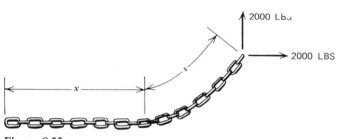

Figure 6.55.

Solution.

(1) Assuming a holding power of 0.75, the length of chain needed to resist the horizontal pull is given by

$$(0.75)(40)x = 2000 \text{ lb}$$

therefore,

$$x = 66.5 \text{ ft}$$

(2) The length of chain needed to resist the vertical pull is given by Eq. (4.12) as

$$T_V = Ps$$

from which

$$(40)s = 2000 \text{ lb}$$

$$s = 50 \text{ ft}$$

(3)   The total length of chain required is, thus,

$$L = x + s = 116.5 \text{ ft}$$

Using a safety factor of 1.5 to account for the uncertainty on the holding power, the recommended length is 175 ft. Adding a small embedment anchor (Danforth) at the end of the chain would add to the reliability of the chain anchoring.

A series of small weights attached to or around a cable constitute an excellent scheme to permit the anchoring of a buoy supported array of the type depicted in Figure 7.11. A "flexible" anchor of this type is easy to deploy—it can even be made to pass through a sheave if necessary—and it will adjust itself to bottom slope and line pull.

Experimental explosive anchors (Smith, Beard, and Taylor, 1971) have received considerable attention in the recent years and should be mentioned as having a great potential for permanent bottom anchoring.

Chapter

Seven

SPECIAL TOPICS

7.1. ENVIRONMENTAL PROBLEMS AND CORRECTIVE MEASURES

Protection of buoys and anchoring lines against wear and deterioration due to corrosion, fatigue, and marine life attacks is a major problem. Measures that will prevent accelerated degradation must often be incorporated in the design of long term buoy systems.

Corrosion

Perhaps the most difficult environmental problem is the corrosive action of sea water on the metallic components of the buoy system, especially wire ropes.

Marine corrosion can be defined as the destructive attack of metals by electrochemical reactions of the metals with the sea water environment. For this destructive process to occur, three reactive agents must be present: a material acting as an anode, another acting as a cathode, and an electrolyte.

Ionized metal atoms leave the anode as cations, going in solution in the conducting sea water. It is at the anode that the deterioration of the metal mostly takes place. The propensity varies for metals to form cations. A measure of this tendency is provided by the electric potential difference existing between the metal and a standard reference potential. Measurements of these potentials are presented in the familiar galvanic series that usually lists the metals by order of decreasing activity.

As the cations go in solution, free electrons flow in the metal towards the cathode. At the cathode, a reduction reaction occurs. For the corrosion process to continue, the rate of reduction at the cathode must equal the rate of oxidation at the anode. Both reactions can be generally represented by

Oxidation $M \rightarrow M^+ - e$
Reduction $O_2 + 2H_2O + 4e \rightarrow 4OH^-$

These reactions will take place in sea water whenever a potential difference exists between two metallic components or two different locations of the same component. Such a potential difference can be created by the contact of two dissimilar metals or by the introduction of physical changes in the metal itself (for example, breaks in coating, part of the surface covered by tape, different stress levels in parts in contact, etc.). Rates of corrosion are difficult to predict, however, means of inhibiting the flow of cations into solution or of electrons between anode and cathode will greatly reduce the deterioration process.

Forms of corrosion most often encountered in the hulls of buoys, anchoring lines, the connecting hardware, and the casings of instruments follow.

Uniform Corrosion

A uniformly distributed loss of metal, taking place generally at a slow and predictable rate is characteristic of uniform corrosion. Rusting of buoy steel plates or cast iron anchors are examples of this type of corrosion.

Pitting

Pitting can be described as a localized type of attack resulting in cavities of variable sizes and depths. Initiation sites might be surface scratches, breaks in protective coatings, or variations in surface composition or finish. Stainless steels exposed to sea water sooner or later develop deep pits especially in locations deprived of oxygen (bottom of crevices, areas covered with fouling organisms, interior faces of nuts and threads, etc.).

Intergranular Corrosion

This form of corrosion is characterized by a localized attack at the grain boundaries of the metal with little deterioration of the crystals in the grains. The attack is often rapid, penetrating deeply in the metal, and resulting in early failure. Improper welding can result in high susceptibility to intergranular corrosion. Welds or zones affected by the welding heat can rapidly decay when exposed to sea water.

Corrosion Fatigue

A metallic part when submitted to repeated stress cycles of sufficient amplitude will develop minute cracks that tend to grow and propagate across the metal until failure of the whole part occurs. Normally this mode of failure can be prevented if the stress amplitude is kept below a known level called the endurance limit of the metal. However, when immersed in a corrosive environment to which the metal is susceptible, the fatigue deterioration of the metal is accelerated and the part will fail in a much lesser number of cycles. Furthermore, the endurance limit will no longer exist and the metallic part will eventually fail no matter how low the stress amplitude. Nicks, cuts, sharp edges, pits, and crevices act as stress risers and often initiate cracks that will propagate when submitted to cyclic stresses.

This combination of fatigue and corrosion effects is called corrosion fatigue. It can be very detrimental to mooring line components that are almost always submitted to cyclic stresses of one form or another.

Stress Corrosion Cracking

Cracks in a metallic part immersed in a corrosive medium and submitted to a constant tensile load can rapidly progress across the grain boundaries until failure of the whole part occurs. This deterioration process that combines corrosion and constant tensile stress is called stress corrosion cracking.

Galvanic Corrosion

As already mentioned, a galvanic cell is created when two metals with different electromotive potentials are connected in sea water. As a result, the production of cations is enhanced at the anode, and the metal anodic to the other one will rapidly deteriorate. This form of corrosion is known as galvanic corrosion. The rapid and severe deterioration of carbon steel shackles when inserted in stainless steel instrument casings or of wires of carbon steel wire ropes when clamped by copper fittings are typical examples of galvanic corrosion.

Practical measures that will prevent or retard deterioration due to corrosion are hereafter briefly reviewed.

Coatings

Corrosion protection can be obtained by placing a watertight barrier between the surface of the metallic components and the surrounding sea water.

Thin coats of highly adhesive and impermeable compounds (paints, epoxy, resins) can be systematically applied to all metallic surfaces. Films of protective and insulating oxides can be deposited by electrolysis on the surface of aluminum instrument casings (anodizing).

Steel wires and hardware can be fully covered by zinc or aluminum by hot dipping, electroplating, or hot spraying. Zinc coating is called galvanizing, and aluminum coating is referred to as aluminizing. There is a definite advantage in using galvanized wire ropes and fittings, for zinc is anodic to steel, and, therefore, the zinc coating will act as a sacrificial anode at the points where the coating may break and the steel surface would be exposed to sea water.

A jacket of extruded plastic placed over wire ropes constitutes an additional barrier between the wires and the corrosive environment. Actual tests comparing the performance of jacketed and unjacketed wire ropes, when submitted to identical tensile loads and environmental conditions, have revealed a sustained tendency for the jacketed ropes to have a far better endurance and a much longer life (Morey, 1973). Jacket material must be hard, but not brittle to resist cuts and abrasions and pass over sheaves without damage. It should not absorb water under high pressure and should retain its properties over the wide range of temperatures encountered in oceanographic applications. High density polyethylene has often been used as a good jacket material.

Elimination of Galvanic Incompatibility

Placing dissimilar metals in contact always results in accelerated corrosion when immersed in sea water. It is, therefore, a sound practice to ensure as much as possible that metallic components of buoy systems be made of the same material. For example, stainless steel wire ropes should have their end fittings made with the same alloy as the rope itself, and the connecting hardware (shackles, links, etc) should also be of the same alloy.

Plastic inserts are often used to separate and electrically insulate parts made of different metals. These inserts (sheets, bushings, etc) cut the flow of electrons between the two metals and thus prevent the galvanic corrosion process from taking place. If two dissimilar metals must be placed in contact, then the size of the anodic part should be such that corrosion does not endanger the system reliability during its expected life.

Cathodic Protection

An effective method of preventing corrosion is achieved when the potential difference between the two electrodes of a corrosion cell is reduced to zero or when a new cell is created with the metal to be protected being the cathode.

In the first approach, an external current of the proper polarity is applied to the corroding metal. This solution is obviously difficult to implement on offshore buoys. On the other hand, sacrificial anodes made of metals more active in the galvanic series than the metals to be protected are often installed on buoy system components. Sacrificial anodes are commonly made of magnesium or zinc or a combination of both.

A detailed review of the theoretical and practical aspects of marine corrosion is certainly beyond the scope of this book. The reader is strongly encouraged to seek further information by consulting the literature on this important subject (Uhlig, 1971).

Fatigue

Surface motion can induce repeated bending and torsion stresses in points of attachment of the mooring line as well as longitudinal cyclic tension stresses in the line itself. The number of cycles reached in a few months of implantation can be very high and fatigue is a serious cause of concern. Deterioration due to fatigue can be reduced by

1. using elastic synthetic fiber ropes that provide mooring line compliance and damping of the surface excitation;
2. protecting the wire rope termination from concentrated bending stresses with vibration dampers as shown in Figure 6.27;
3. avoiding conditions which initiate fatigue failures (stress risers, crevices, nicks);
4. using a large safety factor in all components subjected to high stress levels; and
5. limiting the life expectancy to a safe and reasonable time.

As already stated, fatigue and corrosion are often simultaneous. Early and catastrophical failure will result under their combined effect. Figure 7.1 showing the fracture face of an eye bolt used as the point of attachment to the buoy of a surface mooring illustrates the severity of the corrosion fatigue problem.

Strumming

When a fluid flows past a cylindrical object at a speed such that the wake behind the cylinder is no longer regular, alternately clockwise and counter-clockwise vortices are shed from the cylinder in a manner much as depicted

Figure 7.1.   Bolt fracture face showing effects of corrosion fatigue.

in Figure 7.2. The frequency of the vortex shedding, f, has been found to be proportional to the ratio of the fluid speed, V, and the diameter, D, of the cylinder, that is,

$$f = S \frac{V}{D} \tag{7.1}$$

The "constant" of proportionality, S (Strouhal number), varies with the Reynolds number, Re, but remains essentially constant and equal to 0.22 for $5 \times 10^2 < Re < 10^5$ (Ippen, 1966).

Example.   Find the frequency of vortex shedding of a rope 1 inch in diameter immersed in a 1 knot current.

Solution.   Reynolds number $Re \cong 10^5 \, VD$

$$D = \frac{1}{12} \text{ ft}$$

$$V = 1.69 \text{ ft/sec}$$

$$Re = \frac{10^5 \times 1.69}{12} = 1.41 \times 10^4$$

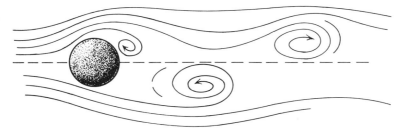

Figure 7.2.   Karman vortices behind cylinder.

Thus, the Strouhal number is 0.22. The frequency of vortex shedding is, therefore,

$$f = (0.22)(1.69)(12) = 4.45 \text{ sec}^{-1}$$

The vortex shedding on alternate sides of the cylinder results in the application on the cylinder of a cyclic force in a direction normal to the flow. As a consequence, if this cylinder is not rigidly supported—as the case would be for a taut mooring line immersed in a current—an oscillatory motion normal to the free stream velocity develops, especially if the frequency of vortex formation is close to the natural frequency of oscillation of the cylinder. This high frequency flow induced vibration is commonly referred to as "strumming."

Strumming of mooring lines is a serious cause of concern for the following reasons:

1. additional cause of fatigue failure of system components;
2. wear and abrasion of line and fittings; loosening of fasteners of system components and instruments;
3. increased drag on the mooring line while vibrating. Up to 50% increase has been measured (Charnews, 1971);
4. introduction of noise due to sensor motion, particularly in acoustic measurements;
5. the possibility that it provides an added attraction for fishbites.

Strumming of mooring lines can be reduced by inserting profiled fairings that orientate themselves downstream of the rope and act as a separation plate, thus preventing the formation of a vortex street. Ribbons attached to ropes as shown in Figure 7.3 have also been found effective in reducing strumming. Effects that the added mass and possibly the added drag of these fairings can have on the overall mooring performance must, however, be carefully considered.

Figure 7.3. Plastic ribbons attached to mooring line to reduce vortex shedding induced line strumming.

Deterioration Due to Marine Life

Buoy systems are fouled by marine organisms, particularly bivalves, that collect on the bottoms of buoy hulls and grow to a certain depth on the anchoring lines.

Fouling can result in considerable additional weight and drag. It is also often the cause of oceanographic sensors failure. The use of special antifouling paints is presently the only standard way of protecting buoy system components from marine growth.

Fouling is often the start of a food chain that rapidly develops at the mooring site, thus increasing the probability of predators attacking the mooring. Sharks, swordfish, and benthic species have attacked mooring lines, entirely severing synthetic fiber ropes or severely slashing the jacket of wire ropes, thus exposing the wires to the environment (Figure 7.4).

Little can be done to prevent fish aggression, yet its effects can be reduced by placing an armor of hard plastic over synthetic fiber ropes or by using wire ropes in areas where fishbites are likely to occur.

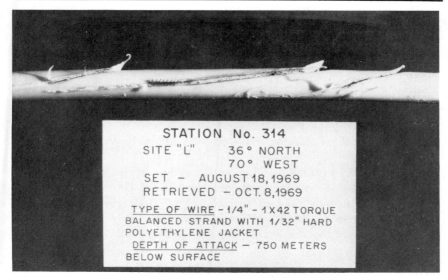

Figure 7.4. Typical damage caused to plastic jacketed mooring lines by fish bites.

7.2. DEPLOYMENT AND RETRIEVAL TECHNIQUES

The deployment of simple buoy systems—single point moored or free drifting buoys, for example—is straightforward, in principle at least. On the other hand, the implantation of complex multileg buoy systems requires careful planning and adequate logistic support. Weather, ship traffic at the implantation site, and available equipment on board the deploying vessel will often set constraints on the deployment and retrieval techniques used with a given buoy system.

Buoy First Deployment

In this technique, the buoy is the first system component to be launched. (Large buoys may be towed to the site rather than launched from the deploying vessel.) Usually, the first section of the mooring line is secured to the buoy as the buoy is deployed overboard and drifts aft of the ship. More mooring line is then paid out from the storing reels, while the ship is slowly moving ahead. When the end of a particular mooring line section is reached, the ship is stopped and the next line section is then connected. Instruments, sensor packages, and ancillary equipment are inserted at preset mooring lengths as the deployment proceeds. When the entire mooring line has been paid out, the anchor is made fast to the end of the line. The anchor is then lowered or dropped overboard and allowed to free fall.

This technique is often used to deploy surface and subsurface single point moored buoy systems. It has the advantage of simplicity and ease of handling of the system components as they are connected to the mooring and deployed overboard even under adverse weather conditions. Certain disadvantages of this method are:

1. Obligation of keeping the ship underway at slow speed during deployment.
2. Difficulty of accurately positioning the anchor on the bottom.
3. Possibility for the tension in the mooring line to become small or zero during deployment, and in the case of subsurface systems, just after anchor bottoming. Mooring slackness may result in wire rope kinking.
4. High transient mooring loads due to the anchor pull. (See Exercises 27 and 28.)
5. Long towing line—sometimes several kilometers long—between buoy and deploying vessel with the danger of possible interference from passing ships.

A particular case of interest is the launching transient of single point taut surface moors. Synchronous measurements of tension at the buoy, at the anchor, and at points in between have been made to obtain the tension history during anchor fall and after anchor bottoming. Figure 7.5 shows a typical sequence of events and Figure 7.6 shows a set of tension records obtained during such a launching transient.

These records indicate that the launching transient can be divided into three phases—the anchor free fall, the pendulum mode, and the mooring relaxation phase. During the anchor free fall, the tension values remain essentially constant in the line. When the depth reached by the anchor is such that the mooring line is approximately straight, the pull of the anchor starts to be felt by the entire mooring, and the second phase begins. The anchor swings somewhat like a pendulum in a complex path determined, in part, by the considerable stretch of the synthetic fiber rope in the line, and, in part, by the motion of the buoy on the surface. As the anchor slows down, the tension immediately above the anchor increases until a maximum value equal to the anchor wet weight is reached. This value is maintained as the mooring line stretches until the anchor bottoms.

Just before anchor bottoming, the tension is maximum at all levels. The maximum tension, $T(s)$, then reached is given by

$$T(s) = W_A + W(s) - B(s) \qquad (7.2)$$

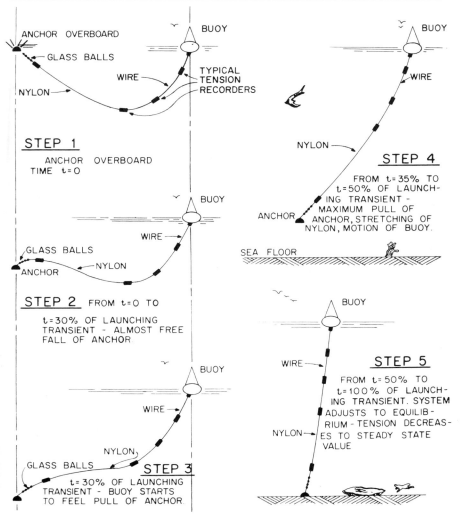

Figure 7.5. Taut surface moor, buoy first deployment—Steps of anchor free fall.

where $T(s)$ is the tension at distance s from the anchor; W_A is the immersed weight of the anchor; $W(s)$ is the immersed weight of all components from the anchor to the point at distance s from the anchor, and $B(s)$ is the buoyancy of all components from the anchor to the point at distance s from the anchor.

After anchor bottoming, the buoy pulled by the restoring force of the

TIME (min.) →

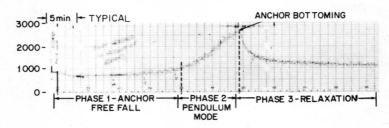

1.) TENSION AT SURFACE BUOY

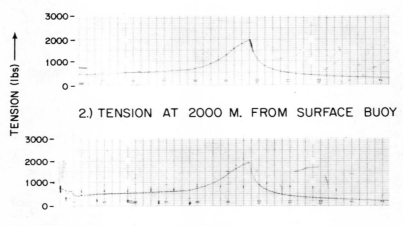

2.) TENSION AT 2000 M. FROM SURFACE BUOY

3.) TENSION ABOVE GLASS BALLS (2500 M.)

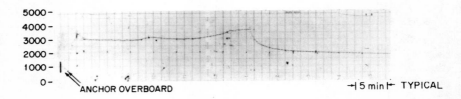

4.) TENSION ABOVE ANCHOR (2600 M.)

Figure 7.6. Taut surface moor, buoy first deployment—Typical launching transient records.

284

stretched line continues to travel towards its equilibrium position. Both the length of the line and, therefore, the tension decrease. A steady-state value, characteristic of the static response of the buoy system to the amount of prestretch in the line and the prevailing current regime, is eventually reached, and the relaxation phase of the launching transient is then completed.

Maximum tension obtained just before bottoming may be a large portion of the strength of the components. If large enough, it will sink the buoy. Furthermore, the initial peak load is an important factor in the subsequent elastic response of the nylon rope.

Anchor First Deployment

In this technique, the anchor is first lowered overboard with the help of the mooring line. The line is constantly under high tensile load, and, therefore, it is normally deployed through a pulley or series of pulleys with the help of a power-operated winch. Attachment of line sections and/or insertion of instrument packages require a stop-off procedure to relax the tension. A standard way to do so is depicted in Figure 7.7.

The buoy is launched last, the tension in the line being progressively applied to the buoy by means of a slip line. Figure 7.8 suggests possible schemes for buoy launches.

Accurate anchor positioning may be achieved using the anchor first deployment method. This technique minimizes the danger of kinking and the possibility of interference from passing ships. However, the probability of high launching loads due to resonant conditions must be investigated for different sea states. Connecting mooring lines sections to one another or to instrument casings inserted in the line is difficult and time consuming. This type of launching is certainly weather limited.

Deployment by Free Falling Anchor

Simple buoy systems may be conveniently and expeditiously deployed by allowing the anchor to pull the mooring line out of a storage space as it falls free to the bottom. The mooring line may be coiled on a freely-rotating drum or carefully faked in a box. The line may be stored on the vessel or inside the buoy itself. Slackness and line fouling may occur if parts of the mooring fall at different rates. On the other hand, snapping may be the result of a sudden slow-down in the line pay out rate. When started, the

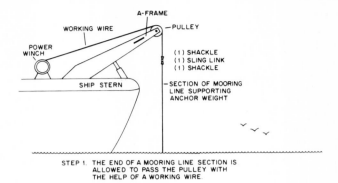

STEP 1. THE END OF A MOORING LINE SECTION IS
ALLOWED TO PASS THE PULLEY WITH
THE HELP OF A WORKING WIRE.

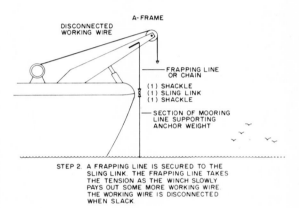

STEP 2. A FRAPPING LINE IS SECURED TO THE
SLING LINK. THE FRAPPING LINE TAKES
THE TENSION AS THE WINCH SLOWLY
PAYS OUT SOME MORE WORKING WIRE.
THE WORKING WIRE IS DISCONNECTED
WHEN SLACK.

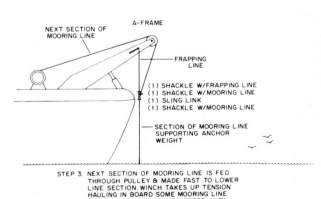

STEP 3. NEXT SECTION OF MOORING LINE IS FED
THROUGH PULLEY & MADE FAST TO LOWER
LINE SECTION. WINCH TAKES UP TENSION
HAULING IN BOARD SOME MOORING LINE.
FRAPPING LINE IS DISCONNECTED WHEN
SLACK.

Figure 7.7. Anchor first deployment—Procedure for connecting sequential mooring
line sections.

286

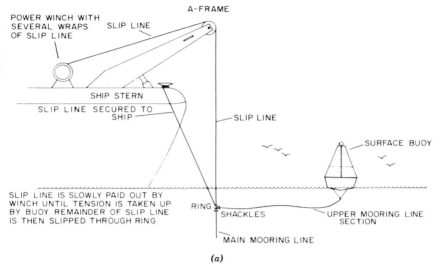

Figure 7.8(*a*). Anchor first deployment—Buoy launching Scheme I.

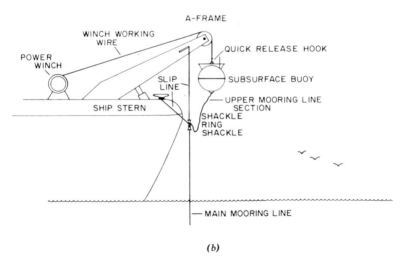

Figure 7.8(*b*). Anchor first deployment—Buoy launching Scheme II.

deployment operation is difficult—if at all possible—to interrupt. Success of implantation of the self-deployable buoy systems is highly dependent on careful design of line storing and pay out components and on quality control at the time of system assembly.

Deployment with the Help of Auxiliary Buoys

Auxiliary buoys combined with remote control releases can be used to advantage in the deployment of certain buoy systems. For example, an auxiliary buoy can be used to support the weight of the anchor during the deployment of a mooring launched anchor first. In this scheme, depicted in Figure 7.9, the high tension due to the anchor weight is practically eliminated during the deployment. After launching the buoy, the anchor is permitted to free fall by actuating a release mechanism remotely controlled by radio or acoustic telemetry. The anchor is normally outfitted with a drogue. The drag on the drogue reduces the terminal velocity of the anchor and, therefore, the amount of energy the line must eventually absorb. Should the course of a passing ship be of concern for the safety of the deployed mooring, the anchor can be left free to fall prematurely. The mooring line will then sink starting at the auxiliary buoy, while the deploying vessel still takes hold of the other end. Deployment will then have to be completed anchor first. The auxiliary buoy is retrieved after implantation of the buoy system.

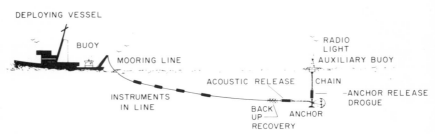

Figure 7.9.   Anchor first deployment with auxiliary buoy assistance.

An auxiliary buoy can also be used to set at a precise depth a subsurface buoy deployed anchor last. The deployment initially proceeds in the waters deeper than the intended site depth. The auxiliary buoy is connected to the subsurface buoy by a temporary mooring line the length of which is equal to the prescribed subsurface buoy depth. A remotely actuated release mechanism is inserted immediately above the subsurface buoy. The auxiliary buoy—launched first—must have enough buoyancy to remain on the surface after the anchor launching (Figure 7.10). The auxiliary buoy supporting the whole subsurface buoy system hanging underneath it is then slowly towed towards higher grounds by the deploying vessel. When the anchor approaches the bottom, the release mechanism is actuated. The subsurface buoy system then free falls a short distance, and the subsurface buoy is implanted at its prescribed depth. These two schemes illustrate the flexibility that the use of auxiliary buoys can introduce in a large variety of launching techniques.

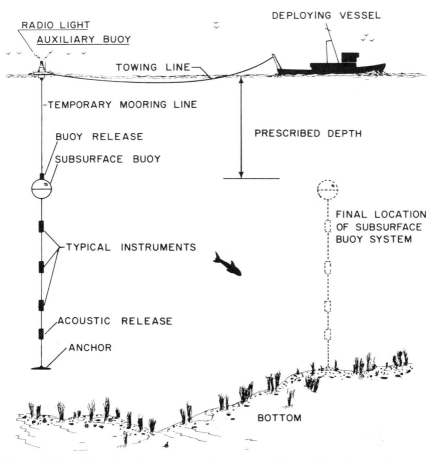

Figure 7.10. Subsurface buoy system deployment with auxiliary buoy assistance.

Deployment Involving Bottom Cable Laying

Information acquired from submerged sensors is often relayed ashore by hard wire connections. Buoy supported hydrophone arrays of the type depicted in Figure 7.11 are a good example of this particular buoy system application. The attachment of the anchor to the electromechanical cable, the lowering of the anchor, and the laying of miles of cable on the bottom represent particular problems that require special attention.

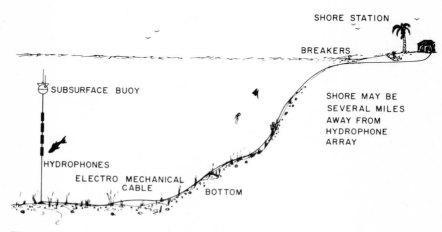

Figure 7.11.   Buoy supported hydrophone array.

A procedure for the implantation of the system depicted in Figure 7.11 could consist of the following steps (See Figure 7.12).

1. Set marker buoys equipped with lights to mark the proposed cable track. These marker buoys can greatly assist navigation during deployment, especially at night.
2. At the launching site, set a temporary taut surface mooring to assist in the buoy system deployment and the anchor lowering. (An auxiliary vessel could be used in place of this buoy.)
3. Make fast to this "tether buoy" a temporary mooring line. A reasonable length for this line is suggested in Figure 7.12.
4. Steam away from the "tether buoy" paying out the temporary mooring line. Insert a release mechanism between the line and the top side of the subsurface buoy. Connect hydrophone array cable to bottom side of subsurface buoy.

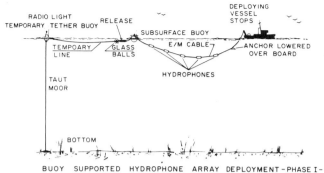

BUOY SUPPORTED HYDROPHONE ARRAY DEPLOYMENT – PHASE I –
LAUNCHING OF SUBSURFACE BUOY AND HYDROPHONE ARRAY

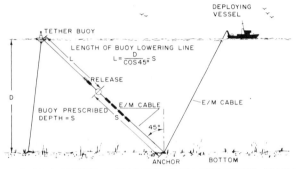

BUOY SUPPORTED HYDROPHONE ARRAY DEPLOYMENT – PHASE II
LOWERING OF ANCHOR

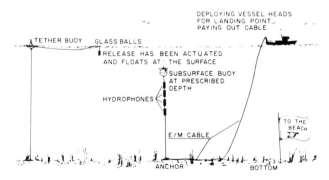

BUOY SUPPORTED HYDROPHONE ARRAY DEPLOYMENT – PHASE III
CABLE LAYING OPERATION

Figure 7.12.   Buoy supported hydrophone array deployment.

291

5. Launch subsurface buoy. Resume steaming while paying out cable and hydrophone array. Attach anchor to cable.
6. Stop ship. Place anchor overboard. Slowly lower anchor to the bottom as ship maintains position.
7. After anchor bottoming, the cable is payed out while the ship proceeds toward the beach landing. Releasing of the subsurface buoy may be done at this time or at a later time.

Determining the pay out rate so as to adequately cover the ground track and yet not run short of cable before the landing point is an important consideration. To help in determining the pay out rate, the track is divided by checkpoints into a number of segments approximating the bottom topography. The pay out rate from one checkpoint to the next can then be computed using the following formula:

$$r = \alpha \left\{ \frac{(b+c-a)V}{d} \right\} \qquad (7.3)$$

where r is the payout rate between the two end points of a given segment (ft/sec); b is the distance between the two end points of the segment, as measured on the sea floor (ft); c is the amount of cable from the surface to the shore end of the segment (ft); a is the amount of cable from the surface to the other end of the segment (ft); d is the distance between the two end points of the segment as measured on the surface (ft); V is the ship speed (ft/sec); and α is the coefficient, greater than unity, given by

$$\alpha = \frac{\text{total allowable length of cable}}{\text{total length of cable track}}$$

The different parameters of the formula are shown in Figure 7.13.

The amount of cable paid out should be monitored as the deployment proceeds and checked against predictions from time to time.

8. When the ship reaches shallow waters, the shore end of the cable is passed to a boat of shallow draft or buoyed off.
9. The ship then returns to the auxiliary tether buoy and if not yet done, actuates release mechanism, thus allowing the subsurface buoy to reach its prescribed path.
10. The recovery of the "tether mooring" and if so desired, of the marker buoys, complete the launching operation.

Emphasis should be placed on the importance of a good analysis of the anchor lowering sequence. Geometry of and tension in the lowering lines should be investigated as a function of the distance between the tether buoy and the ship as it lowers the anchor. This analysis will permit the selection of

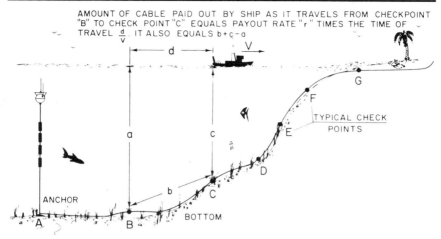

Figure 7.13.   Pay out rate paramenters.

an optimum distance to avoid tangling of the lowering lines. It will also predict the amount of cable payed out at the time the subsurface buoy is pulled under and at the time the anchor bottoms (Walden, Berteaux, and Striffler, 1973).

Deployment of Complex Arrays

Procedures for the deployment of multileg surface and subsurface buoy systems are usually tailored to suit a particular set of logistic and budget constraints and do not follow a general pattern. Some deployments may be accomplished with the help of several ships, while others are performed with the use of auxiliary temporary buoys. Anchors may be lowered by the main mooring lines or may be placed in position with the help of auxiliary lowering lines. Usually the implantation of complex cable arrays requires excellent navigation references to permit the precise implantation of buoys and anchors. Acoustic navigation networks consisting of a number of transponders deployed on the bottom are often used to pinpoint the location of the deploying ship(s) and of the anchors as they are lowered into position.

A detailed analysis of the geometry and the tension in the lines during the different anticipated deployment phases must be performed to establish important deployment parameters like distance between ships, pay out rates, transient loads and corresponding safety factors.

Mooring designers, operation managers and ship personnel usually cooperate closely to formulate detailed schedules of events, including contingency plans. It is often necessary to outfit the deploying vessel with special equipment: winches with large storage capacity, large diameter sheaves, stopping-off devices, auxiliary cranes, spares of long ropes, workboats, and so on. Tension readouts can be extremely useful to avoid the build-up of large tensions in the deployed lines and to confirm bottoming of an anchor. Training of personnel and deck rehearsals are excellent practice for the safety and the success of the operation.

Example. A brief review of the method used for the implantation of the IWEX trimoor (1973) shown in Figure 6.10 can serve as an example of complex system deployment. The trimoor was set in the Atlantic Ocean (28°N-70°W), the depth of the water being 5465 m (18,000 ft). In its final configuration, the apex of the trimoor had to be 600 m (1368 ft) below the surface and the three anchors at the vertices of an equilateral triangle with sides 5964 m (19,500 ft) long. Each leg, also 5964 m long was heavily equipped with recording scientific instrumentation.

Hundreds of buoyant elements to help support the weight of the steel legs and the connected instrumentation had to be attached to the mooring lines as deployment proceeded. Advanced mooring design and deployment analysis, detailed preparation of the mooring components, acquisition of special launching equipment and, when on site, the combination of good weather and excellent navigation were all decisive factors in the success of this 3-day operation.

The different deployment phases are depicted in Figures 7.14 to 7.16. The operation was started by first establishing the acoustic transponders base line. A temporary surface mooring was then set. The anchor end of Leg C was then attached to this surface buoy. The ship then paid Leg C out, launched the apex buoy, and paid Leg B out while steaming toward the anchor B location. When on station, the anchor of Leg B was lowered to the bottom with the ship's crown line. When the anchor was properly positioned, the ship actuated the crown line release and hauled the crown line on board. Leg A was then attached to the apex buoy and paid out as the ship was steaming toward the anchor A location. When on station, anchor A was lowered to the bottom, again using the ship's crown line. The apex buoy started to submerge during anchor A lowering. After properly positioning anchor A, the ship's line release was again actuated, and the crown line retrieved. The anchor end of Leg C was then taken off from the surface buoy and anchor C made fast to Leg C. Anchor C was then lowered and positioned using again the ship's crown line. Retrieval of the temporary surface mooring and of the transponder network completed the deployment. The IWEX mooring was entirely recovered after 2 months on station.

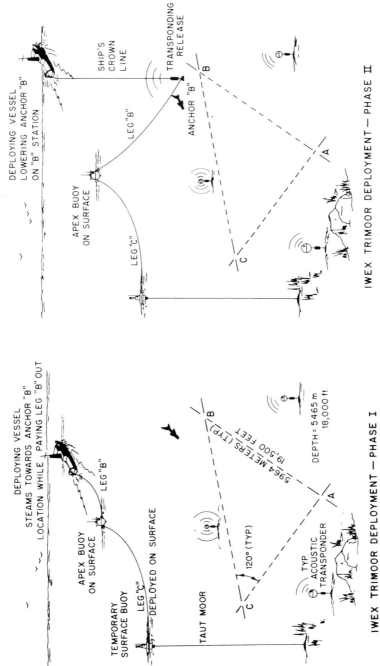

Figure 7.14. IWEX trimoor deployment.

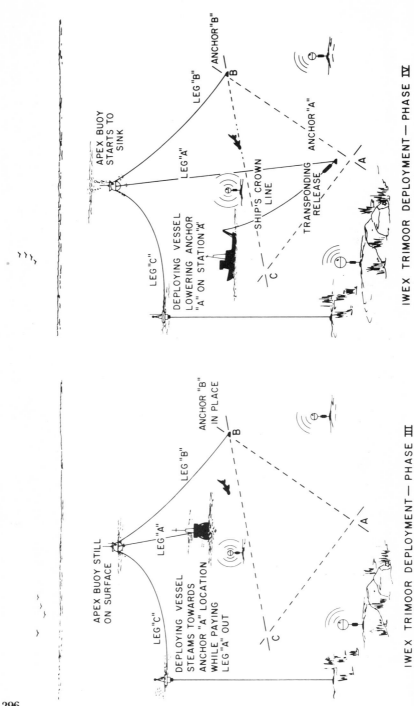

IWEX TRIMOOR DEPLOYMENT—PHASE III

IWEX TRIMOOR DEPLOYMENT—PHASE IV

Figure 7.15. IWEX trimoor deployment.

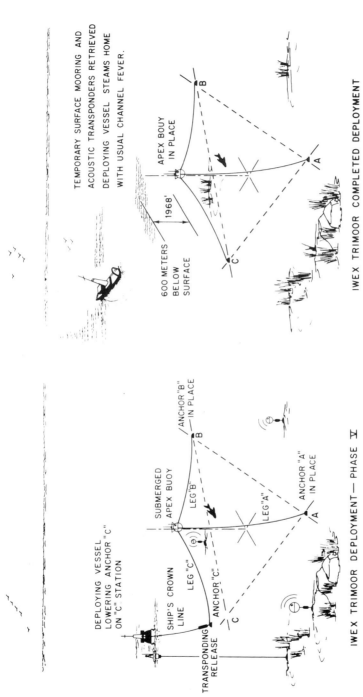

TEMPORARY SURFACE MOORING AND ACOUSTIC TRANSPONDERS RETRIEVED DEPLOYING VESSEL STEAMS HOME WITH USUAL CHANNEL FEVER.

APEX BOUY IN PLACE

1968'

600 METERS BELOW SURFACE

IWEX TRIMOOR COMPLETED DEPLOYMENT

DEPLOYING VESSEL LOWERING ANCHOR "C" ON "C" STATION

SUBMERGED APEX BUOY

ANCHOR "B" IN PLACE

LEG "B"

LEG "A"

ANCHOR "A" IN PLACE

SHIP'S CROWN LINE

LEG "C"

TRANSPONDING RELEASE

ANCHOR "C"

IWEX TRIMOOR DEPLOYMENT— PHASE Ⅳ

Figure 7.16. IWEX trimoor deployment.

297

Retrieval

Recovery of data and recording instrumentation, replacement of buoy system components (batteries, lights, sensors, instruments, deteriorated mooring parts, etc.), system inspection and maintenance are reasons for the retrieval of most buoy systems. Failure of retrieval often means failure of the mission. Attention should therefore be given ahead of time to the design features and logistic details that will insure the best chances for a successful recovery. For example, night, fog, and bad weather can make the search for a relatively small buoy rather frustrating. It is certainly of prime importance to provide redundant means of location (light, radio beacons, radar reflectors, acoustic transponders) to reduce as much as feasible the real possibility of never finding the buoy.

Simple buoy systems are normally retrieved by first actuating the anchor release. In the case of a subsurface mooring, this permits the free ascent of the buoy and its mooring line. In the case of a surface mooring, the anchor weight is left on the bottom for ease of recovery of the buoy and the mooring line.

Usually, the recovery procedure is the reverse of an anchor first launching operation. The buoy is the first component to be brought back on board. The mooring line is then fed through a sheave and hauled in by a power winch. One must remember that due to weight and drag, the line is under considerable tension. Means for easily disconnecting the buoy from the mooring line and subsequently, decoupling line sections or instruments must, therefore, be provided, whatever the deployment technique used. Inserting a sling link below the buoy, at each line connection, and on both sides of the instrument casings can be of great help for "stopping off" at the time of retrieval.

The recovery of complex buoy systems is often facilitated by allowing the system to be broken down at the time of recovery into subsystems that can be independently recovered. For example, the recovery of the multibuoy subsurface system depicted in Figure 7.17 is best achieved by first calling the upper part to the surface and release the lower part at a later time. The retrieval of the IWEX trimoor was greatly simplified by allowing the apex buoy to separate into three independent sections at the time of recovery. Retrieving one leg at a time is certainly easier than trying to haul on board a single buoy with three tangled mooring lines attached to it.

Whenever possible, redundant methods of recovery should be incorporated into the system. Failure of anchor releases should be anticipated. Backing up the main release by a second release or a time device mounted in parallel is a standard safe procedure. When designing subsurface buoys, it

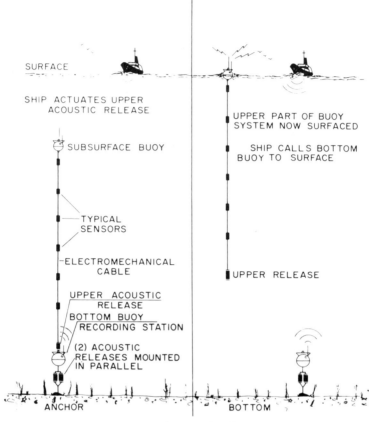

Figure 7.17. Retrieval of multibuoy subsurface system.

is prudent to provide additional buoyancy to account for possible flooding of instrument casings. A ground line to permit recovery by dragging (Figure 7.18) is sometimes used to increase the chances of recovery.

Back-Up Recovery of Deep Sea Moorings

Failure of deep-sea moorings usually results in the loss of valuable equipment, and unless at least part of the mooring is recovered, no information is made available to understand the cause of failure and to initiate the required corrective measures.

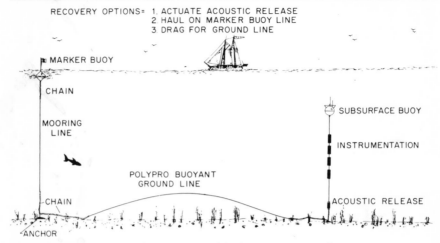

Figure 7.18.   Subsurface buoy system with three recovery options.

After the failure of the mooring line, one part of the failed buoy system rests on the sea floor, thousands of meters below the surface, while the other part hangs from the buoy drifting hundreds of miles away from the site. The odds of a passing ship sighting the buoy adrift are small, and of the ship hauling the lost buoy, even smaller. Inserting enough buoyancy elements directly in the mooring line to permit the failed end to come to the surface upon command release of the anchor provides a simple and elegant solution to the problem.

The buoyant elements can be passive, as the glass balls or syntactic foam floats shown in Figures 6.47 and 6.49, or active like certain gas generators that can on demand provide buoyancy by water displacement. The buoyant elements can be lumped in one package immediately above the anchor release as shown in Figure 6.1, or they can be discretely distributed along the mooring line. The dynamic response of surface moorings equipped with distributed buoyancy packages has been found to cause slackness and kinking in the upper part of the mooring. On the other hand, with subsurface moorings there is no danger of slack conditions due to wave excitation, and the discrete distribution of the buoyancy can be used to advantage to reduce, at desired locations, the mooring line inclination in a given current profile (Figure 7.19).

The amount of buoyancy provided by the back-up recovery system must not only account for the immersed weight of all the mooring components to be retrieved, but, in addition, it must also include enough reserve buoyancy to free the failed mooring from bottom friction and permit its ascent at a reasonable rate.

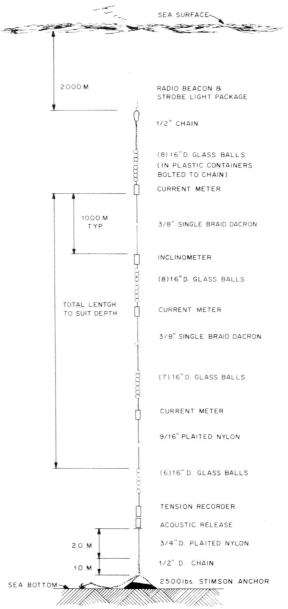

SEA SURFACE

2000 M

RADIO BEACON &
STROBE LIGHT PACKAGE

1/2" CHAIN

(8) 16"D. GLASS BALLS
(IN PLASTIC CONTAINERS
BOLTED TO CHAIN)

CURRENT METER

1000 M
TYP.

3/8" SINGLE BRAID DACRON

INCLINOMETER

(8)16"D. GLASS BALLS

CURRENT METER

TOTAL LENTGH
TO SUIT DEPTH

3/8" SINGLE BRAID DACRON

(7)16"D. GLASS BALLS

CURRENT METER

9/16" PLAITED NYLON

(6)16"D. GLASS BALLS

TENSION RECORDER

ACOUSTIC RELEASE

20 M

3/4"D. PLAITED NYLON

10 M

1/2" D. CHAIN

SEA BOTTOM

2500 lbs. STIMSON ANCHOR

Figure 7.19. Typical subsurface mooring with discrete buoyancy distribution.

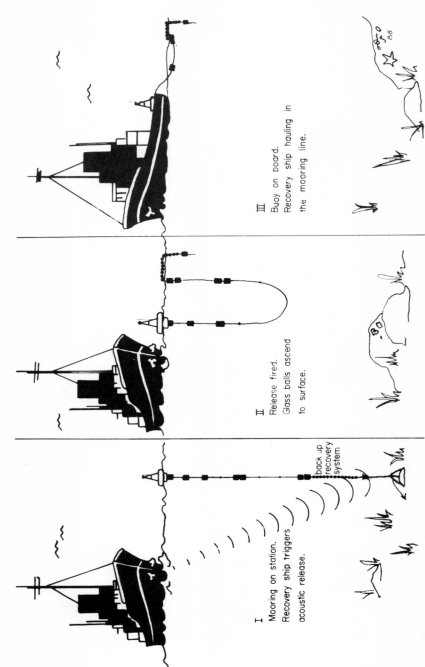

I
Mooring on station.
Recovery ship triggers
acoustic release.

back up
recovery
system

II
Release fired.
Glass balls ascend
to surface.

III
Buoy on board.
Recovery ship hauling in
the mooring line.

Figure 7.20. Normal retrieval of mooring with backup recovery system.

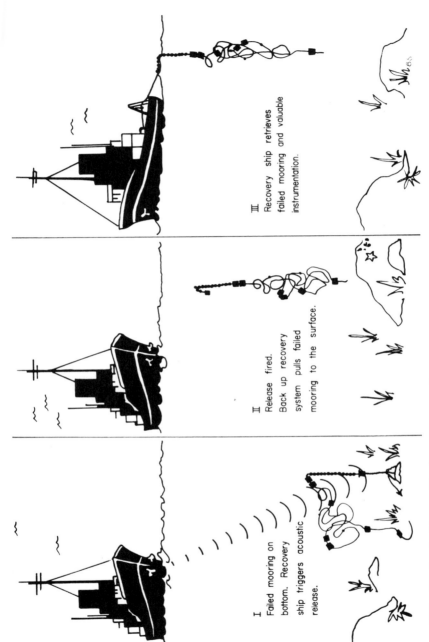

I
Failed mooring on bottom. Recovery ship triggers acoustic release.

II
Release fired. Back up recovery system pulls failed mooring to the surface.

III
Recovery ship retrieves failed mooring and valuable instrumentation.

Figure 7.21. Retrieval with use of backup recovery system

303

Figure 7.22.

Normal retrieval of moorings equipped with back-up recovery systems is straightforward. Figure 7.20 shows a typical sequence of events for a surface mooring. The acoustic anchor release is actuated to allow the cluster of balls to ascend to the surface, lifting the lower part of the mooring. The balls eventually surface a few hundred yards away from the buoy. The float is then picked up by the recovery ship, and the entire mooring line is hauled in, the back-up system being the last to be retrieved.

In the case of a failed mooring, the glass balls may have to lift a considerable amount of weight (Figure 7.21). Their rate of ascent is slow and the time for the back-up recovery system to reach the surface may be considerable. Often the ascent of the balls is monitored with the help of an acoustic transponder, which may be part of the anchor release. The cluster of balls is located on the surface either visually or by tracking the release transponder. The balls are then taken aboard the recovery ship, and the rest of the mooring is hauled upside down. Considerable tangling is always present in a failed mooring (Figure 7.22), and retrieval is no longer straight-forward. However, the extra time and effort necessary to untangle and haul on board the failed mooring is a small price to pay for the recovery of the valuable equipment and of the scientific and engineering data that would otherwise have been lost forever.

REFERENCES

Adamchak, J., and J. H. Evans. *Ocean Engineering Structures*, The M.I.T. Press, Cambridge, Massachusetts, 1969.

Alexandrov, M. "On the Dynamics of Cables with Application to Marine Use," *Marine Technology Society Journal*, 1971.

Beck, R. W. "Anchor Performance Tests," Offshore Ocean Technology Conference, OTC-1537, Houston, Texas, May 1972.

Berteaux, H. O., et al. "Experimental Evidence on the Modes and Probable Causes of a Deep Sea Buoy Mooring Line Failure," Transactions Marine Technology Society Conference, 1968.

Berteaux, H. O., and R. G. Walden. "Analysis and Experimental Evaluation of Single Point Moored Buoy Systems," Woods Hole Oceanographic Institution, *W.H.O.I. Ref. No. 69-36* (unpublished manuscript), Woods Hole, Massachusetts, May 1969.

Berteaux, H. O. "Design of Deep Sea Mooring Lines," *Marine Technology Society Journal*, Volume 4, Number 3, May/June 1970.

Berteaux, H. O. "An Engineering Review of the Woods Hole Oceanographic Institution Buoy Program," *Colloque International Sur l' Exploitation des Oceans*, Theme V, Tome I, Cnexo-B. P. 107, Paris, France, March 1971.

Capadona, E. A. "Establishing Test Parameters for Evaluation and Design of Cable," Transaction of the Marine Technology Society Conference, 1967.

Charnews, D. P. "Drag Coefficients of Vibrating Synthetic Rope," Ocean Engineering Degree Thesis, M.I.T. and W.H.O.I., September 1971.

The Colorado Fuel and Iron Corporation. *Roebling Rope Handbook*, Roebling Wire Rope, Trenton, New Jersey, Copyright 1966.

Dahlen, J. M. "Oceanic Telescope Engineering Program Report on Pilot Project Design, Testing, and Progress through October, 1968," Instrumentation Laboratory, Massachusetts Institute of Technology, Cambridge, Massachusetts, Report E-2320, October, 1968.

Dahlen, J. M. "Oceanic Telescope Engineering Project," Charles Stark Draper Laboratory, Massachusetts Institute of Technology, Cambridge, Massachusetts, March 1970.

Daubin, S. D., and D. S. Potter. "Some Design Criteria for Deep Sea Moorings," The American Society of Mechanical Engineers, New York, New York, Paper Number 63-WA-211, September 4, 1963.

Daubin, S. C., H. O. Berteaux, et al. "The ACODAC System," Woods Hole Oceanographic Institution, *W.H.O.I. Ref. No. 72-87* (unpublished manuscript), Woods Hole, Massachusetts, November 1972.

Devereux, R., H. Q. Driscoll, W. R. Hoover, et al. "Development of an Ocean Data Station Telemetering Buoy," Progress Report, General Dynamics/Convair, San Diego, California, GDC-65-01i, December 1964.

Devereux, R., H. Q. Driscoll, W. R. Hoover, et al. "Development of an Ocean Data Station Telemetering Buoy," Progress Report, General Dynamics/Convair, San Diego, California, GDC-65-018, Revised May 1965.

Ewing, G. C., and F. L. Striffler. "Experience with a Drifting IRLS Buoy," Woods Hole Oceanographic Institution, *W.H.O.I. Ref. No. 70-53* (unpublished manuscript), Woods Hole, Massachusetts, October 1970.

Flory, J. "The Single Anchor Leg Mooring," Offshore Ocean Technology Conference, OTC-1644, Houston, Texas, May 1972.

Froidevaux, M. R., and R. A. Scholten. "Calculation of the Gravity Fall Motion of a Mooring System," Massachusetts Institute of Technology, Instrumentation Laboratory, Cambridge, Massachusetts, E-2319, August 1968.

Haas, F. J. "Natural and Synthetic Cordage in the Field of Oceanography," Transactions of the Third Annual MTS Conference, June 1967.

Haedrich, R. L. "Identification of a Deep-Sea Mooring Cable Biter," *Deep Sea Research*, Vol. 12, 1965.

Hilsher, J. E. "Wire Rope Assemblies," *Machine Design*, August 1961.

Hruska, F. "Calculation of Stresses in Wire Ropes," *Wire and Wire Products*, Vol. 26, September 1951.

Hruska, F. "Tangential Forces in Wire Ropes," *Wire and Wire Products*, Vol. 28, No. 5, May 1953.

Hruska, F. "Radial Forces in Wire Ropes," *Wire and Wire Products*, Vol. 27, No. 5, May 1952.

International Nickel Company, Inc. *Guidelines for Selection of Marine Materials*, 1966.

Isaacs, J. D., G. B. Schick, et al. "Development and Testing of Taut-Nylon Moored Instrument Stations (with details of design and construction)," University of California, Scripps Institution of Oceanography, San Diego, California, SIO Reference No. 65-5, April 15, 1965.

McLoad, K. W., et al. "Torque Balanced Wire Rope and Armored Cables," Transactions of the 1964 Buoy Technology Symposium, Marine Technology Society, Washington, D.C.

Mollo-Christensen, E., and C. E. Dorman. "A Buoy System for Air–Sea Interaction Studies," Massachusetts Institute of Technology, Report No. 714, Cambridge, April 1971.

Morey, R. L., and H. O. Berteaux. "Alleviation of Corrosion Problems in Deep Sea Moorings," Third International Congress on Proceedings, Marine Corrosion & Fouling, North Western University Press, Evanston, Illinois, October 1972.

Morey, R. L. "Evaluation of Long Term Deep Sea Effects on Mooring Line Components," Charles Stark Draper Laboratory, Massachusetts Institute of Technology, Cambridge, Massachusetts, February 1973.

Morton, W. E., et al. *Physical Properties of Textile Fibers*, Textile Institute, Manchester and London, England.

Paul, W. "Review of Synthetic Fiber Ropes," National Data Buoy Development Project, United States Coast Guard, Washington, D.C., August 1970.

Poffenberger, H. E., et al. "Dynamic Testing of Cables," Transactions of the Marine Technology Society Conference, 1967.

Rendler, N. J. "Damage Analysis of Wire Rope from a 34-Month Ocean Mooring," Naval Research Laboratory, Washington, D.C., NRL Memorandum Report 2196, October 1970.

Savage, G. H., and J. B. Hersey. "Project Seaspider. The Design, Assembly and Construction and Sea Trials of a Tri-Moored Buoyant Structure with Neutrally Buoyant Legs to Provide a Near Motionless Instrument Base for Oceanographic Research," Woods Hole Oceanographic Institution, *W.H.O.I. Ref. No. 68-42* (unpublished manuscript), Woods Hole, Massachusetts, June 1968.

Schick, G. B. "The Design of a Deep-Moored Oceanographic Station," Buoy Technology Symposium MTS, 1964.

Smith, J. E. "Structures in Deep Ocean Engineering Manual for Underwater Construction," Chapter 7, *Buoy & Anchorage System*, U. S. Naval Civil Engineering Laboratory, Technical Report 284-7, Port Hueneme, California, 1965.

Smith, J. E., R. M. Beard, and R. J. Taylor, "Specialized Anchors for the Deep Sea," Marine Technology Society 7th Annual Conference, Washington, D.C., August 1971.

Smith, P. F. "A Summary of Recent Deep Ocean Scientific Buoy Performance," NATO Subcommittee on Oceanographic Research, Technical Report No. 19, August 1964.

Starkey, W. L., et al. "An analysis of Critical Stresses and Mode of Failure of a Wire Rope," ASME, Machine Design Division, December 5, 1968.

Stimson, P. B. "Synthetic-Fiber Deep-Sea Mooring Cables—Their Life Expectancy and Susceptibility to Biological Attack," *Deep Sea Research*, Vol. 12, 1965.

Stimson, P. B., and B. Prindle. "Armoring of Synthetic-Fiber Deep-Sea Mooring Lines Against Fishbite," Woods Hole Oceanographic Institution, *W.H.O.I. Ref. No. 72-75* (unpublished manuscript), Woods Hole, Massachusetts, September 1972.

Swallow, H. "A Neutral Buoyancy Float for Measuring Deep Currents," *Deep Sea Research*, pp. 74–81, Vol. 3, 1965.

Thresher, R. W., and J. H. Nath. "Anchor-Last Deployment Procedure for Mooring," Oregon State University, School of Oceanography, Corvallis, Oregon, Reference No. 73-5, June 1973.

Turner, N. J. et al. "The Vertical Distribution of Fishbites on Deep-Sea Mooring Lines In the Vicinity of Bermuda," Woods Hole Oceanographic Institution, *W.H.O.I. Ref. No. 67-58*, Woods Hole, Massachusetts, 1967.

U. S. Steel Wire Rope Handbook.

Uhlig, H. *Corrosion and Corrosion Control*, John Wiley & Sons Inc., New York, 1971.

Vachon, W. A. "Kink Formation Properties and Other Mechanical Characteristics of Oceanographic Strands and Wire Rope," Massachusetts Institute of Technology, Charles Stark Draper Laboratory, E-2497, April 1970.

Vanderveldt, H. H., and R. De Young. "A Survey of Publications on Mechanical Wire Rope Systems," The Catholic University of America, Institute of Ocean Science and Engineering, Washington, D.C., Report 70-8, August 1970.

Walden, R. G. "A Review of Oceanographic and Meteorological Buoy Capabilities and Effectiveness," Proceedings of the 4th ISA Marine Sciences Instrumentation Symposium, Cocoa Beach, Florida, January 1968.

Walden, R. G. "Oceanographic and Meteorological Buoys," *Underwater Science and Technology Journal*, September 1970.

Walden, R. G., H. O. Berteaux, and F. Striffler. "The Design, Logistics and Installation of a SOFAR Float Tracking Station at Grand Turk Island, B.W.I.," Woods Hole Oceanographic Institution, *W.H.O.I. Ref. No. 73-73* (unpublished manuscript), Woods Hole, Massachusetts, October 1973.

Webb, D. C. "A New Instrument for the Measurement of Vertical Currents in the Ocean," Proceedings Conference in Electronic Engineering in Ocean Technology, page 416 and following, September 1970.

Wilson, B. W. "Elastic Characteristics of Moorings", *Journal of Waterways and Harbors Division*, Proceedings of the American Society of Civil Engineers, San Marino, California, Vol. 93, WW4, November, 1967.

INDEX